One of the Family

40 Years with the Krays

Maureen Flanagan

with Jacky Hyams

arrow books

3 5 7 9 10 8 6 4 2

Arrow Books
20 Vauxhall Bridge Road
London SW1V 2SA

Arrow Books is part of the Penguin Random House group of companies
addresses can be found at global.penguinrandomhouse.com.

Penguin
Random House
UK

First published in Great Britain by Century in 2015

www.penguin.co.uk

A CIP catalogue record for this book is available from the British Library.

ISBN 9781784750763

Printed and bound in Great Britain by Clays Ltd, St Ives plc

For my four beautiful granddaughters,
Scarlett, Madison, Jade and Sapphire.

Contents

Part One

Chapter 1

The hairdresser

I pushed the door open and straight away it hit me: the all too familiar pong of the cramped local hairdressing salon. Mostly, you got the awful lingering, acrid whiff of the ammonia we'd use for the cheap perm lotion for the older ladies, mingled with the sickly smell coming from the clouds of sticky hair lacquer. Isn't it funny how quickly you forget all the little things you hated about your job once you've moved on to something better?

I'd forgotten how noisy it all was, too: Carol's salon on the Bethnal Green Road was really far too small. Frequently, she'd run out of chairs for her clients as they waited for their weekly hair-wash: just two tiny sinks, and five big chairs for the lucky customers who were actually being tended to by Carol's two permanently busy young stylists. It was a room full of women nattering, gossiping, swapping tales of Saturday night and men's treachery as they waited – and it was always a long wait – to be 'done'.

A few of Carol's clients were halfway through the tortured process: trapped fast under the big ugly hood-dryers at the back of the salon, merciless humming contraptions under which the women sat for ages, flicking through magazines, impatiently clicking the heating controls if the machine got too hot, waiting for the moment when their heavily rollered, silver-gripped and hairnetted confections would finally be pronounced dry – and ready to be teased or backcombed into stiff barnets. Or, for the younger ones, beehives like busby hats.

Right on cue, the junior, a bored, pimply fifteen-year-old whose mum had pushed Carol to take him and get him off the street, was listlessly pretending to sweep the salon floor that was strewn with all the hacked-off bits of hair, making a complete mess of it into the bargain. It was all exactly as I'd known it, six days a week every week since I'd started work in a salon as a Saturday shampoo girl, aged fourteen.

Not too long ago, this had been my world: I'd been a lively young hairdresser who'd finished a three-year apprenticeship in another busy little salon in North London, on the Holloway Road. I'd enjoyed some things about hairdressing, I admit. I worshipped fashion, clothes, make-up and looking good – I was proud of my long mane of home-bleached platinum hair – and I took pleasure in making other women look their best. I had no problem with chatting to people all day long. It was fascinating how women would tell me, a comparative stranger, all sorts of personal stuff about themselves. One or two questions and away they'd go. Sometimes you'd wish they'd shut up. But, of course, your job was to smile and listen to most of it while you worked away, curling the hair round the rollers, positioning it with pins, teasing the result to the heavens once it was dry.

The trouble was, the money in the Holloway Road salon wasn't anything to get too excited about for an engaged girl who was already saving hard to get married. Even with the occasional generous tip. So when I was nineteen I went 'up West' where me and my sister Iris sold gorgeous expensive Italian shoes made of the finest leather and softest suede in Pinet, right in the heart of swanky Bond Street, earning wages plus commission for whatever we sold. No more smelly, noisy, crowded salons with impatient women shouting 'I'm dry!', just plush carpeting and the refined elegant moneyed atmosphere of one of London's most exclusive shopping streets.

The customers too were much more intriguing. Instead of chatting to ordinary girls like us who'd grown up in a bombed-out, grey, semi-wrecked part of London, Iris and me got to meet seriously famous people. Shirley Bassey was a regular every week: we'd dye her shoes to match the fabulous slinky sequinned outfits she wore each night at the London Palladium, just up the road. American singer Lena Horne came in one day. Smooth, sleek movie actors like Laurence Harvey and James Mason drifted through the doors in beautiful cashmere overcoats en route to lunch with their agents at the Ritz Hotel. The grim post-war stretch of the endless Holloway Road versus magical Bond Street: no contest whatsoever. Especially if glamour and excitement were your heart's desire.

On my twentieth birthday I married Patrick Flanagan, my teenage sweetheart, and was swiftly installed in our little one-bedroom rented flat in Camden. I still did a bit of private hairdressing work, on the side, as it were, usually on Thursdays, my day off from Pinet. Through salon work I'd discovered that some of the older women liked the idea of a girl doing their hair in the comfort of their own home, without all the hanging around – and without the nattering, nosy crowd.

This was the summer of 1961 and the once-weekly shampoo-and-set for Saturday night was becoming a must-have for millions of women, even in the less affluent areas of the country. The salon hairdos were rigid and stiff with the nasty, glue-like lacquer that kept it all in place: girls regularly went to bed in scarves that protected the hairdos – or even with the newer red jumbo rollers pinned into place. But the end result was neat, groomed. They topped off the straight tight skirts or sheath dresses that were worn well below the knee (the miniskirt had yet to arrive) and the pointed-toe stilettos from Dolcis. There weren't as many hair products as we have now. Some of the chemicals we used to mix up would have had the health-and-safety people shrieking with horror today. But some things never ever change – and the desire to look good at the dance hall or in the pub was just as much a feminine preoccupation then as it is today.

So on that day I found Carol busily backcombing and chatting to her customer simultaneously. She flashed her wide grin at me, obviously pleased that I'd turned up. Dark-eyed, petite, chirpy and constantly on the go, she'd worked side by side with me at Holloway Road at one stage. The week before she'd rung and insisted I come down to her Bethnal Green salon on my day off. She had someone she wanted me to meet, she'd said. A potential client for me. A woman everyone knew round the East End because of her twin sons. The name was Kray. Carol had primed me when she'd asked me to meet Violet, one of her regulars. 'She's Ronnie and Reggie's mum, wants someone to go round her house and do her hair.'

'This is Violet, Maureen,' she said, gesturing to a round, fair, good-looking woman of about fifty seated by the door, waiting to be 'done'.

'Vi, this is the girl I told you about – you know, Maureen, the one who'll come round to your house.'

Violet Kray looked up at me with a friendly smile that made me feel instantly at ease. You could see immediately what type of woman she was. I'd been in the hairdressing business long enough to be able to spot The Moaners and The Complainers straight away. Usually they were round Violet's age, discontented with their lot in life, endlessly reminding us youngsters what they'd lived through in the Second World War, sometimes widowed early or abandoned. These were the women who'd toughed out the hard times, struggled to keep home, hearth and family together somehow.

Violet definitely wasn't a moaner. She oozed kindness. She had quite thick spun-gold hair, light blue eyes and a handsome face. Quite immaculate in her floral print dress and cardi, a thin gold chain round her neck, a small diamond ring on her right hand. Fairly high heels too, I noted. I guessed she was around the same age as my mum, Nell. There was something about this woman: perhaps my instinct told me that she was a woman who loved her kids, and lived for her family. Just like my dear mother. In fact, Violet reminded me a lot of her.

Within a minute or two we could have been old friends. That, in essence, was Violet Kray's personality: a sociable, well turned-out motherly East Ender with a manner that compelled you to talk to her, to tell her your stories. The Italians have a word for it: *simpatico*. Ten minutes talking to Vi and you felt you'd known her for ten years. In time I'd understand that a lot of people around the East End's Bethnal Green area felt that way too about Violet. She was a much-loved presence in an area of familiar faces.

I had, of course, heard of Ronnie and Reggie, the Kray Twins, had even had the briefest glimpse of their older brother Charlie in an Islington pub one night. Although I wasn't an East Ender and had grown up in North London, around the Islington area, the Kray boys' reputation as the East End's hard men, vicious street fighters running all manner of protection scams and nightclubs, wasn't exactly a glowing reference. The fact that they enjoyed a great deal of notoriety around the East End – and, increasingly, beyond – didn't trouble me in the least, I guess because I had married into a family that had a similar reputation around the area we lived in.

Back then different groups of 'faces' or gangs were known to 'run' criminal activity around different parts of London. They each stuck to their manor: the rule was that you didn't attempt to 'do business' on anyone else's patch. Islington, where I'd grown up, was for the Nash family. And the East End was for the Krays. Feared. 'Naughty', to use the euphemism of the times. And talked about constantly, mostly by people who'd never even clapped eyes on them.

In my childhood, violence and aggression were far from being a way of life for me, the eldest of three kids, in our home. But you knew it existed around you: it was what men did sometimes. I'd seen it for myself in my teens, the vicious fights that went on between street gangs, outside local dance halls or nightclubs. Why they felt compelled to fight each other I couldn't tell you. It was a boy thing. My husband, Patrick, was a Flanagan, one of eleven children who included a pair of identical twins, funnily enough: Noel and Chris. As far as the Flanagan Twins were concerned, being Patrick's wife meant I knew there was always a soft side to these men. In those days, men fought each other for all sorts of reasons – and quite often the police were never involved because no one would dream of contacting them.

The Flanagan Twins were so fond of fighting each other that in the end I became the only one in the family who could step in to prise them apart. You couldn't say I didn't know about men fighting.

Of course, it had always been that way in the tougher, meaner streets of London. Locals gossiped about the doings and crimes of local gangs or villains all the time, who was 'inside' and who was 'coming out'. People had the telly and the newspapers, of course, but most such talk about what the 'naughtier' members of the community were up to went on in the local pubs. The stories of their misdeeds spiced up other more mundane yet respectable lives, in a way.

Violet, of course, was an innocent victim of this kind of gossip.

According to Carol, the Kray Twins had now become so well known around the East End that it had started to make it somewhat difficult for Violet to go out and about. It was OK if she stopped to chat briefly with the neighbours around Bethnal Green, people she'd known since she was young. 'Twins all right, Vi?' they'd say. That was fine. Every neighbour knew the code of behaviour. She'd reply politely, glad they'd asked her. But you didn't ask pointed questions, you exchanged pleasantries. If you did derive a scrap of information to pass on, all to the good.

But Carol's salon, alas, was much trickier, simply because all Carol's customers had to sit around there for a couple of hours. It was a trap. There was no appointments system, you just turned up and waited your turn. No easy escape if virtual strangers chose to seize a golden opportunity to corner the Kray Twins' mum.

'I can't come 'ere any more, Maureen,' Violet Kray told me that day, shaking her head. 'Women I don't even know come up and start talking to me about their families,' she continued. 'Well, of course I don't mind that, of course I don't. But then they start asking me for favours if they're 'avin' a bit of trouble with one of their sons. They ask me to get my Reg to sort it out for them!' Which meant could she use Reg and Ron's violent reputation to solve their problem?

'I get that all the time now, Maureen, and I don't want to be rude but it's not for me to get involved if their boys are up to no good, is it?'

So there it was: me, a twenty-one-year-old girl, talking with a fifty-something mum. Me, not an East Ender and her with 'naughty' twins who were now so well known that people were trying to use their mother's influence to deal with their family woes. A bit unfair, to say the least. And embarrassing for her. You could see straight away that she was a decent, protective sort of woman. Respectable in many ways. She'd never dream of getting involved.

I'd taken to Vi straight away and, if I am honest, I liked the idea of the extra work. Still, I wasn't 100% sure about all this: something held me back, so I played for time. 'Couldn't someone from Carol's salon go round to your house and do your hair?' I asked cheerfully, as if that seemed like a better idea.

'No,' she said. 'I've thought of that already. I even asked one girl. But she turned me down.'

'OK,' I said as I made a snap decision. To hell with the 'naughty' sons and my brothers-in-law. This was my life.

'I'll come round and do it next week and then you can see if you like it. What's the address?' I said, opening my bag and scrabbling around for a bit of paper as Carol, hovering, rushed to grab the pencil she kept by the till.

'It's 178 Vallance Road,' Violet dictated.

I didn't have a clue where the hell that was. Bethnal Green isn't very far from Islington in terms of distance, only a few miles. You have to remember that, in those days, Islington in North London was a world apart from the East End. Or any other area. The different areas of London were all completely separate fiefdoms. By then, I'd saved up hard to buy myself a little Mini Minor to whizz around in. But not everyone had that kind of mobility in London at the dawn of the 1960s: the majority of women didn't drive. They tended to stick fast to their little patch. It's always claimed that London is a series or collection of villages and back then that was exactly how it was: you lived with your family in your bit of London, maybe you ventured 'up West' for a night out with your friends or worked there. But you only travelled to someone else's area if you were invited round – or if they were related to you. As a teenager, you only went out with boys from the area you lived in, that sort of thing. South London? The outer suburbs? Unknown territory.

So that was how it all started with me and the Kray family. Vi and I set a price. I asked for seven shillings and sixpence – cheeky of me because it was quite a lot. I knew that other girls charged five bob for home hairdos – but I was lucky because that suited her fine. The following Thursday afternoon I'd go round to her house. Everything was agreed just as the shampoo girl appeared with the black gown, ready to wash Vi's hair.

I had a couple of regular Thursday clients but one more would be nice if this worked out, I mused on my way home. Seven and six . . . easily enough for two new pairs of seamed stockings and some earrings off a favourite stall in Chapel Street Market. The girl I was back then, lacking experience in some ways but streetwise in the way of young London girls who'd already been out working for quite a few years, would never seriously worry about whether it was wise to be visiting the home of men who were already famed for what was politely known as 'getting into trouble'.

Chapter 2

Meeting the family

I wouldn't say I was totally naive: I knew how to think on my feet, stand up for myself. We'd lost my lovely dad, Leo, when I was fifteen and my mother needed help looking after the three of us. That same year I'd been asked to leave convent school. It suited me fine as I wanted to be at home to help out. In an act of rebellion, I'd dyed my hair platinum and started wearing make-up, much to the horror of the Mother Superior. Only 'bad girls' dyed their hair back then, but in a way this act of rebellion set me on the path as it led me to become a hairdressing apprentice.

I did a little bit of 'homework' that weekend when Patrick and I met Noel and Chris, his brothers, for a drink in a Camden pub. Noel's talk, as usual, turned to the 'insider trading' of info about London's other 'naughty' boys and their respective territories. Perhaps not so surprisingly, the Kray Twins cropped up: something to do with a gambling club, Esmeralda's Barn. Noel said something about it being in Knightsbridge, an area we'd never set foot in.

'I thought they weren't allowed to run places outside the East End,' I said innocently.

'Yeah, well, they do now,' snapped Noel. 'They're making a hell of a lot of money. But that Ronnie . . . he's out of control. The other one's almost as bad.'

Then Chris chipped in: 'Good people to stay away from, eh?'

Patrick, my husband, nodded and ordered another round. There'd be no conversations with any of the Flanagans about my new client Violet Kray, I decided. Definitely a subject to avoid.

Thursday afternoon came in a flash and it was time to go see my new client. I popped my portable Ronson Escort hood dryer, zip-up bag of rollers and pins, bottle of Vosene shampoo and little puffer lacquer spray into the back of the Mini and set off.

I had to stop and ask for directions a couple of times but eventually I found 178 Vallance Road, a little 'two up, two down' four-roomed Victorian terraced house, one of many in a long row. You saw houses just like this round where I lived: some had been bombed badly in the war but this street seemed to have just about survived, though by then the authorities had already earmarked streets like this for demolition. Slum clearance they called it. Each house had a yard at the back, many cluttered with all kinds of junk and debris, plus a small outdoor cubicle containing the only toilet. Yet the windows of the houses were clean, the doorsteps scrubbed. People round here were poor. But boy, were the women house-proud.

And this was no slum dweller who answered the door and ushered me into the narrow hallway. It was Violet who opened the door, wearing a knitted dress with a 'pinny' over it. Violet was as neat as could be, and the house itself, you could see, while certainly modest, was spotless. The lino on the floors was shiny and the net curtains at the window were whiter than white. I knew the layout of these houses as Violet led me past the closed door of the front room into the kitchen, where everyone congregated. The kettle was already on and whistling.

The first thing to catch my eye in the somewhat drab kitchen, which contained just a sink, a narrow gas cooker and a table in the middle that was covered by a tablecloth, were the photos, proudly lined up on the tiled mantelpiece above the fireplace – which was obviously never used.

I didn't want to stare or check out the photos, but a quick glance revealed that they were all of men. I presumed they were her boys. Then I noticed the white shirts, freshly washed and ironed, all hanging up. There must have been about a dozen decorating the kitchen. Maybe they're for her husband, I thought to myself. Perhaps she was getting him ready for a trip. Yet their presence was puzzling because everything else was so neat, ordered really. I wondered why she didn't hang them elsewhere.

'I've got us some nice sponge cake,' Violet told me, getting out the dark green plates and cheerfully cutting the cake up for us to have with our tea.

'Hungry, Maureen?' She smiled, looking at me. 'Say if you want a sandwich, don't be shy.'

Suddenly I was overcome with shyness and said that I didn't want a thing. I was sure that had I requested a big fry-up she wouldn't have blinked an eye. This was a very ordinary East End home but you couldn't mistake the generosity of this woman. Mothering people, even if she hardly knew them, was second nature to her, and I immediately felt safe here at Vallance Road.

After we finished our tea and cake, I suggested we get cracking.

'I'm going to wash your hair now, Mrs Kray,' I said, gesturing to the kitchen sink where I'd do the shampoo and rinse with a jug of water. Like so many homes then, the house had no bathroom. All it boasted was a tin bath hanging on a nail in the yard outside. People took themselves off to the local baths, once a week, for a proper bath. There's still one in Bethnal Green today.

'Don't be silly, Maureen. Please call me Violet,' she said, smiling.

Violet had fantastic hair, really thick, a joy to do. I gave her the same hairdo that my mum had – lots of backcombing and lacquer once the rollers were out and it was dry. You could see she was a very feminine sort of woman: clothes, hairdo and make-up were important to her. As I did her hair, we chatted away and I got the distinct impression that she welcomed the female company, someone to share her thoughts with.

Beyond the rumours, and knowing that Violet had three sons, I knew virtually nothing of the Kray family history. And at that stage I was a bit wary about revealing too much of my own life. I'd already told her in the salon that I hadn't been married long. But my decision to keep my visit to Vallance Road a secret from my husband and his brothers made me reluctant to say much more. As I put the rollers in I noticed that her hair had really dark roots.

'It's because I can't go anywhere these days, Maureen,' she told me yet again as I fixed the Ronson dryer hood over the rollers and started it up.

The drying always took ages, which gave plenty of time for me to hear more about Violet's life.

Violet couldn't even go to a market stall and buy a pound of King Edwards without the stallholder trying to grill her about Ronnie and Reggie, and what they were doing, eager for any interesting titbit of information to pass on down the pub later on. Violet was unfailingly polite, too polite in my opinion. She wasn't the type of woman to tell someone to 'eff off'.

In the end, she told me, it had become easier to get a lot of her food delivered to her front door. I didn't realise it then, of course, but this home-delivery thing was all part of the Kray Twins' local business.

It wasn't exactly neighbourly kindness that made local shopkeepers offer to deliver. Some people in the area were actually eager to do favours for the Krays, to get 'in' with these local celebrities whose pictures now cropped up in the local paper regularly, showing them at some sort of charity event where they'd raised funds for young boxers or underprivileged kids. Fish, fruit, veg, you name it. All delivered, Ocado-style, right to the door.

'I don't want people giving me things, Maureen, but of course people know the boys, so they don't mind doing it,' she told me. 'I 'ave to pay them but sometimes they say they don't want the money.'

My mind was already going in an entirely different direction, of course.

'Look, I can bring the bleach here and do your roots for you, Violet. It's no trouble. I do my mum and my sister's hair with the bleach, anyway. It wouldn't be any bother,' I argued.

I could tell she was chuffed with this as I promised I'd do it the next time. Then, as I carefully removed the rollers and started the comb-out, I told her how I'd once met her older son, Charlie, at a charity function in an Islington pub. That was before I got married.

'Your boy Charlie's a bit of a handsome charmer. I realised that the one time I met him. He's not just good-looking, he's really warm and friendly, like you are. Looks like you too, doesn't he?' Vi went all quiet when I said this. She seemed a bit taken aback that I had met him. She didn't seem to be expecting it.

After a moment's pause she laughed. 'Oh, yes, he's always been one for the girls – all the women like Charlie.'

I was drawn into Violet's world completely on that first day. She told me everything from the start. Her life, growing up in Bethnal Green in the 1920s, hadn't been that tough. The Lees, her parents, hadn't known grinding poverty like some families from that generation. They made sure there was always enough to eat for her and her two sisters, Rose and May. They were the prettiest girls in the area. As she told it, she'd been a happy, smiling, young girl of seventeen when she'd first met handsome Charlie Senior, two years older than her. Her family were dead set against her marrying him, so Violet defied them and carried on meeting him in secret. There were terrible rows with her dad, she told me.

'He definitely didn't want me to marry Charlie. So we just did it one day,' she said.

I was a bit shocked at this but quickly I realised that Violet had discovered she was pregnant. I understood about her going against her dad because fathers were very strict then and I'd already doubted if my dad would have let me marry Patrick if he – dad – had not died so young. I knew all too well that he'd have put his foot down about me marrying into the Fighting Flanagan clan. But not to have had a white wedding . . . I felt for Violet. To me, back then, every girl had to have a white wedding . . . I kept the questions to myself as she got up and filled the kettle for the umpteenth time.

'Heart of my heart, I love that melody,' she sang at the top of her voice. Once I got to know her better I saw how much she loved to sing. She had a great voice and would get up and sing sometimes in the local pubs. In those early years of our friendship she'd often be singing what I call Pearly Queen songs, the ones everyone knew the words to and sang along with round the piano in the pub. But 'Heart of My Heart' was her particular favourite.

I'd been there for more than two hours and my work was nearly finished yet Violet gave no sign that she wanted me to leave. I was anxious to hear more about this husband she'd run off with, had defied her dad's wrath to marry.

'Charlie home from work soon?' I hinted.

'Work? 'E doesn't do any work,' came the response. 'He's out. On the knocker.'

I had no idea what this meant. I'd never heard that phrase before. She must have seen I looked confused because then she said, with a sigh, 'It means going round people's 'ouses, knocking on doors, to see if they've got anything to sell. Sometimes they ask "Any old gold or silver you want to sell?" '

I thought that sounded terrible. My husband's family had grown up in dire poverty, yet I'd never heard of them doing this or anything like it.

What I didn't understand, of course, were the traditional ways of East End people: they were poor but entrepreneurial in survival terms, using their wits to buy and sell whatever came their way, working for themselves rather than being a slave to a factory owner or shop proprietor. Being 'on the knocker' meant that Charlie could, in theory, earn good money sometimes. But the buying of gold and silver still puzzled me.

They're not jewellers, I thought to myself. How could they know the value? The truth is that he probably didn't. He just learned as he went along. Charlie, his wife said, bought whatever he could get. Sometimes he would even buy old wardrobes. They'd be lugged into their tiny back garden so he could mend them. And sell them on.

I was learning fast. The Flanagans had come to London from Limerick, Ireland. There were originally fourteen children in the family, but three had died in Ireland. They'd had a very hard life there, with not much food to eat and no shoes to wear. They were builders, roofers, asphalters, jobs typical for the Irish of the time. In London they could earn by manual labour. But here was this very different brood, a woman with three sons, two of whom were twins and with a very powerful 'don't mess with 'em' reputation, a husband who didn't work in any official capacity – and she had defied her whole family to marry him. All this, to my mind, was totally fascinating.

There was more. Violet told me she had split from her

family after marrying Charlie. It seemed that her mother had come to terms with it but her father could never forgive her.

'You see, I was very pretty when I was young. That's why Charlie liked me, Maureen,' she said proudly. 'These days, though, he's never here. Now weeks go by before I see him.'

That didn't sound good. It was easy to see the pretty girl she'd been, with her lovely face, strong features and thick hair. Now middle-aged spread had set in – she was as people were more or less expected to look in their fifties back then. No gyms, Botox, massages or nips and tucks. Women just looked their age, especially if they'd had a tough life.

At the end she gave me a tour of the front room, with its big dark green sofa and odd patterned wallpaper depicting birds and trees, complete with three flying ducks on the wall, a standard lamp in one corner and a little glass-fronted sideboard in the other. I commented on the ducks – you saw them in a lot of houses in those days.

'Oh, they're my three boys,' she laughed.

There were also a few reproduction pictures – landscapes, as I recall – hanging on the wall, plus a pink-tinted mirror into which Violet peered, patting her new hairdo, clearly delighted with the result.

But it was the sideboard that told me the most about this family. It was crammed with family photos which I could now examine more closely: there were Violet and

Charlie Senior looking smart and much younger, he in a slick suit, she with her wartime hairdo, two combs on either side, holding her blonde hair back. And two skinny young men in boxing gear.

'That's the twins when they was fifteen, boxing champions they was.' She gestured proudly.

The black-and-white photo didn't tell you much. But the youngsters were uncannily alike. Identical. I hadn't heard about this resemblance the twins had had when they were young.

'My God, how did you tell them apart?' I blurted out.

'Oh, sometimes I'd be the only one that could tell,' Violet told me. 'They came out ten minutes apart, Reggie first. Of course they talk the same, walk the same and they've both got the same terrible temper. And they're always fightin' each other,' she added. 'But they're very close. They stick together. They're very good to me. I don't go out much with their dad but the boys take me out sometimes. One day you'll have to come with us, Maureen.'

By now I should have been halfway back to Camden. I was already cutting it fine timewise. But it was difficult to tear myself away. I was fascinated by everything I'd learned about this household. I was definitely ready to know more.

'Have they all got tempers, then?' I enquired, thinking of the Flanagan men and their shared fighting spirit.

'No. Charlie was always quieter. No trouble – ever,' she

24

said matter-of-factly. It crossed my mind briefly that if you did have a row with one of these twins you wouldn't know which one it was, anyway. Confusing, to say the least. Let alone dangerous.

Violet didn't attempt to show me round the rest of the house – people wouldn't back then – and anyway, upstairs consisted of just three rooms, two bedrooms and one which was, I gleaned later, effectively the twins' operational base, the room they used for business meetings. Three hours had flown past so quickly and already I had begun to be drawn willingly into the lives of the inhabitants of this house.

Of course I wanted the extra cash for doing Violet's hair. It'd be useful for buying that new three-piece suite on the HP, from the furniture shop at the Nag's Head. But if, as I'd heard, these twins were ''ard bastards', Violet was right to be very careful what she said and to whom. It wasn't rocket science to work that one out. Yet I realised straight away that she trusted me, a virtual stranger, to talk to. She needed it in a house that was essentially dominated by men's needs. And, from what she'd been saying, she adored her three sons.

In the kitchen Violet took out her purse and handed me the seven and six. We arranged my next visit for the following week, when I promised to bleach and trim her hair. I'd done lots of people's hair over the years at the salon, but as I left it occurred to me that my new client was definitely one of the nicest women I'd ever come across.

Most of the people I visited for home hairdos were friendly: cups of tea and, yes, sometimes there were confidences exchanged about family or secret woes. That, I'd known for ages, was just part of hairdressing.

But somehow, I thought, as I drove away from the East End, this woman was quite different from the rest. Though I couldn't then have put my finger exactly on why the house at Vallance Road held so much attraction for me.

That afternoon, I was a newly married girl who firmly believed that her destiny was already mapped out: in time I'd be a housewife with a couple of kids, doing a bit of part-time work as a travelling hairdresser, fitting everything in around the needs of my husband and children. At that point, even the idea of switching to another kind of job would have been unthinkable to me.

But my future – and the fate of the family at Vallance Road – were destined to be totally different from anything that any of us could have predicted back then. I would go on to share some small part of Vi and her family's good times. But that wouldn't last and afterwards I would bear witness to much of the heartbreak that would come to dominate all their lives. Especially the life of the smiling, friendly woman who was positioned at the very centre of it all . . .

Chapter 3

Raising the twins

The following week, purely on impulse, I bought Mrs Kray a little bunch of flowers from a florist in Holloway and put it alongside my hairdressing bag on the back seat of the Mini. As we stood in the kitchen at No. 178, Violet pouring water into a vase, clearly delighted with my offering, the kitchen door swung open and a man in a beautifully cut Italian suit walked in. He was a bit surprised, to say the least, to see an unknown woman standing there with his mum, holding flowers.

I knew who it was so I introduced myself.

'I'm Maureen. I'm doing your mum's hair,' I said, teasing. 'You must be Charlie. Your mum's told me all about you.'

'Didn't know you 'ad your own 'airdresser now, mum,' the man said cheerfully, flashing me a wonderful smile.

'We've bin tryin' it out, Charlie,' said Vi, not noticing our familiarity. 'You know 'ow fed up I get with all those

27

people asking me questions about the boys and Maureen don't mind comin' round on 'er day off work,' she told him, reaching out to fill the kettle.

'Wanna cuppa?'

'No, thanks, mum. I've got someone waitin' outside in the car,' he said, still smiling at me. 'Just wanted to make sure you was all right.'

'So,' he said, turning to me. 'We'll be seeing you again, Maureen, right?'

'Looks like it, Charlie,' I told him, already quite smitten with this charming blue-eyed Kray who looked like his mum.

'OK, mum, I'm off,' he said, giving her a swift but warm hug. 'See ya, Maureen!' And off he went through the front door.

I couldn't help it. I had to say something.

'Your eldest boy's gorgeous, Vi,' I told her.

It was true. Charlie Kray, at that point in his mid-thirties, was jaw-droppingly good-looking. He was tall, immaculate, with a lovely build and wavy blond hair. He reminded me of a younger version of Burt Lancaster, a very big movie star of the 1950s. He was what we called a head-turner.

Vi had already told me that he'd been married to a woman called Dolly for thirteen years and that they had a nine-year-old son, Gary, Vi's only grandchild, on whom she doted.

'Charlie's always been a good boy,' she said. But that

was it. There was no mistaking the genuine warmth between mother and son but you could tell that Vi had other things on her mind that she wanted to talk about. Whilst I could have talked about Charlie till the cows came home, Vi just wanted to talk about her number one topic of interest: The Other Two – or The Two Ones, as the twins were sometimes called by their family.

That day, over the rollers and hairpins, she told me all about the twins' childhood. Apparently they had started earning a reputation quite early on in their life. Local notoriety had started in their early teens, when it looked like they might be professional boxers. (They could have been, had it not been for brushes with the law for serious street fighting, which the boxing authorities weren't too keen on.)

'I always thought Reggie'd be a famous boxer,' Vi told me wistfully. 'My Ron was a slugger but Reg had the way with him not to lose his temper in the ring.' They could have been world-famous boxers. It wasn't just Vi who thought that – everyone always used to say what a shame it was that they didn't continue with the boxing.

I always got the impression that if Violet doted on one twin more than the other, then that was definitely Ronnie. And that day, sure enough, she told me what had happened to her Ronnie. When he'd been about three years old she had nearly lost him to a grave illness. And this brush with death, it turned out, had made a huge impact on all their relationships afterwards.

At the time both boys had contracted diphtheria, though Vi didn't know it at first.

'Ron was burnin' up, crying, wouldn't eat, we didn' know what to do. In the end we took Ron to the hospital. 'E was in a terrible state.'

At the hospital little Ron was crying for his twin until Rose, Violet's sister, arrived with an ailing Reggie. He too was now getting worse. Until Reggie arrived, Violet told me, Ron wasn't getting much attention from the doctors. But at that point, seeing these very poorly identical twins brought on a swift change of attitude.

Soon there were three doctors by the twins' beds. That was when Mrs Kray learned that the twins had caught diphtheria, a highly contagious respiratory infection that is now rare but was often fatal during the 1930s.

'The best thing you can do, Mrs Kray, is leave them with us and go home,' she was told by the doctors.

'I wasn't going to leave my boys, ' Violet recalled. 'No way would I leave 'em with them doctors.'

One, two, three doctors at the twins' bedside, yet she'd stayed put by the bed. She obviously didn't care about the normal code of behaviour. In the 1930s, most people, especially working-class families, put all their trust in doctors. Doctors were high-ranking people, way above 'ordinary' folk on the social scale and the class divide was still very rigid then. So if a doctor said 'go home' you did it: you didn't dare question their authority. They knew best, didn't they?

But Violet just wouldn't leave that hospital. There she remained through the night. She told me that she had 'a feeling' that something dreadful would have happened to the twins if she had left. Violet said that she had part-gypsy blood and she often 'saw' things, just like her mother: her family, the Lees, she told me, were quite psychic.

By the following day, Reggie had improved a great deal and was taken back home by Rose.

But things were not going the same way for poorly little Ron. He was hallucinating, crying, pining for his brother, so Violet thought.

'He desperately wanted his twin close by, Maureen. Until then, the twins had never been separated.' Later that day, one of the doctors called Violet into an anteroom to tell her that he was sorry but that her son was getting worse. There was nothing more they could do for Ronnie.

Violet had already made her decision. If they couldn't do anything, she could.

'I'm taking my son home,' she told the bemused doctor. 'He needs his mother and his brother. I'm taking 'im now.'

The doctors, of course, insisted that she was wrong but Violet wouldn't hear of it. Undaunted, she picked up her son, bravely wrapped him up as well as she could and walked home to Vallance Road with him in her arms. Once home, she put him straight into bed next to Reg. Immediately, she sensed that he had settled a little bit.

'You see?' she told her sister Rose. 'That's what he wanted: his twin.'

Another sleepless night followed where Violet sat up all night watching over her boys. Yet within a couple of days the improvement was visible. Vi's old Granddad Lee came round to take Reggie for a while – but Reggie started crying. He wouldn't leave his twin on his own.

Violet Kray's life, you could tell, was marked dramatically by this event. She had obviously been scared witless at the thought of losing the twins, so much so that I got the impression that had she lost them she'd have wanted to do away with herself.

'Oh, I couldn't live without 'em,' she said more than once when reminiscing to me about their early years. 'I was the proudest woman in the East End when they were born.'

As they got a bit older, she continued to telling me, they could be obsessively jealous of each other. There'd be rows at the dinner table over the smallest things. Like the shelled peas, for example. I was intrigued.

'Reg would count the peas on his plate. And the peas on his twin's plate,' Violet said. '"Mum, he's got twelve and I've got ten," he'd shout, and when I ignored them he'd kick up a terrible stink.

'"Oh shut up, Reg, don't be such a baby," Charlie would say.

'But then Reg'd keep going on about it. So I'd have to go and get him the extra peas, exactly the same as his brother, no more, no less.'

There was, I learned, an uncannily eerie aspect to their twinship.

'If one would come in from boxing out in the garden and say: "I've got an earache," then the other would come in a bit later, saying exactly the same thing.'

Twins, in the era before fertility drugs, weren't that commonplace so people didn't know very much about the similarities between them. But it was the attention that Violet obviously lavished on the twins – and the way in which Charlie tended to be excluded because they were so demanding – that struck me most of all.

Vi explained how bad it could get: 'The minute I'd show little Charlie any attention at all, the twins would just plonk themselves down in a chair, either side of me, like two little guards. They didn't want anyone, whoever it was, to have any of my attention.'

That's what they were like. Everyone except their mother was an outcast as far as they were concerned, it seemed.

You can't help but make comparisons with your own life when people tell you their stories. Violet's stories of the twins' childhood and her fascination with them led me to think about my mum and how she loved all three of us: me, my brother Leo and my sister Iris – all equally. There weren't any favourites in our house. When Violet told me all this I understood perfectly who the favourites were in 178 Vallance Road. Whenever the subject of her children came up – as it did, of course, frequently – it was always the same: a brief mention of Charlie, then she'd go on and on endlessly about 'my Ron' and 'my Reg', kings of their little domain.

Reg, she said that day, was always 'very clever'.

'But after the diphtheria got him, I always made a bit more fuss of my Ron.'

What Violet failed to tell me then was that in his twenties Ron's uncontrollable paranoia and scary violent outbursts had led to him being sectioned and certified insane. At the time the doctors had said he was a paranoid schizophrenic, someone who needed medication at all times to control the frenzy and keep him stable. So there had been something wrong with Ron since the battle with diphtheria. Yet to Violet, her son had merely been very ill and it had left him with a weakness that had affected his behaviour later on.

I don't think Violet ever really thought that Ron was insane. Or perhaps she successfully convinced herself that this was not the case. Her view was that no one really understood him because they didn't know what had happened to him when he'd been a tiny tot.

Later, when I knew them all much better, I'd often hear Charlie refer to Ron by saying: 'Well, you know 'e's not well, mum.'

The answer was always the same.

'Yes, well, it comes from when 'e was a baby,' Violet would retort. She was an old-fashioned mum, making excuses for her son's behaviour. It wasn't madness to her. It was just his temper.

This woman, whom I really liked, and who so worshipped these twins, fascinated me and I wanted to know more about how they felt about their mother. Were they like Charlie, nice and gentle to her? Or did they behave like the tough, hard men I'd heard about?

The stories I'd heard about them were legion. Some quite scary, yet I really wanted to meet these two men. I'd never known any family like this. The Flanagans, for all their fighting, seemed quite dull compared with this family at Vallance Road.

I only had to wait till the following week to meet them, the week I'd arranged to do Vi's roots. She wanted me over much later, around five p.m. I got there just before that time and immediately set to work. In the kitchen, with my kit on the table, I started working quickly: it didn't take long to mix up the peroxide solution and get started on bleaching her roots with the toothbrush that I always used for such sessions. Then, once the bleach was on, we stopped briefly for our usual cuppa.

'You'll be meeting the boys today,' Violet announced proudly. 'They'll be in for their cup of tea, and their clean shirts.' She trailed off as if she was ticking off things that she had to do.

Hanging by the dozen in the same place as when I'd seen them on my first day were the shirts. They were a permanent feature of the house at Vallance Road: white, crisp, washed to perfection, beautifully starched and ironed, they always festooned the kitchen and the hallway, waiting, like priest's robes, for the twins to religiously don them when they came home in the early evening to change.

They had an unchanging routine: out and about during the day, slickly suited and booted, coming home to change into fresh clean shirts and another smart suit early every evening. Two freshly pressed suits, four clean shirts every single day of the year. I never saw any sign of Vi producing these laundered clean shirts for their dad: I figured he must have had his own routine, what with him being away so much.

'I don't know any woman that does more shirts than me, Maureen. Sundays I'm doing them all the time,' she'd told me cheerfully.

And that, for Violet, was an expression of her undying love: constantly replenishing the boys' endless supply of clean ironed whites. A one-woman Chinese laundry – no washing machines back then – for two men approaching thirty whose crisp whites would sometimes wind up bearing the marks of their chosen career: stained blood red from the punishing violence they doled out to others.

I would never dream of talking to Violet about the stories and rumours I often heard about the twins' brutal fights with those who had crossed them. But it was pretty obvious that those sparkling white shirts didn't stay that way all the time.

Yet their proud mum, blind to such vices, never saw the bloodstains because the boys, ever concerned about upsetting her, were cunning to a fault. They'd never dream to give her any nasty ones to wash, craftily making sure that any stained clothing was left in the various 'safe' houses or flats they had dotted all over the place; places or homes where their trusted associates could be relied on to keep shtum. The twins would change there if they had a spot of blood on their shirt. At some houses they kept more shirts and even spare shoes.

I found all this out later on. Even when a puzzled Violet would notice that the twins' laundry was 'missing' a shirt here or there, she didn't choose to connect the disappearance with any kind of trouble or interrogate the boys. The more I got to know her, I realised that even if she did discover the occasional shirt with a telltale red dot on it, such was her devotion that she'd shrug it off and say that she had to get rid of a few shirts because there were stains 'the boys must have had another fight.'

'Mum!' came the voice in the hallway.

'Oh, that's Reg.' Violet smiled – the twins' voices were similar but she knew the difference between them.

And there he was, at the kitchen door and, just like

Charlie, he was taken aback to see a strange young woman with platinum hair sitting in his kitchen.

By the way everyone went on about them, you would have imagined the twins to be giants, at least six-footers. So it was a bit of a shock to see that, in the flesh, Reg Kray was of only average height, around five foot nine inches, very well built and with sleek dark hair, a bit gypsy-looking. Yet the man definitely had presence, an aura about him. He held himself like someone who understood that he was special. He didn't strike me as someone scary.

To me, he was an attractive man in his late twenties. He was an immaculately dressed man whom many women would go for. Even if you hadn't heard about the violence, mind you, there was still a hint of something quite sinister about Reggie Kray. But it was just a hint. You couldn't quite put your finger on it.

As he entered the kitchen, my first thought was that he was rather handsome. Sharp suit, white shirt, neatly knotted tie – what's he need to change for? I wondered.

'Who's this?' he said. His voice was very quiet and low.

'This is Maureen – she's doing my hair now. She's a friend of Charlie's.'

Of course, Violet had to get that in quick. She was careful: the twins didn't want any strangers in their house, hanging around their mum, asking nosy questions. Violet knew that. What's that saying from the war: careless talk costs lives?

'Want tea?' she asked, changing the subject quickly.

'Nothing to eat. I'm meeting Ron, I just wanna wash and change.'

Then he sat down at the kitchen table as Violet jumped up to boil the kettle for his cuppa. The stranger had to be interrogated.

'So . . . where do you live?' he asked slowly.

'Camden Town. I'm married. And I think you know my brothers-in-law, they're identical twins too,' I blurted out, hoping to hide my nerves.

Reg had black hair, combed back, and a prominent nose. But it was the eyes that held you, dark brown, not hazel, an intense, penetrating stare. You couldn't look away.

It was most unusual.

'Identical? I don't think so. Not like us.'

'Yes, they're identical too,' I said, pleased that I could hold my own.

'What's their name?' he continued, still holding his gaze.

'I'm married to Patrick. Patrick Flanagan,' I told him, 'but his twin brothers are called Noel and Chris Flanagan,' knowing full well he'd know who they were.

Whatever these men thought of each other, they all knew exactly who the other gangs were, where they hung out. Provided every gang stuck to their patch or territory it was fine. Cross borders, however, and there could be serious problems.

'Oh yes, I know those twins. Met them in a club in Highbury once.'

Well, that was news to me. Noel hadn't said that they'd actually met the twins. I figured it was 'business'. But I wasn't going to say so.

Then he frowned. His eyebrows knitted. A quizzical look, one that I came to know so well, as if he was trying to work you out, wondering how useful you'd be, followed by another barrage of questions.

'Where does he live, that twin of yours?'

I told him.

'What does he do?'

'Oh, a bit of wheelin' and dealin',' I said and laughed.

Reg laughed too. He knew perfectly well that he wasn't a bank manager or clerk.

'Are you a hairdresser, then?' He seemed to ease off at this point.

'Well, I was until I was nineteen, but now I do it in people's homes. I've been here twice, haven't I, Violet?' I said, looking to bring her into our conversation.

Violet merely nodded, placing the cup of tea before Reg, not wishing to interrupt The One With The Brains as she regularly referred to him.

'You've met Charlie, then?' he said, looking up at Violet as if to say thank you.

'Yes, I've met the handsome Charlie,' I quipped, trying to keep it light.

'Well, I'm handsome, aren't I?' Reg said without a trace of humour.

'Yeah, but he's more handsome!' I told him.

He didn't seem to get that, either.

Maybe he wasn't accustomed to women actually saying out loud what they preferred but it didn't seem to bother him that much.

''Ave you seen Ron? Is he coming?' Violet interrupted, sensing the tension.

'No,' Reg said, offering me a cigarette from his pack of Players. I shook my head.

'That's good – you don't smoke,' he said, lighting up and finishing his cup of tea.

Getting up to go upstairs, he turned to his mum. 'Ain't she got lovely blonde hair, mum?'

'See, you're into blondes as well!' I said, nipping in smartly.

I got a half-grin. His older brother Charlie would have turned it all into a joke, would've had everyone chuckling: 'blondes, brunettes, love 'em all' or some such nonsense. But this Kray boy was quieter, he wasn't that congenial. Well, not in his mum's domain, anyway. Politely, he asked Violet what she'd been doing all day.

'Shopping,' she said. 'I bought some nice ham and cheese if you want something to eat. Make it in a minute.'

No, Reg said again, he really didn't want anything. He excused himself and went upstairs while I started to wash the bleach off Vi's hair. About twenty minutes later, as the rollers were going in, he strolled into the kitchen again, looking like the immaculately clad, slick club owner that he was at that time. He'd changed his tie as well as his suit, I noticed. Talk about fussy.

'I'm off, then, mum. See you again, Maureen,' said Reg.

'You definitely will. Your mum wants me to come every week,' I warned him, not sure how much Violet had told them about our new arrangement.

'Well, mum, it's a bit of company for you, eh? You've made a new friend,' he said as he briefly pecked her on the cheek before heading for the door with what was always his farewell riposte: 'I'll be very late, mum, but don't worry.'

Phew. I'd definitely got the seal of approval as the new friend. And this was the clever one who could have been a champion boxer. One thing I did notice was that he had beautiful hands. Not a boxer's hands at all. They were slim, well-shaped, sinewy hands – strong, too. They weren't bruiser's hands at all. And he wasn't at all what I had expected. Vaguely, I'd imagined that he'd be one of those cheeky chappies, all 'Allo, darlin', maybe a bit flirtatious, quite friendly in a lively cockney way.

Not Reggie. This man was well mannered, softly spoken and courteous, but there was no indication that he was flirting with you. He seemed quite detached, perhaps even a little calculating or a bit edgy. But he was incredibly polite. I'd spotted that he'd even picked up his cup and saucer from the table and placed it carefully by the sink. Once he'd stubbed out his ciggy, he'd thoughtfully removed the ashtray from the table too. A careful man. The good manners impressed me, to tell the truth, especially after all the stories from the pubs and the neighbourhoods. I thought our first meeting had gone quite well.

Yet Mrs Kray obviously thought I'd gone too far.

'Oo, what about when you said Charlie was more 'andsome. 'E didn't like that, Maureen,' she warned me.

'Well, to me he is.' I said always determined to hold my own.

'Wait until you see Ron.'

The Favourite – she obviously thought he was even more desirable than Reggie and Charlie. I wondered if she was right. But it didn't matter to me. I was glad I'd got the nod because I was really enjoying my new Thursday job.

It was to be another few weeks before I got to meet the two twins together.

I'd just finished washing Violet's hair when the kitchen door opened and there they were, accompanied by another man, a blond guy who they politely introduced by his full name.

'This is Ronnie Bender. He's our driver.' (When I knew them better I discovered that Ron didn't even have a licence and Reg was such a terrible driver that they had both been using drivers for years – it helped enhance their image to be driven around by a chauffeur, of course.)

The three men were all slickly dressed. But when you saw the twins side by side you had to do a double take. They'd been identical as youngsters but now there were obvious facial differences: Ron was much fleshier, not as physically fit-looking as his twin, though they still were astonishingly alike. Like two peas in a pod. But whereas Reg's physical presence and manner only hinted vaguely at something sinister, Ron's appearance told you straight away that he could be a threat to any equilibrium. His eyes bulged slightly. Ron Kray, everyone had said, was the more fearsome twin. That was true. Just like his twin, he had that aura of being different, set apart from other men. Yet actual menace positively oozed from this twin.

'This is Maureen,' Reg said to his sibling. 'Mum's 'airdresser. Married to a Flanagan. You know, those twins we met at 'Ighbury.'

'Oh yeah, I remember,' said Ron, sitting down at the kitchen table. His voice too was quiet, but he spoke slowly, very sombre. Then the kettle went on, Ronnie Bender left and Violet served the tea with a big plate of Crawford's Custard Creams, Ronnie's favourites.

I was ready to start her hair but then Violet went into fussy mode around the kitchen. Did Ron want a suit laid out upstairs? Where had they been, what time were they going out again? Silly little inconsequential questions. It was like she was desperate to start a conversation.

Ron wasn't in the mood. He gave either one- or two-word answers, short and simple. He preferred to just sit there, staring at me. The same penetrating dark-eyed stare as his twin's. With a far more obviously unnerving look. Why didn't he just go upstairs and let me get on with what I was there to do? It was deeply unsettling. Finally, Violet sat down beside me and I could start with the pins and rollers. I felt relieved, hoping this would stop the questions. But Ron wanted answers.

'Oh, you bring your own gear, then? Do you do this for a lot of people?'

'Yes, I'm what they call a travelling hairdresser,' I said nervously, putting in the first pin.

'You should be a model,' said Ronnie out of the blue. I wasn't expecting that sort of personal remark at all. And it definitely wasn't flirting.

'We can 'elp you. We know lots of photographers, don't we, Reg?'

Reg merely nodded. He was taking it all in, too. Maybe he was as surprised as me at the comment but he didn't show it.

'Well,' I started, 'it has been said before—'

Ron cut me short. 'You should do it,' he said.

He wasn't making a polite suggestion. Ronnie Kray had decided. He was telling me what I should do.

Therefore I should obey him. Go and do it.

'Oo, Ron, I don't wanna lose me 'airdresser,' Violet chipped in.

'Nah, she should do it,' he persisted.

Then, thankfully, just as quickly as it had started the conversation switched away from my future as a model. More questions from Ron, though, one after the other. I was being grilled as though I was being given the job interview from hell. But I found that somehow I could hold my own.

Did I ever go out for an evening with my husband? Would I like to go over to his club?

I nodded and agreed with what Ronnie was saying. But I knew I could hardly go home and tell Patrick: 'Hey, guess what? Ronnie Kray wants you and me to go to his club.' I didn't care to think about what the reaction would be. So Patrick and our respective families remained blissfully ignorant about my new hairdressing client.

'When my husband gets home from work, he just wants to stay in,' I said somewhat weakly.

'What's he do, then?'

'He's in asphalting – his family is Irish.'

'Are YOU Irish, then?' Ron had to know.

'No, my dad was. He was a professional dancer in Ireland. But he died on my fifteenth birthday.'

And so the interrogation, worthy of MI5, went on. Did I have any brothers or sisters? What did they do? Where did I come from? It wasn't from the East End, was it?

'No, I don't really know the East End. I'm from Islington.' I told them a bit of my story. 'I was born in Hemel Hempstead where my mum had been evacuated in the war. I went to a convent school up in Holloway.'

'A convent? What, with nuns 'n' everything?' said Ronnie, visibly impressed. Oh, so I wasn't just some silly hairdresser. I'd had nuns to teach me. That, it seemed, made me a cut above the rest in his eyes.

'Yes, the nuns were our teachers. But, as I said, I had to leave at fifteen,' I told him.

Then Ronnie harked back to my in-laws.

'Do you get on with your in-laws, then?'

'Oh yes, they love me.' I laughed as I said this. It was true to a certain extent.

Then, somewhat unnerved by all this, I started telling him how they were always fighting each other.

Bewilderingly, Ron started laughing. I'd obviously amused him and in a flash I twigged. It was the violence. This was Ron's kind of entertainment.

If I thought that The One With The Brains was inquisitive, his twin was doubly so.

He wanted to know everything. That was how it was with them, right from day one. There was, I came to understand, a motive behind every single question. They weren't just making polite chit-chat or even just being friendly.

Information, to them, was power. The twins would store the tiniest, seemingly inconsequential bit of conversation in their minds, like they were living computers. I had no idea that this relentless questioning, endlessly using their own 'spy network' of informers and tipsters, was an important aspect of running their criminal activity and maintaining their reputation as the East End's most vicious hard men.

For the Krays, this desire for more information wasn't anything to do with knowledge for its own sake. The more they knew, the better they could operate. Knives, guns, fists were their weapons. But, in a sense, this endless desire to know everything was equally useful to them.

Many people tend to forget half of what they're told. Not these two. They would remember everything. And, as I found out eventually, they had to be informed of everything at all times. All their lives it would be like this. Who drove that car? Who is so-and-so's brother? How much money is that one making? It never stopped – they could be very manipulative.

My brothers-in-law were scallywags; Ron Kray and most of Finsbury Park knew that already. The interrogation of their mother's hairdresser had a real motive: to try to weasel out more about what was going on with the Flanagan Twins, store it all up. Just in case there was money to be made off the back of whatever the Flanagans were doing.

Both twins could stare at you and damage your equilibrium, particularly if you were a nervous type of person. Ronnie's 'look' was terrifying to those who already knew his reputation for unpredictable violence. It might seem odd to say it, but all this still didn't really unnerve me. I understood what it was all about. I could see I had to keep these guys in the loop. Whatever the question, in the end it was all about them, and how it related to their world. It was nothing personal, just business, and I had to comply.

My grilling over, they both trooped upstairs to ready

themselves for the night ahead. More preening, smoothing on of Brylcreem, careful knotting of expensive silk ties, fixing their chunky gold cufflinks, changing their highly polished footwear. They lived in one of London's most deprived and bombed-out areas. The evidence of grim poverty, tough living, was all around them. Yet they dressed and carried themselves like princes. Or, better yet, movie stars.

Later on, Violet would tell me, with a great deal of pride, how the twins were 'friends' with the famous people who came to their clubs, glamorous women like Judy Garland, Barbara Windsor, Diana Dors. How the twins delighted in introducing these rich and famous people to their mum, even bringing one or two round to meet her at Vallance Road. Their celebrity locally knew no bounds. Violet even kept scrap books of all their press cuttings, the stories about their donations to local charities and their court appearances on various charges for crimes they'd been accused of – yet, as Violet mentioned, they frequently managed to walk free.

I finished drying Vi's hair and just as I was starting the comb-out the twins' driver, Ronnie, came back to collect them.

'See you, mum,' they said through the open door, smiling at me. And off they went, suited and booted, into the night.

'Don't they look lovely?' their mum sighed as the door closed.

'So smart,' I commented.

Well, it's mostly because you're washing and ironing for them all the time, I thought to myself. I couldn't exactly bring myself to disagree with her.

'Lovely-looking' might have described their older brother Charlie back then but you couldn't use the 'lovely' word in connection with these immaculate twins with their penetrating stares and their barrage of questions. Unusual. Unnerving. Even fascinating. But definitely not lovely.

Up to that point, I'd said nothing to anyone about my visits to Vallance Road, not even to my own mother, who would have worried – and would've wanted to know why I hadn't told Patrick.

But I was bursting to tell someone about it all so the next time I saw her I told Iris, my closest girlfriend who was also married, how I'd met the three Kray brothers. She'd been my bridesmaid. We'd gone to Sunday School together. I knew she'd never tell anyone, not even her husband.

Iris's reaction was predictable. She thought I was risking far too much by just being around that house.

'What's going to happen when Patrick finds out?' she asked. 'You're gonna be in real trouble if he finds out.'

I fancied my chances. 'He's not going to find out, is he?' I snapped back.

Iris clammed up then. She was determined to keep well

out of it. She'd heard all the stories about the Kray Twins.

Of course I knew it was risky for me to keep going to the house behind my husband's back. It wasn't as if I didn't know how Patrick's Flanagan temper could erupt over relatively minor things. But I was a headstrong girl back then and, anyway, I liked Mrs Kray a lot. She was such a cheerful, happy person to be around.

Sometimes I'd arrive at the house to hear the radio playing at full volume and Vi singing her heart out to whatever was playing.

Matt Monro's song 'Portrait of My Love' was one of many favourites at the time. Vi was a big Matt Monro fan. He too was an East Ender who'd found fame and fortune beyond the bombed-out streets of Shoreditch. Vi identified with all this because her twins, I realised, had shown that East Enders could rise up from the grime, make an impact in that world, cleave a path to successful, comfortable living. I guess she was right in a way. It's called aspiration nowadays. You hear it all the time. But back then, in Bethnal Green, it wasn't a word that most people would recognise.

I was living dangerously by not telling Patrick and I knew it. Yet I told myself that Vi would be upset or disappointed if I suddenly told her that I couldn't do her hair any more. But really, that was just me finding a justification for what I was doing. The truth was that I just wanted to continue this relationship.

Looking back, I can see that right then there was

something else going on with me. Without even realising it, by deceiving my husband I was feeling my way towards some kind of independence.

Very slowly, through my weekly visits and chats with Violet, I was starting to think differently about myself. It didn't happen overnight and it wasn't entirely born out of Ron's comments but at that point I was beginning, gradually, to feel that modelling might possibly be an option for me – and I desired it, mostly in secret.

I knew too that my husband wouldn't be too pleased about my huge ambition. Patrick hated change. Patrick hadn't grown up in a world used to change. Liberated women weren't exactly running up and down the streets of London then. He knew where I was, what I was doing, most of the time, and that was how he wanted it to stay.

So I just thought I won't say a word to him about Vallance Road. I'll just leave it like that. For now . . .

Chapter 4

The lost baby

I must have been to the house in Vallance Road about half a dozen times before I finally met Charlie Senior. By then, I'd told Violet a great deal about my marriage. Patrick had been my second boyfriend, one of the big Holloway Road crowd I used to hang out with at the famous Royal Dance Hall in Tottenham when I was seventeen and mad about jiving and rock 'n' roll. He was the most popular one in his crowd, a bit of a hard man, three years older than me. We courted for about a year, then we got engaged and by the time I was twenty I was married.

Of course, in those days you had no idea what sort of man you'd signed up with until you actually tied the knot. Young couples like us didn't live together beforehand or go away on weekends or sleep together. We weren't practising Catholics or anything but Patrick not only expected a virgin bride, he wanted a wife who obeyed her husband, who did as she was told. He was very traditional.

As a fiancé, Patrick had been warm and loving, yet

once domesticity set in I soon discovered that he had a terrible temper. Which was bad news because I wasn't Miss Mouse in any way – I'd argue back all the time. So the rows and the shouting started in our first year of marriage. Socially, he didn't trust me and he didn't trust other men. I was a bit of a flirt – it came naturally to me – but it was totally harmless. I wasn't going to run off with anyone. Alas, Patrick could never see it that way. So it was a relief to be able to open up to Vi about all this. My mum and my sister knew some of it, but I didn't tell them everything, not even when he lost his temper and I'd fight back. It wasn't exactly a happy situation.

Naturally, in turn Vi talked at length about her marriage. She too had married a man with a ferocious temper. This was Charlie Senior.

'But he's not a fighter, Maureen, he's a worker. Hardly ever here. Doesn't like to be here when the boys are here. When they were small,' she said, 'they didn't see him much. He gave them a few wallops when they were very young but, now they're grown up, I think they still remember what he did to me,' she continued. 'The truth is he'd given me "a few wallops" several times.

'There'd been bad times when my sisters had to come round to intervene, put a stop to it. Yet once the boys were teenagers, things changed and he stopped. Because Ronnie caught him one day. Ron was upstairs but Charlie Senior didn't know 'e was there. So 'e 'ad me pinned against the wall and started 'ittin' me, layin' into me, because I'd said 'e'd 'ave to wait a bit for 'is dinner to warm up.

'I must've been yellin' out really loud because Ron 'eard the racket, came runnin' down the stairs and pulled 'is dad off me.

'Got 'old of him by the scruff of the neck and said: "If you EVER touch our mother again, I'm gonna KILL you!"'

(For some reason, the twins always said 'our mother,' not 'my mum'.)

Vi told me that Ron had made extra sure that Charlie Senior knew precisely what he was up against.

'That goes for BOTH of us,' he'd snarled at his dad. 'Either one of us will kill you 'cos I'm gonna tell Reggie about it.'

In my mind I was thinking, how could anyone want to hit such a lovely, kind woman? But then again, I had friends I'd worked with whose husbands weren't at all reluctant to raise their fists against their wives. A couple of times I'd had to go round to friends' homes to calm things down. After all, I wasn't a stranger to all this.

Violet said she'd tried to protect the twins from Charlie Senior's violence when they'd been small, but he'd been 'walloping' *her* quite a lot. Strangely, it always tended to happen after Charlie Senior had been away for some time.

'But he was a good worker,' she told me. 'We was never hungry. There was always food in the house.' And that was the way it was for many families back then.

You couldn't help but feel sorry for her. She lived for her family, kept the home spotless, and adored her boys. Yet she was with a man who'd walk through the door and start hitting her if his meal wasn't on the table straight away. Then off he'd go again.

Growing up, Violet said, she'd had a very strict father. When the family sat round the table, no one could eat until he'd carved the meat up. That sounded so typical of the times. The woman served, the man carved. That was all they did, carve the meat. So young, pretty Violet had run away from home and her strict dad to be with Charlie – who turned out to be even stricter!

One weekend – it wasn't a hairdo day – I'd driven to Bethnal Green on the Saturday afternoon to have a wander round the market stalls. I decided, on the spur of the moment, to pop round to see Violet.

I knocked on the door and there he was. Charlie Senior opened the door. The first thing I noticed was the twins' resemblance to him, especially Ronnie. Dark staring eyes. No smile. Dark, smoothed-back hair, lots of Brylcreem, just like the twins, darkish skin like he'd been out in the sun. Wearing just a shirt and trousers, definitely in for the day.

'Yes?' he snapped.

'Oh, you must be Mr Kray – is Violet in?' I asked timidly.

'Who are you?' he rasped.

'I'm Maureen, Mrs Kray's hairdresser. She knows me.'

Then Violet called out, all warm and friendly. 'Come in, Maureen!'

She was delighted to see me and she quickly put the kettle on and got the biscuits out.

Charlie Senior still had a sour look on his face. He made no attempt to brighten up and engage with his wife. He was definitely not happy to see me. The twins, I reflected, were more like their dad physically. Their older brother took after their mum.

We talked for a bit, all together round the dining table. Charlie too was surprised to learn that I wasn't an East Ender. From that point on, however, he became quite talkative. When I mentioned that I'd married into a family of 'naughty' brothers he made a curt but pointed comment.

'Hm. We've got a couple of them 'ere.' Then he laughed, in an unmistakably sarcastic way.

Like his sons he too was very inquisitive about me and my background. But then again, I thought, if he was buying and selling all the time, that kind of man can find out your life story in five minutes. It was easy to imagine him knocking on doors, conning women out of their little bit of gold or silver – if they had it. And, of course, Violet had told me how he'd gone on the run from the authorities during the war, hiding under the stairs when they'd come to the house. A deserter dad. Had I met his sons?

Yes, I'd met Charlie, I said quickly, thinking of the breezy and cheerful one.

'What about The Other Two?' he asked, surprised.

'Reg is handsome. He takes after you.' I flirted, which was wrong, of course, but I couldn't stop myself sometimes. I was still very young.

'So say you,' said Charlie the elder, looking quite annoyed.

Sometimes I was just too outspoken for my own good. He was their father and you could see that he didn't relish their reputation for being 'naughty' one bit.

I was desperate to lighten the atmosphere, so I turned to Violet.

'No one home, Vi?'

'Not till six o'clock,' she said, her usual refrain while looking up at the clock.

But Charlie hadn't quite finished questioning me. 'What car do you drive?'

'A white Mini,' I told him.

Then he got up, went outside and had a look. He came back in, not impressed at all.

'Hm. Bit small, innit?' he said as I got up and readied myself to leave.

'It's got a good boot, Mr Kray. For all my equipment,' I said chirpily, hoping for a smile.

None came. At the door, Violet pecked me on the cheek, quite apologetic for her surly old man.

'Come on Thursday as usual, Maureen?' She looked at me. 'When Old Charlie's not 'ere.' She waved me off and closed the door.

So that was Violet's husband. Definitely not the kind,

loving man she deserved. Not one pleasant word to her or to me. There was no affection in sight. But most revealing of all was that he did not like his twin sons' activities. He didn't seem to like me much, either. It helped explain a bit more about this family: why those two boys, spoilt rotten from birth, were the entire centre of their mother's universe, every hour of the day. And why her husband and her other son were never going to get a look-in. Though I could understand why she felt that way about Old Charlie, I never quite understood why she was the way she was with Charlie junior.

Weeks turned to months and Violet and I would chat in the kitchen about anything and everything: movies, music, the stars, etc. She told me more about the places where the twins would take her, not just to their own clubs but to really posh nightclubs like the Astor. Before I knew it we were like the oldest of friends. We had a warm routine and I was beginning to feel more at ease at her place and in her presence.

I hadn't mentioned it on my early visits but I suppose it was more to try to comfort myself than anything that one afternoon I found myself confiding in Violet about what had happened to me. After being married for just nine months – and just before I'd met Violet – I'd lost my first baby. I'd miscarried after about six weeks of pregnancy. It was an ectopic miscarriage and I was left devastated.

Physically, I'd bounced back but mentally I hadn't yet

got over it. I desperately wanted a little girl. Patrick fully expected us to start a family immediately, so he'd been initially upset. But, coming from such a large family, he believed that when you were young one miscarriage was a mere blip. Which turned out, in our case, to be wrong. But it still troubled me frequently, the thought of this baby that I'd never be able to cuddle and protect.

I guess I probably just needed to share it with someone other than my family, someone who understood the power of being a mum, nurturing children. But also someone who wouldn't judge me. And Violet would always listen and be sympathetic about everything. So it all came tumbling out that day: the loss, the what-ifs, all the complicated and confused feelings that miscarriage can engender. I had to let it out.

Violet said exactly what I needed to hear as she reassured me that it'd be fine, that I was young, and that there'd be another baby soon. But after a brief moment's pause to catch our breath, Violet started talking, as if she was carrying on our conversation. It was totally unexpected.

'I 'ad a little girl, Maureen,' she said very quietly, as if she didn't want anyone else to hear the story. 'She died.

'I must've been about six months into the pregnancy and Charlie was about five then. I was upstairs one afternoon on me own when it 'appened, all of a sudden, a miscarriage, there and then. Oh, it was terrible. I gave birth to a baby girl but she only lived for a couple of hours.

She didn't stand a chance. You don' expect to see your own little baby lying there in front of you, dead.' Violet trailed off as if talking to herself.

I didn't know what to say to her. What could you say? What a dreadful thing to happen to this lovely woman with the miserable, uncaring husband.

'So . . . what did you do, Vi?' I managed.

'Oh, we 'ad a proper funeral for 'er and everythin'. Violet, we called 'er.

'She was so pretty, Maureen, big dark eyes and dark hair,' she said, lowering her voice almost to a whisper. Then Vi started to rub her hand back and forth across her mouth, as if she'd said too much and she didn't dare speak of it any more.

Yet the sad, longing expression on her handsome face told you all that you needed to know. The loss of little Violet was something that Violet Kray still struggled to come to terms with.

'After I 'ad Charlie, I always used to dream about 'avin' a little girl. Just give me my little girl and I'll be 'appy, I'd say to meself when I woke up. She'd 'ave been company for me with old Charlie bein' away so much and little Charlie always runnin' in and out of the place. It would have been a perfect family.'

It was only eighteen months after the tragic miscarriage when the twins arrived. I knew that this was why the twins had become everything to Violet, had won all her time and affection. It was partly because of the little girl who'd died after only two hours of life.

Ronnie and Reggie weren't replacements, of course, but she'd certainly done everything to make the twins look and appear feminine when they were very small. She grew their hair long and dressed them in cute angora dresses, like two little bunny rabbits. As a consequence, even as babies, they drew attention wherever she took them. Right from day one, the twins were in the spotlight.

'They was like two little dolls, Maureen,' she said, brightening at the memory. 'Everyone round 'ere used to make a fuss of 'em. I'd take the pram down Bethnal Green Road and people would stop me all the time, they was so lovely. Oh, I was so proud of 'em. Ron at one end of the pram and Reg at the other.'

Of course. She'd treated the twins like small, pretty dolls in the pram, rather than baby boys, because in some way her heart was still longing for her beautiful little girl.

After Ronnie's illness, when it was obvious that he was going to be a bit slower and less confident around people than Reg, she'd doted on him even more, always fussing around him because she knew her son needed his mum very badly. Which was true – the adult Ronnie Kray was, in many ways, very fortunate that he had so much protective love and support: a mother utterly devoted to him and a twin who couldn't help but look out for him all the time. Without that kind of support, other people with

Ronnie's kind of mental-health problems could have easily wound up in the gutter, rejected by the whole world.

The more I knew her, the more I understood that she knew perfectly well, in her heart, that she hadn't given her eldest son much attention as he grew up, because the twins were so incredibly possessive around her.

I often wondered whether, had that little girl lived, Violet would have given all that love and attention to the twins? They'd have had to share their mother, in the normal way, like other kids learn to do. How different would it all have turned out if that had been the case? But, then again, she might never have had them.

But as it was, those two, they didn't want to share Violet with anyone. She was theirs and they were hers. Violet was their possession and, as twins, they were each other's possession.

Everything the two boys saw they wanted, they had to possess. And, in turn, for Violet the twins always had to come first.

As for Charlie junior, it was as if Violet knew deep down that her oldest son was a far kinder, more sympathetic person than her idolised twins.

She would sometimes say to me, 'We'll tell Charlie but we won't tell the other two,' knowing instinctively how they'd react to any situation. As for the pain of losing that little girl, it remained with her for good, as I would discover so many years on. A love unspoken and unacknowledged. Nowadays, of course, we all talk openly about emotions and feelings but for a woman of Violet Kray's generation with an unsympathetic husband who was never there, you just bore it. And kept quiet.

After that day, we never talked about the lost baby again.

Yet the twins' childhood was a topic she often returned to – for example, how she'd been called in to see the twins' teachers on several occasions because they'd been fighting in the playground with bigger, older boys. They were about seven or eight at the time.

Violet's rationale, of course, was a protective mother's interpretation of events.

Her sons weren't vicious little buggers, unafraid to take on older boys because of the sheer power of their double act. Oh no.

'It's obvious. They were being picked on because they're twins. And they're different,' she used to tell me whenever she'd recall that time.

This, sadly, would be Violet's mantra for the years ahead. It was always the other people. Never her boys.

Round about this time, the Kray stories started to spread. You'd go to parties on a Saturday night and someone would be regaling a group of people with tales about what one of the twins had done to so-and-so outside the pub. Or you'd hear nasty things that had happened at their new gambling club, Esmeralda's Barn. Some of the stories were awful: brutal slashings by Ronnie with razors, and terrible things like that. How ordinary, common people knew so much about these things I never quite understood. The Kray Twins were a scary proposition as far as most people were concerned. But still, people loved talking about them.

This made it quite difficult to maintain too many illusions about it all: the contrast between the warmth and kindness of that lovely lady in the kitchen at Vallance Road and the ugliness of what her twin boys were rumoured to be capable of. Of course, you could see that none of the violence would ever go on while their mother was around: she'd schooled them, as kids, to be polite, respectful to adults, to never fight each other – and to stick together.

They'd conveniently ignored the fighting bit, of course. Fighting each other, to the twins, was as natural as breathing. They just made sure their mother didn't see them. As for sticking together, I doubt if they'd have been any different even if she hadn't instilled that into them as kids. Maybe some identical twins don't choose to stick together. But the Krays did.

Violet always said that the reason they do and think alike was because they were one in a thousand.

'They're identical, it isn't possible for them to do things differently. The egg splits in the womb, they're one person in two bodies,' Violet would often point out.

In some ways, though, the twins were no different from other 'naughty' boys or villains of their generation. I knew that from my own experience of my husband's family.

Outside the home they'd be violent, effing and blinding, very naughty. Yet in their mother's house it was the 'not in front of mum' rule. You showed respect.

Mrs Kray didn't go out to work – she had her hands full with kitchen life and the endless washing and ironing of shirts, anyway – but Mrs Flanagan was up at dawn to scrub floors, cleaning out a couple of the cafes in the Caledonian Road before breakfast. In her sons' eyes she was the one that kept it all together.

My own mother had struggled to bring up three kids alone at the age of forty-nine. She was exactly the same, getting up early to clean out the hairdressers' salon, and she had to be back home by 7:45 a.m. to get my younger brother to school. These were tough lives. Yet as far as their children were concerned, there was always love and respect for them as mothers.

By 1962, Violet and I knew quite a lot about each other. Yet up to that point she'd never said anything about her twins' courting habits, girlfriends, things like that. Or her romantic aspirations for them. It had never come up in conversation. She'd talked about Charlie's wife, Dolly, briefly. She didn't say it in so many words but I didn't get the impression that she was crazy about Dolly. But one day, as I was trimming her hair, I learned more about Reggie's private life.

'Reggie's got a girl, she's very pretty,' she told me.

'Is she blonde?' was my typical reaction.

'No. She's got auburn hair. Everyone says she's the prettiest girl in the East End.' She said proudly, 'She's very young.' Then she trailed off before continuing.

'But he's known her a long time, she's from a family we know.'

That sounded right to me. People often went out with neighbours, boys or girls from the same street or a few streets away. Families all knew about each other.

Having met Reggie it all made sense to me.

He's the type that would have a very pretty, very young girl on his arm, I thought to myself.

She HAD to be very pretty because you could tell that Reg liked everything to be perfect. He'd always comment on what you wore – your hairstyle, earrings, your dress. But I knew he definitely wouldn't have wanted a girl who'd had a few boyfriends. I knew that because this kind of thinking was typical of my brothers-in-law. And of my husband, come to that. It was a very macho world. They didn't want the girl they were with to have been with anyone else.

That might sound funny nowadays but these men just couldn't stand the idea that another man would have had you, been intimate with you, before they came on the scene. Patrick wouldn't have even considered marrying me if I had not been a virgin. Not a chance.

One day, I went round to do Vi's hair and there the girl was, seated in the kitchen. Auburn hair, extremely pretty, a little blue dress and jacket, mesmeric big brown eyes, nice smile, trim and petite. Yes, she was immaculately turned out. Frances Shea was just as lovely as I'd been told.

At the time, she'd have been about eighteen or nineteen, fully ten years younger than Reggie. What I didn't know, because Violet had never mentioned it, was that Reggie had started courting her a few years before, but much of the courtship had been conducted from a prison cell for over eighteen months when he'd been serving a two-year sentence for his role in a protection racket. This was just before I started doing Violet's hair in 1961.

Frances, for all her beauty, seemed quite timid. We chatted briefly but you could see that she was a shy, nervous thing. At one point she got up and attempted to make us all tea while I got on with Violet's hair. She was clattering around, nervously picking things up, putting them down, frowning a little bit. She didn't seem to be in any way domesticated. Just making tea for three people was too much, it seemed. I'm not domesticated myself, you see, so that was how I knew the signs.

As I put the rollers in, I realised that Violet had also picked up this unfamiliarity with domesticity. Yet she didn't say anything to Frances or try to help her. She just let her get on with it.

By the time she'd done it and we'd all managed to have our tea, Frances relaxed a bit. She asked me where I worked, so I explained I was working in a shoe shop in the West End.

'I want to go to work,' she said wistfully, almost childlike.

'Oh, there's plenty of jobs around here – are you any good at hairdressing?' I said.

She shook her head. But before I could continue Violet cut in.

'Frances doesn't have to work,' she said, smiling at her.

Frances had been working as a bookkeeper in an office in the West End when Reggie first started courting her. But, in time, he'd managed to convince her that she didn't need to work.

Violet, of course, knew all too well her possessive son's attitude to his girlfriend going out to work and having a life independent of him. He wanted to know where Frances was every minute of the day. A job, therefore, was out of the question. She'd gone to a grammar school but, like me, had left at fifteen. She didn't speak like a typical little East End girl, didn't drop her aitches or use slang. She had a nice way of speaking. You had to like her.

But she was one of those girls who really needed drawing out. I tried my best. Did she like dancing? Me and Patrick went dancing quite a bit, to the Downbeat in Manor House or Barry's at Highbury or our original meeting place, the Tottenham Royal Dance Hall. We'd gone dancing since our courting days. He didn't jive, only liked the slow dances. But I was allowed to jive with a couple of his friends. I told her all of this. Dancing was a big part of my life then. Mrs Kray had told me that Reggie was a good dancer too – he'd even had ballroom-dancing lessons. Ron, I learned, never danced. He just sat there, watching other people dance.

Frances said she didn't really go dancing with her friends. 'Reg always took me to his club in Knightsbridge or sometimes to the posh West End clubs like the Embassy or the Astor.' It all sounded pretty upmarket and flash for a teenager from Hoxton, which was a very poor part of the East End in those days.

To break the ice, I'd already offered to put Frances's hair up when I'd done Violet's hair. I'd do a pleat, with a bun on top, which was very fashionable at the time. She seemed hesitant but she agreed. When I finished fixing it with liquid glue, I was a bit surprised at her reaction when she looked in the mirror in the front room.

'Will Reg like that?' Frances asked nervously. 'Maybe I look too old.'

'No, you look lovely,' Violet assured her.

'It's sophisticated,' I added.

It was all about Reg. It didn't matter whether she liked it or not. Reg had to approve.

I only got to see Frances a few more times after that first meeting. The next time I saw her at Vallance Road, in the kitchen, she was a bit more forthcoming.

'I had an argument with Reg yesterday,' she told me and Violet.

They were going out to a movie when Reg had phoned Ronnie and Frances overheard him telling Ron he was taking her to the cinema that night.

Ronnie's reaction was extreme, to say the least. He went potty.

'He was screaming so loud, you could hear him down the line of the telephone,' she told us.

Then, she said, Reg had slammed the phone down. Relieved, she got her coat on. They'd go to the cinema, whatever Ron thought.

But for what would prove to be the umpteenth time, the bond of twinship triumphed.

'I'd better go to see Ron,' Reg told his girlfriend. 'No telling what he might do if I'm not there.'

'It's like blackmail,' Frances said sadly. You could see how much this row had upset her. 'He knows Reg won't let him down.' She tried to explain it all somehow.

'Don't worry,' Violet said, anxious to make it right. 'They have to go to their clubs or they won't have any money.'

She was being naive, really. No one knew exactly what kind of money the twins were earning by then – years later, when it all came out, it was revealed that they'd been doing very nicely, thank you, back in the early 1960s – but anyone would have known, in a cash-only society as it was then, that the clubs they ran, especially Esmeralda's, raked them in quite a lot of money, let alone all the other protection rackets they had going for them. All she'd really wanted was to have her Reg to herself for a night, just like other couples.

This couldn't happen because Reg was always too worried about what Ronnie *might* do if he was in a temper and Reg wasn't around to calm him down and stop the tantrum turning into serious violence.

Only once did I myself witness Ron's possessiveness of his twin as something truly frightening. I'm not the nervous type but it shook me, the way Ron could explode into a fearsome rage without any warning.

Frances, Vi and I were in the kitchen with Reggie when Ronnie came downstairs. Their driver, Ronnie Bender, was already hovering in the hallway, ready to go. The twins were heading off somewhere.

'Looks like a mothers' meeting in 'ere,' grunted Ron as he entered the room.

Then Frances, holding Reggie's arm, piped up: 'Reg, will you be long?' she asked him.

Ronnie's face turned to thunder. He glared at Frances and his eyes seemed to bulge even more than usual. It was truly horrible. Any minute now, I thought, and he's going to whack her.

'HE – WILL – BE – AS – LONG – AS – IT – TAKES! WE'VE GOT BUSINESS TO DO!' he spat out, his face already contorted with rage.

So this was what happened when Ron lost it, I thought. I realised, in a flash, that all the stories about him lashing out with knives and killer punches weren't just exaggerated gossip. They were real. This was Ron right on the edge of losing all control. Then, miraculously, he looked over at his mother. Just that glance alone seemed to calm him down a fraction.

'Mum, tell 'er! Tell 'er we gotta go!'

Thank God Violet was there. She didn't get up or do anything – she just sat there calmly. Frances by then was looking absolutely terrified, like a trapped animal. She must have been quaking inside. Yet Violet had been here, in this dreadful situation, so many times before. She knew the drill. She turned to her other son.

'Reg, Reg, you won't be long, will you?' she pleaded with him. In other words, do what he says, Reg, and we'll all be all right.

Reg too had been here before. He knew what would defuse the violent outburst before it boiled over into messy chaos. He just turned to his girlfriend and gave her a nervous little kiss on her cheek. Then, without another word, he followed his twin and Ronnie Bender out of the house.

At that point I was ready to go home. I'd seen enough for one night. But before I could say anything, Frances turned to Vi.

'What time will he be back?' she asked as if she hadn't heard any of what had gone on. They'd only just gone out the door and there she was like a child at the school gate.

But in another way it was scary, too. We'd all had a brief

glimpse of the frightful terror that Ronnie Kray could generate without warning. Vi and I were just relieved it hadn't turned into all-out war. Yet I sensed that, for Frances, this fear of Ronnie wasn't going to stop.

'I think they've gone to pop into their club,' Vi said, trying to soothe Frances. 'Don't worry, he'll be back soon.'

I'd already wondered why she talked to Frances in that very motherly, soothing way. Frances really was a child – she was too young. And that night, before Ronnie's explosion, I'd also noticed that Reggie seemed quite shy and different in front of Frances, as if he was afraid of upsetting her. He was polite and well mannered, sure, but he also had to tiptoe round his girlfriend like she was some precious fragile object that might break at any time. At the same time, he knew that she wanted him to be with her, not with Ronnie. But Ronnie always won.

It was all very odd. As I say, these were just very brief glimpses of Reggie and the girl he so loved and you never really know what's going on with a couple, do you, even if you think you know them quite well. Outwardly, all you saw was a very pretty girl on the arm of a handsome older man. And the explosive anger of his very possessive twin, a man rumoured to be violent in the extreme, who didn't want anyone to come between him and his other half. It did not look good to me.

Yet their mother, ever supportive of her boys, didn't venture to interfere or impose her own opinion on the situation. If Reg was happy with this girl, that was great.

One of the Family

If Ron was unhappy, she – Violet – would still be there,
as she'd been when he was tiny, when his life had been
in peril. Only she knew how to soothe him, calm him
down . . .

Chapter 5

A Kray night out

Sometime in 1963 I switched jobs. I left Pinet and went after a job at Dickens and Jones, the big ladies' department store in Regent Street. The money was a bit better for a sales assistant.

But at the interview the buyer asked me to try on a few dresses. They liked the way I wore the clothes and asked if I'd like to be a house model for them.

In those days, big department stores and fashion show-rooms regularly used house models to show the clothes to their customers. It wasn't a case of tripping down the huge long catwalk we know today, accompanied by loud or dreamy music. I'd just have to walk around a small, carpeted area so that the customers could scrutinise the clothes more closely. By twenty-first-century standards it was all very low-key and modest. But to me it was a fantastic break, virtually a dream job, getting paid to show off clothes. And, truth be told, I quite liked the attention: it was a step closer to my dream of becoming a real model.

One of the Family

Back then and soon after my wedding, Don McCullin, who knew Patrick and was then a fledgling young photographer (today he's an internationally known veteran war photographer) had suggested that we go over to Highbury Fields where he could take some shots of me. He had a hunch that I might be photogenic. The results, he assured me, were excellent . . . I should definitely go for modelling. But, newly married as I was, I'd ignored all this. Now here I was, actually modelling dresses.

In those days the store put on afternoon shows for their customers to watch the fashion parade. The more I did it, the more I loved it. But, with an eye to upping the ante as usual, I spotted an advert for C&A, another big Oxford Street chain store. They too needed a house model but there was an added incentive: a small commission paid to the model. If you modelled a dress and a big order came in from one of the buyers, the house model received a tiny cut. It wasn't much, just a few pounds extra. But it made a difference to me. I kept my Thursdays off. I always worked on Saturday. So it didn't make any difference to my arrangement with Mrs Kray. She, of course, was thrilled to hear all about my new working life.

But at home, I was still playing The Lying Game. I was more or less covered for my Thursday afternoons at Vallance Road because Patrick was at work all day and didn't know where I'd be going. I could have been anywhere – my best friend's house or doing her mum's hair somewhere else, for instance. But the Vallance Road sessions took far longer than if I'd stayed in North London. Apart from getting there and back – which didn't take long, because there wasn't so much traffic on the roads then as there is today – even if I got to Violet's house after lunchtime, I often didn't get away until five or six p.m., which meant a mad dash back to be home in time for Patrick's tea.

Violet's life, of course, was dominated by the twins' habits. She loved to cook and meat pies were her speciality – the family, she told me, had always eaten well, even when times were tough before the war. But, as far as I could see, they ate very little. I never saw her prepare a meal for Charlie Senior, for instance. Most of Vi's cooking seemed to be for herself – or when any of her family dropped in. As for the twins, their usual breakfast, I gathered from her, was tea and ciggies. If they fancied a cooked breakfast, they'd head down to Pellicci's, the Italian café in Bethnal Green Road. Six p.m. was when the twins arrived back at the house from whatever they'd been doing during the day before going out for the night. They didn't have any sit-down meals at home. But they were generous hosts: if they did organise a party or a bash in a pub, there were always fabulous buffets laid on for the guests, so it was said.

Vi told me that they tended to eat whenever they were hungry, usually late at night, eating in the clubs and pubs where they were known. This was more or less their eating routine, apart from when they took a trip somewhere: from what I heard from Violet, they'd often go away on trips down to the country or, unusually enough for those days, on trips abroad. Ronnie, she'd told me, loved Morocco in North Africa. That sounded pretty exotic to me. I'd never been anywhere outside England at that point.

So while I was working in the West End and being the 'good' wife much of the time, it was inevitable really that I'd be invited out to socialise with the family. So the lies that I told to my husband needed to become more creative.

The first time I went on a Kray night out was a birthday celebration in August for Violet. The party was taking place at one of the twins' regular haunts, the Grave Maurice pub. I told Patrick that I'd be going out 'with a couple of girlfriends' and that I'd be back by eleven definitely. In those days I didn't drink at all. But, of course, I'd never once had a night out in the East End. To me it sounded exciting, something different. And Violet was always telling me: 'Oh, the girls all dress up lovely, Maureen, when we have a night out.' I wasn't going to miss this chance to join the family celebration.

The Grave Maurice was just along Whitechapel Road, one of many pubs that the Krays frequented, not far from the Blind Beggar, which would be elevated from just an ordinary 'local' to the most well-known pub in London by 1966, thanks to Ronnie Kray.

The Grave was a much smaller, more intimate pub than some of the other locals. Some people thought it was a bit depressing and dingy. Yet such was the reputation of the Krays locally that on that night the publican would have had to warn the pub's regulars, in advance, that the Krays would be having a party night for their mum – so any locals who didn't want to be around could go somewhere else for the evening, apart from the odd older customer who knew and liked Violet.

Sure enough, when I arrived there was a big table for eight, specially reserved for the Krays' female guests. There was no sign of Frances, I noted. Or of Charlie's wife Dolly, for that matter. Dolly was nicknamed 'Jackie Kennedy' because she was always smartly turned out in Chanel-style suits or pillbox hats. I was looking forward to seeing her so I was disappointed that she wasn't there.

Apart from Violet, I didn't know the women, who were wives and girlfriends of the twins' circle of 'close associates'. Just like Violet had said, the other women at the table had got themselves dolled up for the night: big bouffant hairdos, heavy pancake make-up, slinky taffeta dresses, high stilettos. Everyone looked 'brushed up'. It was a typical East End bash.

Except there was no sign of Kray Senior, either. He was nowhere to be seen that night, nor was he even mentioned. A bit odd for a married couple, since it was Violet's fifty-sixth birthday, after all.

There were plenty of other men there, of course, clustered around the bar, paying court to the twins. Women weren't allowed to stand there – the drinks were sent over to the tables. That was the general pub rule wherever you went then. Ronnie had two younger men in smart suits alongside him. He looked like he was in a good mood. All in all, Violet's birthday was turning into a really good evening. The atmosphere was kept quite light-hearted, with lots of jokes and friendly chat. There was just a bit of local gossip thrown in round the girls' table – who was expecting, whose husband had 'gone away' – but not a word was breathed about the twins, of course. That was another rule.

As I sipped my pineapple juice and looked around, I noticed something that spoke volumes. I spotted Ronnie occasionally looking over from the bar at the women's table, just making sure that everything was OK with his mum, that no one was bothering her.

How possessive can you be? I remember thinking to myself. As if the woman wasn't capable of holding her own in conversation with people.

But, sure enough, when one man, someone I didn't recognise, stopped at our table to talk to Violet for a few minutes, Ron spotted them straight away and beamed his scary glare straight across the pub.

He was watching, waiting, like an animal crouching there, on the alert for an opportunity to intervene. It was a shame because Violet was getting quite merry and had started singing 'Over the Rainbow', her favourite song, at one point. She'd had a few drinks: she enjoyed her gin and tonic on nights out, though I never once saw her drunk in all the time I knew her. But, luckily, the man saw Ronnie looking – and moved away. Quickly.

Every now and again I noticed Violet too glancing over at her twins. She'd be puffed up with pride. I knew exactly what she was thinking. Aren't they smart, my boys? Aren't they the smartest boys in the East End? She probably didn't see what I saw, that they were most likely more feared than liked.

The Krays called it respect. But it was something quite different. You could sense it in the pub. People were scared to say or do the wrong thing around them. If Ronnie said something funny – which he was more likely to do than was Reg – people would all hold back, waiting for the first person to laugh. Then they'd all join in. This tension at Kray pub celebrations was exactly the reason why the publican always gave his regular customers due warning of the impending presence of the twins. It was a juggling act: protecting his business and keeping the twins on side.

Towards the end of the evening, a man in his thirties and quite scruffy, not part of the Kray entourage, started getting a bit too loud and raucous. Then he started shouting at no one in particular. I spotted Ronnie glancing at Reggie, their instinctive telepathy at work. The man, the look said, had to be stopped. Before it got nasty. By now, the man was unsteady on his feet. He was weaving from side to side. Reg just walked over to the man, took his arm and marched him out of the door. Ronnie Bender followed them, just in case.

One of the Family

There were many nights when things would happen but on that night at least there was no trouble. The man didn't try to force his way back into the pub, or get really stroppy for being thrown out. He just went off, weaving from side to side, down the long dark avenue of the Whitechapel Road – a lucky escape, I thought. It had all been done in a very calm, quiet way. That was Reggie Kray's method: deal with it quickly before you have to use force. Ron would have just exploded, hit the man in the middle of the pub, there and then, regardless of the consequences. So Reggie too could never quite relax when they were out in public together. He had to be constantly alert for any shift in Ron's mood, recognising all the signals – the frown, the sneer – instantly. It must have been emotionally exhausting. Reg was the permanent guard of a powder keg. Combustible's the word.

Violet loved everything the twins planned that night. They in turn, I guessed, wanted their mother to go where they wanted her to go. Or even to have friends they knew about. It was always their call: they had to be in control.

I'd been accepted into their little world because they liked the idea of me, a married woman, nicely turned out, being their mum's hairdresser and friend. They liked the one-upmanship of someone attending to their personal needs at home: Ron, I found out, would have the barber come round to the house at times. Mafia men did that, he'd read. So Ron had to follow suit.

All Violet's friendships outside her own family were

vetted by the twins. The only other female interaction she had was with the neighbours. Violet knew exactly how much – or how little – she could tell the neighbours about the twins and their lives. But, unlike many of them, Violet didn't get to go on bingo outings or cheery coach rides to the coast or even round to friends' places for a meal. She adored seeing her only grandson, Charlie's little Gary. But only when the twins decided to take her somewhere did she go out socially. A night out alone with Charlie Senior was a very rare event.

It was an odd life, but it didn't seem to make her resentful or unhappy. She was a happy prisoner of their love, really, besotted with their looks, their success and their fame across the East End as she was. Of course, she never saw herself as locked into their world. Not even when they became prisoners themselves. Independence? If you'd asked her about it in the Vallance Road years she would have said, 'I'm all right here with my boys. They look after me.'

As for me, I'd been longing to go to the Astor Club for months, ever since Violet had started going on about it to me: how posh the place was, how the staff and the maitre d' bowed and scraped to her when the boys took her there for a special night out.

But, of course, in my world I was never going to get inside the front door of the fabulous Mayfair nightclub, the haunt of all the top faces in London and their wives or girlfriends: trotting into Bertie Green's Berkeley Square club on the arm of my husband Patrick was never likely to happen. He hated nightclubs, anyway.

'That family are scum,' I overheard him saying to my brother-in-law one day when the K-word cropped up in the pub yet again. I knew better than to say anything at all about the Krays by then. There were plenty of other things for me and Pat to row about, anyway.

So when Charlie Kray, sitting in the kitchen one day, said right out of the blue, 'Maureen, come and have a night out with us at the Astor' as I was finishing up Vi's hair, I almost jumped up and threw my arms around him in sheer delight. But I didn't, of course. I played it cool.

'Oh, Charlie, you know my husband won't come,' I told him.

By then, I'd also told Charlie quite a bit about my not-very-happy marriage. Like Violet, he was a good listener, not like Reggie who usually gave you the impression he was thinking of something else when you talked to him.

A few weeks before the Astor invite, Charlie had popped round to Vallance Road to see his mum briefly. A friend had dropped him off: Charlie's car was being repaired. I'd been ready to leave as he came in and offered him a lift in my Mini down to the Mile End Road.

Before we drove off, I was complaining as usual about Patrick and his obsession with me getting home on time.

Charlie just looked at me and laughed. 'Maureen, you

can't blame the man for bein' jealous. You're a blindin' good-lookin' girl.'

'Of course, Charlie,' I quipped. 'We all know that!'

More laughter followed. Then, as I put the key in the ignition, Charlie shook his head in disbelief. 'Know what, Maureen? You're the sister we never 'ad!'

And we drove off, still laughing. Of course, I didn't mention the lost-baby conversation to Charlie. Yet I was quietly pleased because I felt the same way about Charlie.

Charlie never stopped repeating that comment down the years. He'd introduce me to people as 'the sister I never 'ad' all the time. Years later, he'd say to me: 'I wish you 'ad been my sister.'

Of course, in time I'd become the twins' good friend, too. But it wasn't acknowledged by them as a sisterly-type relationship, probably because they were too self-obsessed to look beyond their relationship with each other – and with Vi.

That day, when he invited me to the Astor, Charlie merely brushed off my worries about my husband. It was easy.

'Maureen, don't worry about 'im. You can come to the club with Vi, that'll be OK,' Charlie assured me.

So by the time I'd got home that night, I'd already worked out what I'd be wearing for the Astor – and what I'd tell Patrick. He wouldn't get shirty, I reasoned, if I told him I was having a Friday night out with the girls the following week.

One of the Family

I was dead right. Not a peep out of him when I mentioned it, just his usual shrug and 'Yeah, OK.' He was going to be drinking with his mates that night, anyway.

That Friday, I took a cab to Vallance Road to find Violet already dolled up, wearing a beautiful blue satin dress and a white mink stole that the boys had, of course, 'bought' for her. She also sported a lovely diamante necklace and earrings – more gifts from the twins – and wore make-up: bright red lipstick, face powder and eye shadow too.

I'd done her hair the day before and although she'd slept on it, it was still immaculate: my backcombing-and-lacquer skills, plus her beloved hairnet, saw to that. I'd be desperate to know the details but I never ventured to ask Violet where all the good evening gear she wore came from: I figured all the pricier stuff came from the twins' inexhaustible supply of expensive clothing, obtained gratis from God knew where. Violet Kray from Bethnal Green looked like she was going to a Royal Command Performance to mingle with the highest in the land every time she stepped out with her boys, whether it was to an East End pub or a West End haunt of high society.

As for me, naturally I'd put the effort in too: I had a pale blue skintight sheath, very high black slingbacks and a little mink bolero. I'd had to borrow that from a girlfriend. It wasn't anywhere near as nice as Vi's mink stole but still, I felt good as we left the house and climbed into Reggie's Mercedes, driven by Ronnie Bender who seemed to be a constant presence round the house.

Ronnie dropped us right outside the club in the famous West End square that had inspired the song, 'A Nightingale Sang (In Berkeley Square)'. There was a uniformed doorman outside who smiled at us and opened the glass-panelled door with a flourish. Inside, a very smartly dressed man with a bow tie was standing there to greet us.

He greeted Violet like an old friend. They were on first-name terms. 'I trust you are keeping well, Violet,' the man cooed while ushering us down the stairs into the inner sanctum of the Astor, a beautiful plush interior with tall hanging drapes of dark, rich-looking velvet and tiny gilt wall lights, candelabra-style, placed all around the walls.

Of course, I'd never seen this kind of thing before. So as far as I was concerned, all this spelled luxury, class – and grandeur. Afterwards I checked it out, asked around, and found out that those wall lights were called sconces: not something you'd be likely to find in the average home round where we came from.

Small round tables with starched white cloths and little gilt-edged chairs were all dotted on either side of a much lower central area which was obviously used as the stage or dance floor.

'Ooh, Maureen, Lita Roza's gonna be singing tonight,' Violet told me, as excited as I'd ever seen her, while the maitre d' guided us, with a flourish, to our table, which already had a huge silver bucket on it that contained a bottle of iced Dom Perignon champagne. (I knew what this was because Violet used to tell me that was what they always had to drink at the Astor.)

Oh, this is living, I thought to myself as I settled into my little gilt chair and tried my best not to stare around me at the other people sitting nearby. This would definitely be a night to remember. I loved Lita. She was what they used to call a torch singer, singing mostly sad love songs about men that got away, though she'd made her name in the 1950s with that silly record about a doggie in the window.

Being part of the Kray-family entourage in a posh nightclub was exactly how you imagined it'd be if you were invited to dine with royalty. You dared not lift a finger. This was a world where you were cosseted, pampered. Chairs were instantly pulled back and ciggies swiftly lit for you: your every wish was their command. Somewhat stupidly, and probably out of sheer nerves from excitement, I promptly picked up my champagne glass and went to reach out to pour myself a drink from the big ice bucket.

But Violet, quick as a flash, stopped me, grabbing my wrist with her hand.

'No, Maureen, you mustn't,' she hissed. 'Let them do it for you.' Without a word, a smartly attired waiter glided over and poured us both our first glass of bubbly. Sipping mine, wallowing in the glamour of it all, I took it all in: I'd never ever seen so many beautifully dressed men and women in one place. Clothes, of course, were my obsession. So, for me, this was heaven.

In those days, wherever you came from, everyone

made sure they did themselves up nicely for a night out in the pub or a special family 'do', like a wedding. Sharp Italian suits for the men, smart, tight dresses or little two-piece suits for the girls. Matching accessories: shoes, bag, even little gloves. But the Astor, I saw immediately, was worlds away, major-league smart, straight out of the pages of *Vogue* magazine. You could see, just by the cut, the costly fabric of the outfits of the people seated around us, mostly couples (a lot of balding or grey-haired older men sitting with pretty, much younger women) or small groups of men, that what they wore was not just expensive – it was the best that money could buy. Diamonds. Flash gold watches and chunky gold signet rings. The opposite end of the social spectrum from what I knew around our local pubs.

I pretended to know it all, but really I was quite a naive girl then. I didn't quite understand what all the Mafia-style table-hopping that went on that night was all about but later I realised: everyone in the Astor who knew the twins – which meant most people – had to come over to Violet's table at some point to pay tribute to her. That was the twins' rule: pay your respects to our mum.

One by one, people dropped by our table to honour the matriarch of the Kray family. This went on for much of the evening. Most of them – they were all men – I didn't know. But people like Freddie Mills, the boxer, of course I knew – everyone knew who he was. He came over and spoke to us briefly, though it was just an exchange of pleasantries rather than an actual conversation. Then, after Freddie, Charlie arrived, dressed to the nines as usual, with two male friends. Again, there was no Dolly with him. He sat down with us in the chair next to mine.

A bit later, just as the crowd went silent, Reggie came down the stairs with Frances on his arm. That night, Frances looked amazing: despite her initial fears that Reg might not like it, she'd gone for the upswept hairdo, and a sleeveless blue brocade sheath dress, just past the knee. She too had a mink stole with all the tails hanging down. This had been the fashion at the time but it was a bit 'old' for a teenager, I thought.

Reggie's made sure you've got the right mink, just like his mum, I thought to myself. But that, I knew by then, was Reggie all over: the girl on his arm had to turn heads. Not because she looked too sexy, oh no, she had to look very ladylike yet perfectly groomed to fit with his and Ronnie's image: in their minds, they were celebrities now, right up there with the famous movie stars. Which was probably why they were always so keen to hang out with them. Stardust was addictive. (In the twins' case, it also proved to be highly infectious.)

It was like being at Grand Central Station. There was no let-up. Everyone wanted to bow and scrape to the twins: people came over, stopped briefly, said hello and then went off. The whole evening was like that.

Reggie never stayed at our table for long. He kept

jumping up and disappearing for ages, leaving Frances sitting there alone, not saying a word. She hardly drank anything, I noticed. Now and then, Violet would lean across to her and say 'All right, Frances dear?' or something similar. Frances would just nod in a mute reply. Not a trace of a smile. Conversation was obviously out of the question.

I considered trying, but I figured it was a waste of time. She knew me – I was the only person at the table who was close in age to her – but it didn't seem to matter. It was impossible to tell whether she was just in a bad mood that night. Maybe they'd had a row. No one could know for sure what was going on with them.

Again and again Violet kept asking 'Where's Ronnie?' but no one seemed to be sure. It was as if his mum couldn't relax until she saw both her twins on parade. In the end, Charlie briefly left the table in search of an answer for his mum and came back to tell her, 'It's OK, mum, he's coming.'

Finally, Ronnie arrived, also immaculately dressed – in a double-breasted Prince of Wales check suit – with one of his minders, Albert Donoghue. Then, from nowhere, a very good-looking young man called Bobby Buckley, came in to join him. Bobby was slim, about mid-twenties, with very bright black eyes, dark brown hair and an incredibly sweet face, almost a baby face but not quite.

They spoke to Vi and said hello to me. All very polite and friendly as if they were at a garden party: Bobby seemed really charming. Then they wandered off. They weren't going to sit with us.

Violet sat there, beaming proudly, finally aglow with the satisfaction that both of her handsome princes were strutting their stuff at court, as it were. I tried to talk properly to her a couple of times but now she was just nodding at me, still smiling, her gaze darting around the room, drinking it all in, pleased as punch to be at the centre of it all. Queen Vi.

It was a very strange scenario, with everyone dressed to the nines, acting charming. I wasn't sure what it all meant but, impressed as I was, it seemed like we were all on show in some kind of masquerade. The 'masks' were the slick suits and elegant shiny dresses. Yet I could also see that in the furthest corners of the club, at a few men-only tables, the guys were huddled together, sharp-faced and sinister. Plotting.

Through the haze of cigar smoke and the din of chatter I realised that 'business' was the real point of this place for the twins. Wealthy non-criminal people came here too because they were used to being fawned on in Mayfair nightclubs. But certain key players, like the Krays, were here because their lives revolved around 'naughty' business. The business of violence.

All of a sudden, the lights were dimmed right down and Lita Roza wafted onto the stage, and into the spotlight. The show was about to start.

She'd been on the telly a lot when she was younger.

Now she was in her mid-thirties, still looking fabulous, very sultry, dark-eyed, with upswept hair. Surely they'd had to sew her into the exquisite orangey-coloured sparkling sheath dress that went right to the floor, Shirley Bassey-style.

She told us a bit breathlessly that she'd just come back from America. In Las Vegas, she said, she'd sung in cabaret at the famous Flamingo club. 'I met everyone – except Elvis,' she announced to us. We all laughed, enthralled. Meeting the sexy phenomenon that was Elvis was every girl's fantasy then.

Then the music started. Lita had an amazing voice. I'd heard her records, of course, but she was even better in this intimate nightclub setting. The one song I always remember her singing that night was 'Hey There', a very romantic song, full of meaning.

Perpetually curious about other couples' relationships, I sneaked a glance across our table to see Reggie and Frances's reaction to Lita. After all, they were supposed to be engaged and in love. I was expecting to see them holding hands as they listened, at the very least. But Reggie had disappeared yet again, gone to 'talk business' with Ronnie at someone else's table.

I did my best to look discreetly, but all I could see was a truly lovely girl with a completely expressionless visage. Nothing registered on that pretty face. The romantic song didn't seem to affect her at all. She was just sitting there, waiting for her Reg. All the time she'd sat at that table, she'd made no attempt to say anything to me. Had she been turned to stone, I wondered? Or was she too scared to speak?

Then, when Lita finished her act and swept off the stage to much clapping and whistling, Violet leaned across to me. 'We'd better be going now, Maureen,' she said. 'Your Patrick won't like it if you're home late.'

Her being motherly never failed to surprise me. I hadn't realised it, but it was nearly midnight. I'd been so engrossed in everything around me that I'd forgotten all about being home in time to avoid my husband's suspicions. Now I'd have to tell him I'd gone round to one of the girls' places after the pubs shut.

'Oh Maw, just as we're starting to get going, you go home,' Charlie wisecracked. One quick look from me was enough to make him understand about my bad-tempered husband. The Astor was renowned as a late-night haunt. All the men, of course, would stay there drinking until three or four in the morning. Me and Vi were going to be whisked back to Vallance Road by Ronnie Bender. Reggie suddenly appeared and sat down next to Frances, who looked at him as if to say 'Can we go home too?', still behaving like a toddler at a grown-up gathering. But as we farewelled them, they were still sitting there, looking like the perfect couple – but saying very little.

I dropped a few not-so-subtle hints to Vi on the drive back about getting back to Islington and, sure enough, Ronnie Bender offered to drive me there once we'd got Vi home. It had been so exciting, but it had all happened far too quickly as far as I was concerned. Finally, I'd had my little peek into the world of the Astor. I had a lot to think about when I finally got into bed next to a now-snoring Patrick. Unusually for me, it was ages before I even got to sleep that night: I was so wound up, stimulated by it all.

Yet a couple of things stood out for me that night: I'd already seen it in the East End pub but at the Astor Violet had positively wallowed in the glory of all the 'respect' that the smartly suited men had paid to her, all the table-hopping that had gone on because of her boys' scary reputation. I knew all too well what Patrick would say if he heard that his wife had actually been hobnobbing with them socially. His wife, out in public with the Kray Twins. In the West End! He'd have a fit.

I'd sensed it, of course, before that night. But Violet Kray, you could see, was totally immersed in the reflective glow of being the twins' mum – no matter what people said in the pubs when they gossiped about the evil things her Two Ones were supposed to have done to others. Her boys were successful and, in public, everyone treated them like kings. That was what mattered to Vi. Success and recognition. The power of fame. Even if it was born out of blood and intimidation.

The other thing, of course, was the weirdness of Reg's relationship with his girlfriend.

There she was, as glamorous and beautiful as they come, in a place that every girl I knew would kill to be taken to, especially by a good-looking boyfriend with plenty of money to splash around.

I understood the darker side of it all but I still couldn't get enough of this dazzling nightclub world. I had a hunger for this type of thing, for glamour and bright lights, and my presence in Vallance Road was, very gradually, feeding into that hunger. At that point in time, if someone had offered to take me to the Astor several nights a week, as Reggie did with Frances, I'd have been ecstatic. Why oh why didn't Frances look like she was enjoying it?

But the following week, when I went round to do Vi's hair, the atmosphere in the house didn't really encourage me to ask her any questions. I picked up on it as soon as she came to open the front door.

'They've been fighting,' she whispered to me as she walked into the kitchen to put the kettle on for my first cup of tea. No one else was around that afternoon, though I guessed that Charlie Senior was asleep upstairs.

I knew, of course, that she meant the twins. I'd gathered from her that there were times when they fought ferociously in the house, usually upstairs. Verbal battles, perhaps, but still scary to hear. But I could tell by her closed expression – and Violet Kray was normally a very chatty person – that today was not the time to ask her anything. So I just started burbling on about a film I'd seen, and then got on with doing her hair.

This was a house full of incident, with people coming and going all the time at all hours of the day and night, family and 'friends' of the twins. But as I was to discover eventually, even though I'd already learned much about her family from Violet it was still, essentially, a house with unspoken secrets. Bit by bit, over the years, many of those secrets would be revealed to me. But not today. Today I'd have to keep quiet and relive my night at the Astor.

Briefly, just by being there, surrounded by the trappings of luxury and money, the place made you feel you were Someone . . .

Chapter 6

Secrets and lies

I'd heard about the twins' prison history. My brothers-in-law had mentioned it, though they hadn't gone into detail. But what I hadn't heard anywhere in the rumour mill was that Ron was gay.

To tell the truth, I'd never have imagined that Ron was a gay man. He and Reg did have soft, very quiet voices but there were no effeminate actions or body language that hinted at homosexuality. I'd worked with gay men in the shoe shop and those guys were quite effeminate in their hair, their dress. They camped it up all the time. They didn't look butch, not by a long chalk.

But, of course, I was quite ignorant about gay men, mainly because male homosexuality was still illegal in the early 1960s (it was not decriminalised until 1967) and men could go to prison for it, so same-sex relationships existed within a secret world. Most people I knew didn't know much about it, or they talked about it in whispers. So I could be forgiven for expecting gay men to be somewhat effeminate. Which, of course, is often very far from the truth.

I found out about Ron's 'secret' from Violet one afternoon when she was harking back, yet again, to when Ron had been a child, telling me how much she'd spoilt him. Then she revealed that Charlie had told her, one day, that Ron was homosexual – or 'a poof', which was a slang word people used then to describe a gay man.

She hadn't talked to Ron about it at all. The Krays were quite prim and proper on the topic of sex which, again, wasn't that unusual for the times. Very few people then talked openly about sex the way they do now. Despite the 1960s having the reputation as the sex, drugs and rock 'n' roll era, it was only towards the end of that decade and the start of the 1970s that things really started to change – and even then it was mostly younger people who were diving headlong into the new freedoms, not their parents.

I do remember saying to Vi: 'Well, you can't tell, can you?' I was trying my best to be tactful. What else could I say to her? She'd never been out in the world beyond the East End. She hadn't worked alongside gay men in a posh salon or shop like I had.

Underneath it all, I could see that she'd been quite bemused about it when Charlie had told her. She certainly hadn't had a clue about it until then.

'He had a couple of girlfriends as a teenager, you see,' she told me. Then she went quiet for a bit and added, 'But 'e was always a little bit different.'

What I would soon realise, of course, was that Violet totally accepted all this. Nothing in the world could change her utter devotion to the boy who needed her so much. If her Ron wanted boyfriends, that was fine with her. As long as he was happy.

Charlie Senior, I gathered later, wasn't at all comfortable with Ron's sexuality. Again, pretty typical of the times. It was yet another reason for their dad to dislike his twins.

No one who came into that house received anything other than a warm welcome from Violet. There were times when I'd go round and the twins would be hosting their 'meetings' with the men they conspired with in the room upstairs.

Vi would cheerfully prepare and take up the trayloads of tea and biscuits for them, as they discussed their plans for God knew what. If any of the men came down to the kitchen, she'd chatter away to them as if they were little boys. To her, they weren't hard, tough men, scheming criminal activity or ready to dish out violence whenever necessary. They were her sons' friends. Why wouldn't she be nice to them?

And, of course, it wasn't just hard men who had trooped through the front door of Vallance Road. From the time when they started to make it big in the late 1950s, the boys would occasionally bring home the celebrities they rubbed shoulders with in their clubs, specially to meet the mother they were so proud of. Vi had frequently told me about all that.

Dazzling names like singer Judy Garland or the actor George Raft had sat drinking tea with Vi in that modest little kitchen. 'George Raft didn't have a nicer shirt on him than my two,' she told me proudly.

Violet had, of course, been thrilled to bits to meet Judy – 'Over the Rainbow' from *The Wizard of Oz* movie was one of her favourite songs. But the young girl in the 1930s movie wasn't the woman that Violet met.

'She was a frightened little thing, too skinny,' was Vi's description of Judy. The boys had told their mum that Judy was a drinker. So Violet believed, quite rightly, that it was the drink that made her so frail. (Sadly, Judy died in London in the summer of 1969, just a few months after the twins' 'reign of terror', as the papers called it, had finally ended.)

Yet it wasn't just the showbiz names that turned up at Vallance Road. Ronnie, in particular, loved to rub shoulders with the privileged and powerful. Much would be made over the years of Ronnie's friendship with Lord Robert ('Bob') Boothby, an acquaintance that would go on to rock the British establishment and, in a way, reveal to the public a glimpse of the truth about the twins even before their downfall. Vi told me, at one stage, that Ronnie had brought Lord Boothby to Vallance Road, for some reason.

'Funny old man with a bow tie,' Violet told me. 'Didn't like to ask 'im in front of Ron, but I asked 'im later who he was,' she continued.

''E's a Lord, mum,' came the reply.

If she was sometimes puzzled by all this high-level networking – politicians of any hue could never have as much cachet for Vi as movie stars – the eclectic group of visitors to her house were, in the end, all equal as far as Vi was concerned. They were friends of her successful sons. So of course they were treated like royalty.

Around the same time, she also opened up to me about the twins' long stretches 'away' in prison. Ronnie had received a three-year sentence for grievous bodily harm in 1956 and Reg had spent nearly two years in prison for his role in a protection racket in 1960. Cheerfully, Vi had gone off to visit them, took them whatever they needed, ran back and forth, doing whatever the regulations permitted. Of course, the charges for which they'd been sent away were, according to Violet, complete miscarriages of justice. The police had stitched them up. To their mum, her twins were always the wronged victims of the authorities.

I started to get more of an insight into Ronnie's way of thinking one afternoon when I'd turned up early at Vallance Road. I'd knocked and knocked but got no response.

I was halfway back to the car when Ronnie opened the door. His mum was out shopping, he said, ushering me in. Then he got me to make the tea and we had a little chat. For some reason, the topic of sport cropped up because I was – still am – a diehard Arsenal fan.

'Oh, that's because you come from posh 'Ighbury,' he

told me, which did make me laugh. Maybe Highbury sounded posh if you lived in Bethnal Green but the truth was that there were just as many hard men and villains walking around there as there were in the East End.

'Only one sport worth watchin',' Ron informed me. 'Those twenty-two men on a pitch all fallin' over with a ball, can't be bothered to watch it. Boxin's the only sport worth watchin',' he said with pride. 'Two men facing each other, no one to help them, having a good fight until someone flattens the other one.'

Every man I knew loved football. Where I lived, everyone was a fanatical Arsenal follower. Violet had told me the story of how the teenage twins had won bout after bout professionally, only for their boxing careers to end after a big fight at the Albert Hall. All three Kray brothers had fought professionally that night: fighting there meant, in those days, that a younger boxer had really 'arrived'. And, she'd said, while the older Charlie had much more experience in the ring, the twins had got to that level after a relatively small number of fights.

'We was the first three fights on,' said Ron wistfully. 'I 'ad to fight a bloke from King's Cross called Bill Sliney – Reg'd beat 'im on points a coupla months before. I mauled 'im in the first round and 'e didn' wanna go on, but they talked 'im into it and 'e wound up winnin'. On points.'

Ron gave his scary sneer at this point and I could only imagine Sliney's relief when the match was over. 'Then Reg won 'is fight on points over some bloke from Clap'am.

And then Charlie got mullered by this bloke from Aldgate. Punch in the guts finished Charlie in the third round.'

'Did you get paid, Ron?' I wondered.

'Yeah, you got twenty-five quid. But none of us ever boxed again. I didn' wanna and Reg 'ad been up for assaulting a copper. So 'e lost 'is ticket.'

I knew a little bit about boxing. So I knew that 'lost 'is ticket' translated as: the boxing authorities weren't having it. They didn't want pro boxers who went round bashing the 'filth' as they were known then. Violet Kray had filled me in on some of the details but hearing all this from Ron himself made me understand how he'd loved the idea of being a pro boxer.

'So how come you liked boxing so much, Ron?' I asked, just to hear what he'd say.

'Only two people in the ring. No one to 'elp you. Just you and 'im, face to face. I love fightin',' he said, chain-smoking his beloved Players, sipping his tea.

People were terrified of Ronnie Kray, but on that day he seemed pretty normal to me. OK, so he never took his gaze off you as he talked. But that was the only thing, really – he was having a good day, I guess. And, of course, every time he wanted another cup of tea I'd have to get up and make it. New Men didn't exist then. Everyone would have thought you were crazy if you suggested, just once, that the men serve the women or make a cuppa for them.

Then Violet came in, followed by Reggie. Before I started shampooing her, I mentioned football to Reggie.

'Don't like football,' he grunted and proceeded to tell me why *he* loved boxing. Everything he said mirrored exactly what his twin had told me. In time, you did get used to that. The same opinions, the same words, sometimes the exact same phrases. It was quite uncanny if you hadn't heard it before.

Then Reg said something different.

'It's a pity I couldn't do my cigarette punch in the ring.'

I just laughed. I didn't know what he meant and I didn't ask, just busied myself with Vi's hairdo. Later I found out what he meant: it was a trademark trick that he liked to inflict on his victims. The trick of the cigarette punch was this: Reg would offer someone a ciggy with his right hand and the person would open their mouth to put the ciggy in. At that point, the person's jaw went slack. Giving Reg the opportunity to deliver his punch from the left. He was famous for that.

The twins had long established themselves as generous supporters of local charities and at that stage fund-raising events, usually in pubs, were already a part of my life. Me and Patrick would sometimes go to charity dos in a hall in Islington to raise money for the Islington Boys' Club where I'd sell the raffle tickets. This eventually cropped up in conversation with Vi so one day I asked: did she think the Twins would help out, donate anything to give us as raffle prizes? The message was passed on. In due course, I'd arrive at the house to find a big teddy bear waiting for me, the sort of toy you win at a funfair. It didn't stop at one. I lost count of the times they'd leave a teddy bear with their mum for my fund-raising. Always teddy bears, mind you. Nothing else.

When I look back on it all, it was really Charlie who drew me into socialising with them. He was an incredibly sociable kind of guy, a party person. He'd always be saying: 'Oh, you ought to come down to so-and-so's place.' But, of course, apart from Vi's birthday and the memorable night at the Astor, the married lady would usually have to decline. Regretfully.

Yet some months after the Astor night, Charlie suggested that I should go to the Grave Maurice again, this time on a Friday night: 'You might meet some nice people there, Maureen,' he said with a wink.

Like his brothers, Charlie had quite a few good contacts in the showbiz world. Perhaps he was genuinely trying to help me with the modelling thing. This time I promised I'd try. But I needed to do some crafty planning: I couldn't go on my own, that was the main problem. An unaccompanied woman walking into a pub was frowned upon in those days. Then I remembered a friend, Diana. Of course, she'd be perfect to come with me. She too worked as a house model, loved dressing up in the latest gear and making a big impression socially. So one Friday night I took Charlie up on his offer. Diana and I got dressed up and off we went to the Grave. We walked into the pub together in our most head-turning gear: I wore a short, sleeveless minidress in gold brocade, paired with gold boots: Lulu- or Cilla-style. Diana too wore a very short black dress in a shiny fabric, paired with dark boots, quite stunning with her contrasting long mane of fair hair. Charlie, so in his element when new, young good-looking girls were around, rushed out to take us to the part of the pub where the Kray group were sitting, to show us off.

Before we could finish our first drink, however, Charlie wanted me to meet one of their guests that night. She was a girl of around my age, seated at another table with Ronnie and a few people I didn't know.

'This is Maureen,' he said, ushering me towards the girl.

This girl was a real stunner. Gorgeous high cheekbones, a seductive smile, shoulder-length auburn hair, a very slim body dressed seductively in a pale sleeveless dress. A million-dollar babe, the sort men go crazy for.

'Hello,' she said and promptly gave me a kiss on the cheek. 'Are you a model?' she enquired.

'Er . . . yes, a fashion model,' I responded, not expecting the question really. She was so attractive that she could only be a model herself. Or an up-and-coming actress. I was eager to find out more about her but suddenly one of the men said something that distracted her. She turned away and that was the end of our conversation.

Back I went to our table where Diana was already in full flow, all the men around her entranced by this new face, trying their best to chat her up and not really succeeding.

Charlie had mentioned the other girl's name to me but I hadn't really taken it in, I'd been too busy checking her out. The night rolled on and it was turning into a really lively evening but, as usual, I had to do my Cinders bit, leave early to be home in time.

It wasn't until the following week when I turned up at Vallance Road that I discovered more about the lovely girl the Krays had been entertaining.

'Who was that good-looking girl at Ronnie's table?' I asked the twins when they arrived at the house in the early evening. Violet had gone upstairs for some reason.

'That was Christine Keeler,' Reg informed me proudly. 'She's a very good-looking girl, isn't she?'

I was stunned. I'd read about her in the papers but somehow I hadn't connected the incredibly attractive young girl with what I'd read about her. Before I could say any more, his twin butted in.

'They're not good girls, them girls. Sleepin' around, givin' secrets away. If she was a man, she'd be DEAD.'

Ron referred, of course, to the sensational Profumo Affair of 1963, the affair between a teenage Christine and the former Tory War Minister John Profumo that had gone on while she was apparently simultaneously sleeping with a Russian spy, Yevgeny Ivanov. It was a scenario that eventually led to the resignation of Harold MacMillan and resulted in the suicide of Stephen Ward, who'd been at the very centre of the scandal. 'Them girls' of course were Christine Keeler and Mandy Rice Davies, the two party girls who'd been befriended by Ward at one stage. Christine had even gone to prison for six months for perjury.

Reg, for once, didn't share his twin's view.

'I thought she was a very sexy lady,' Reg said.

'Sexy lady? Wotcher talkin' about? You don' wanna be mixed up with any of 'em,' Ron snapped at his twin, though as far as I'd seen that night he'd been playing Mr Polite and Attentive Host to Christine: she hadn't wandered into the Grave off the street, had she?

These types of scabrous comments from Ron were slowly becoming indicators of his paranoia, and of his intense jealousy. He was scared that his twin might actually go off into the night with someone like Christine – which I suppose Reg was capable of doing, given the way the twins mingled all the time with the famous and the infamous in the clubs. I'd seen some of it for myself at the Astor Club, hadn't I?

Of course, as club owners they were accustomed to playing the role of super-polite host, yet when it came to the opposite sex Ronnie didn't want his brother getting too close to any glamorous, attractive female who might tempt him, lure him away from his side. Reggie liked women, was drawn to them – and could be incredibly charming and polite. Ron was capable of that kind of behaviour too. But with him, so much more of it was an act to further his own aims as a major-league gangster and a person of power.

Frances, of course, had been outwardly accepted into the family because she was a 'good' girl, an innocent young virgin. An experienced and infamous party girl, a 'bad' girl, was something else, hugely threatening for Ronnie.

Dolly wasn't so lucky in her position in the Krays' estimations. While Violet had always been quite discreet in her dislike of Charlie's wife, Ron made no secret of the fact that he didn't like his sister-in-law. Dolly's name didn't crop up much, but when it did Ron was dismissive, jeering, 'Oh 'er, we don' want 'er round 'ere,' that sort of thing.

Ronnie obviously saw any wife of his brothers as an intruder into their world, rather than someone to welcome into the close-knit East End family.

Ronnie had his boyfriends, sure, but he wanted his mum and his twin there for him at all times. Maybe Violet had spotted this dislike of Dolly early on in Charlie's relationship with his wife and simply sided with Ronnie to keep the peace.

Someone told me much later that Ron would often tell Reggie that 'women are dirty and they smell', one of his favourite taunts. Underneath it all, Ronnie just couldn't stand the idea that someone – anyone – could come between him and his twin. Sex is a very powerful distraction, isn't it?

*

Before long, my friendship with the family created yet another social dilemma for me. 'Esmeralda's Barn' often cropped up in conversations with Charlie or the twins. It was their club. I really ought to come down there one night and see the place, they all kept saying.

They'd taken it over in 1960, not long after the country's gambling laws had changed and a number of smart casinos had started to open up in central London. Their clubs in the East End – the Regency, the Kentucky, the Double R – had been successful at various points but Esmeralda's was on another planet. It was in Knightsbridge, a real posh people's area. Suppose I went there one night and someone spotted me and it got back to Patrick? There'd have been all hell to pay.

Recently, on Friday nights I'd started going with girl-friends to Tiffany's, a big club in Shaftesbury Avenue, when Patrick went out with his friends. That was fine because I'd go with his brothers' wives, three sisters-in-law and another friend. We'd all go home and tell the same story to our respective husbands, so I was covered. But Knightsbridge was a different matter. How could I wangle a night out there?

Diana, yet again, proved to be my solution. I concocted a story for Patrick. Diana had invited me to a birthday party in the Knightsbridge area. It was still 'be home by midnight', of course, and I knew all too well the consequences of going over my late pass. On one occasion I'd arrived home from a night out with the girls at 12:30, late because I'd driven all the other girls home and at one stage had got lost (no Satnavs or mobile phones in those days). To my horror, when I arrived home I found that Patrick had angrily locked the front door.

Down the stairs I went, back into my car, driving off to my sister-in-law's place in Finchley where I slept on her sofa.

The next day I took my brother-in-law and his one-year-old baby back to our place in Highbury. Poor old Cinderella had to take her relatives with her, complete with baby, before facing her jealous husband. But I had guessed right: he had to open the door to us – and he couldn't start having a go at me in front of them.

Why, you wonder, was I telling even more lies, risking Patrick's wrath? The truth was, by then I was solidly determined to get out there and have a good time. I really wanted to go to these places and rub shoulders with glamorous well-known people, and the Krays' social life was awesomely sophisticated for a young Highbury girl who'd been taught by nuns. I wanted in, even if it was just for a fleeting couple of hours. I didn't have any babies at home. Patrick went out regularly with his friends. I could go out too.

That night Diana and I got to Esmeralda's early, around nine p.m. There were only a few people there. Reggie and Charlie greeted us in the front area, where we had a drink.

Esmeralda's was SO impressive, something out of a

movie – gold chairs, beautiful expensive antique furnishings, a truly plush setting. When I think about it now, it wouldn't look out of date even today. OK, the Astor had dazzled me – but the flock wallpaper and red lamps on the tables there were not in the same league as the Barn's décor; they'd worked really hard to create the right upmarket environment. Or rather, the twins had found the right people to create it. There's no way those two know about antiques, I thought to myself.

Did we want something to eat? We were constantly watching our weight so the answer was always no. However, did we want some champagne? Well, that was certainly allowed. As he poured the champagne, Charlie fed us another little titbit: 'You know we've got a Lord here? He's called Lord Effingham.'

I genuinely thought it was one of his jokes. 'You're having me on,' I told him, nudging him in the ribs.

But no. Lord Effingham was on the board of directors of Esmeralda's.

'How did that happen?' I asked Charlie.

He shrugged. 'Oh, Ronnie can make anything happen.'

'This place is beautiful,' I told Reggie at one point. He gave me a half 'told you so' smile but you could see that he wanted to hear it.

'Yes, it's all right – as long as Ron doesn't spoil it,' he said. Oh dear. It sounded like they'd just had one of their rows.

Secretly, I thought Diana and I fitted in there much

better than we did in the Krays' East End pub haunts. East End girls dressed carefully and they were style-conscious but they didn't wear their skirts as short as we did by then. Also, the girls' hair back 'East' tended to be shorter, neater. Ours was much longer, more flamboyant, King's Road-style. Two different worlds, one with exactly the right 'look' of the moment, the glossy luminosity of the fabulous miniskirted blonde icons like Julie Christie or Marianne Faithfull, always in the newspapers and the magazines; the other desperately trying to catch up in an environment where women weren't anywhere near 'swinging', experimenting sexually or taking the pill, but still trapped socially in the place where they'd been for ever: dependent on men.

In the East End pub, we'd been stared at a lot, which seemed to delight the Kray men. Yet at the Barn no one batted an eyelid at us because we looked like most of the women round the area, young, fashionable, straight long locks – the fashionable look of Swinging London, I realised, was really a Chelsea look, when it came down to it. More groomed. Expensive. Go down the King's Road today, check out the women, and you can still see something of what I mean.

At one stage, Charlie escorted us into the gambling area. I'd never been to one in my life, of course, so it was a real eye-opener for me, watching all those elegantly dressed men and women in evening gear, sitting there, intently staring at the green baize table with its huge pile of gambling chips. In there, the atmosphere was much quieter. Gambling for big sums of cash is a fairly tense business. Even if you're rich.

Ronnie was in there, checking everyone out, walking around, fag hanging from his lips, with his funny little sideways sneer whenever he saw someone winning. He couldn't hide his true feelings. You could see he didn't like anyone winning in *his* club: he hated gambling, never took part and hated the gamblers who moaned when they lost.

Our Esmeralda's night out was impressive but only in the sense of going somewhere glam, to a place that everyone talked about. We didn't gamble, so in the end we left at about eleven, well in time for Cinderella's curfew.

The Barn, it turned out, had been a huge source of cash – a pot of gold – for the twins. But within a few years it all changed and it was closed down some months after we'd visited.

Ronnie had treated it all as a huge joke, dipping into the proceeds and blowing huge sums of money – frequently giving money away for no good reason. Ronnie would always have a hugely generous streak, all his life. But, as was his way, he couldn't moderate it. If he wanted to chuck money around for no good reason, he did so.

Reggie had seen it as a serious business but, as he had predicted, his twin blew it for them. In many ways, Esmeralda's was the fulfilment of a dream for the pair, two East End boys running a high-rolling Knightsbridge casino. In the end it was a disaster.

But, away from all this, my life was heading towards a disaster of my own. By the mid-1960s, Patrick and I were not on good terms. He was intensely possessive, and he had to know where I was at all times. He didn't even like the idea of me having the odd afternoon free and, because of the modelling job and the way I looked, he was increasingly jealous of the attention that he knew I was getting. It got so that he started grilling me all the time.

'So . . . what happens when you do that catwalk thing?' he'd ask, never having bothered to come down to the West End and see what went on inside a big department store. Jealous though he was, he'd never offer to meet me from work – curious though he was, too.

'Are there other girls there?' he'd say.

'Of course there are,' I'd tell him, 'usually four of us on the catwalk, showing off the clothes to the customers perched on their little gilt-edged chairs.'

But he did not understand the clothing business, showing off fashionable clothes and tempting customers to spend. He worried about sex-crazed men stalking the store, popping up at every corner, all with one thing in mind and, of course, ready to whisk me off to have their wicked way with me. He'd always been a jealous guy, right from the start. But now the jealousy about what I did was threatening my job and our much-needed income. And, of course, all this was aggravated by the fact that I didn't conceive.

I'd tried. I'd had two dreadful operations in the four years after my miscarriage to try to remedy the problem. (I'd lost my right-hand fallopian tube during my miscarriage, so there was much less chance of success.) But neither of the ops worked. This was devastating news for Patrick because he'd been so keen to start a family as soon as we got married. We were the only married couple in his big family that didn't have children. Everyone had babies except for us.

One night, as I'd turned away exhausted from yet another screaming match, he'd lashed out with a ferocious slap. I saw stars, as the saying goes. This was a fifteen-stone man. A man who could usually contain his temper somehow – but as soon as his wife turned round to walk away he would blow up. Then, the next time we had a big row, it happened again. And again.

One day I took the plunge, and told Violet about it. I'd held back for ages, scared about what she might say to me. I hadn't even told my mother, sister or brother.

'Don't you ever tell the boys that anyone hits you,' she told me straight away, before I even had time to finish my sentence. 'If you do, they'll go out and do something to them.'

That didn't sound good at all. Starting a punch-up between Krays and Flanagans was not a scenario that any sane woman would contemplate. But by now I was living in an unhappy situation. It was a relief to be able to share it with someone.

Things didn't improve but I couldn't keep quiet, and more importantly I could never stop asserting my independence from my husband, doing what I wanted to do behind his back. That, I realised much later, was because I was a strong-willed girl who'd already got a taste for an exciting, glamorous way of life and was never going to let a man boss her around, tell her what to do.

Patrick, sadly, would have been better off with a very different kind of girl. I'd been far too immature when we married to understand who I really was. I just wasn't cut out to tread the path that I'd blindly embarked on as a relatively ignorant teenager.

In a way, being around the Kray family made it all seem much worse. Vallance Road was the shabbiest of settings but the three boys and, to an extent, their mum were hooked on glamour, shiny surfaces, bright lights and the reflective glow of celebrity.

I was too. I couldn't have defined it that way then, of course. I just knew I wanted, in a small way, to be part of all this glamour. I fitted in with them, if you like, a female friend for Violet, who was turning into a bit of a surrogate mum for me, and a 'sister' for the boys, especially for Charlie, so genial and different from his tense and edgy 'naughty' brothers with their endless supply of teddy bears.

I wasn't the only one. Many people, over time, got sucked into the Kray orbit, one way or another. Some would still tell you, to this day, they regret that. I would never wind up regretting my friendship with this family. I had my own life and identity and could remain detached from the uglier elements of the Kray story. Like their mother, I would stay 'protected' from the worst of their behaviour, from the crime, the scheming and manipulating.

For me, then, as it was for many other 1960s twenty-somethings in London, it was all about exploring an exciting new world that seemed to be opening up for me. The Krays, through force of circumstance, happened to be part of it. It really was as simple as that.

Chapter 7

The wedding

By the dawn of New Year's Day 1965, me and Patrick were just about as shaky as could be. He'd been in a terrible mood all through Christmas. There was even more shouting and slamming of doors but no punches were thrown this time, thankfully.

I'd seen Vi just before Christmas. As usual, I went to Vallance Road late afternoon on Christmas Eve for her hairdo. She loved Christmas, said it always reminded her of when she was a kid. She'd decorate the house with big fat red candles with gold tinsel round them, positioned all over the mantelpiece. Tinsel and mistletoe everywhere. She often cooked a big traditional Christmas dinner or they'd go round to her sister May's place, two doors down, on Christmas Day. Even Old Charlie put in a seasonal appearance in his home. I'd asked her once if she exchanged presents with him but she said that he'd just bring her some flowers. Over the years there had always been several big bunches of flowers and stacks of cards on show. Boxing Day they'd all go for a drink in the Carpenter's Arms. New Year's Eve was usually spent in one of the boys' clubs or somewhere like the Astor. The boys gave her bits of jewellery for Christmas. Her fur coat and stole, she said, were Christmas gifts from the twins.

One year, Charlie asked me to get him 'something nice' for Violet's Christmas present. I got him a beautiful cardigan wholesale, a £25 cardigan for £8. It was pale blue angora with little pearl buttons. Vi simply loved it. It was her colour.

Obviously, I couldn't give the game away when she showed it to me.

'Angora, Vi. Looks expensive,' I cooed.

She did look lovely in it. Pale blue was perfect for Vi.

For various reasons it wasn't until a couple of weeks after the New Year when I returned to the house to find Vi looking somewhat downcast.

She was as neat and tidy as ever in her round-necked loose patterned dress, the same pale blue cardigan and cosy red slippers. But today, I could see straight away from her miserable face that something had gone wrong. There was no sign of anyone else around, either.

'How about I cut it today and paint your nails for you afterwards, Vi?' I asked chirpily in an attempt to perk her up. Vi's hair had been longer when we first met but now we made sure I cut it regularly and the shorter length really suited her.

'Oh Maureen, let's do that next time,' she told me,

filling up the kettle for our first cup. 'Just wash it today. I've got to go to Brixton with Charlie tomorrow. The twins've been arrested,' she said finally.

I wasn't expecting this. Then I heard the rest of it. A couple of days earlier, the police had turned up at the Glenrae Hotel in Finsbury Park to arrest the twins. They were being held in custody.

Vi didn't know much about it. Charlie had simply told her 'it was to do with a man and a club, mum' – anything to make it easier for her.

It was true: the twins had been charged with demanding money with menaces from a man called Hew McCowan, a posh bloke who owned a club in Soho called The Hideaway.

McCowan, unusually for a Soho club owner – others usually kept quiet about the Krays strong-arming them for cash – had actually approached the police and complained that the Krays had been demanding protection money.

At the time, the police had been looking to nail the slippery Kray Twins once and for all; the McCowan case looked like a good opportunity to get them behind bars. Or so they believed.

As it turned out, I saw very little of Violet while they were 'away' for the next three months. We fitted in the odd hairdo but most of the time she was being driven to Brixton by Charlie or Charlie Senior, running back and forth to the prison, making sure that the boys had whatever they needed.

From behind bars the twins were able to successfully hire top lawyers and private detectives, enforce, by threats, the silence of key witnesses – and the case collapsed. Of course, the case made all the papers, with lots of newspaper photos of everyone in Vallance Road, including Vi and Frances, welcoming the boys back to the East End at the beginning of April.

Violet had been cheerfully positive about the twins' prospects of getting off throughout the time they were away. Mainly thanks to her sons' assurances that they'd be out very soon. So when I went round to see her a few weeks before they were finally released, she'd passed on more news: Reg had told her that he and Frances were getting married as soon as the twins got out. The pair had been mostly on and off for quite some time. But now it was going to happen.

'They've held off because of her family but now Frances has said yes,' Vi told me.

I already knew that Frances's mum and dad were dead set against the relationship. Violet couldn't fathom it. 'Why don't they like my lovely Reggie? Who wouldn't want him for a son-in-law?' she'd protest, completely at a loss as to why anyone would object to marrying her boy. The one with the brains.

'He's kind, 'e treats her like a lady, buys her presents all the time. Must be because of her age,' Violet concluded.

Learning of this impending wedding, I'd mumbled something appropriate to Vi. But I was a bit taken aback by her complete lack of understanding of the situation.

She was putting it all down to the ten-year age gap when, quite obviously, Frances's family didn't want her marrying a man with a growing public reputation in the newspapers as a crime lord, let alone all the other stories about the twins' violence and prison history. Not everyone in the area saw them as generous benefactors of the underprivileged and the elderly.

There were plenty of other reasons for the Shea family to be concerned about the prospect of their daughter's marriage. The national newspapers had made a big deal of the McCowan case, partly because of the huge scandal that had erupted the year before when a story about Ronnie with 'the funny old man with the bow tie' – Lord Boothby – had appeared in the *Sunday Mirror*, much to the horror of the people running the country.

The paper had to apologise for the so-called 'libel' and pay out £40,000 in damages to Boothby because they'd claimed in the story that Boothby was a homosexual friend of gangster Ronnie. (Which was, in fact, close to the truth, though technically Boothby was bisexual.)

Boothby, of course, had denied everything. He was far too powerful and well connected to let one newspaper story damage his considerable reputation as a politician and TV personality, so he'd called in the best lawyers. Yet because the newspaper had had to pay out so much money for a so-called 'libel', all the other newspaper proprietors were far too worried about being sued for libel to allow their reporters to write exactly what they did know about the Kray Twins and their activities. The papers couldn't call them gangsters after the Boothby scandal. Just 'successful businessmen'.

Violet had, as I said, briefly mentioned Boothby to me long before the *Sunday Mirror* story. But I didn't dare bring it up in conversation when the scandal broke and I saw it in all the papers. Not a hint of the Boothby affair was ever mentioned to me at the house. Not even Charlie mentioned it.

There was so much that neither Vi nor I knew anything about in those days. There were some pretty sordid stories about the sex parties that Ronnie threw in his Cedra Court flat for groups of his male friends – including leading politicians like Boothby and Labour MP Tom Driberg – that only came to light many years afterwards. But, even if Vi had been confronted with those stories at the time, I'm pretty sure she'd have blanked it out and said it was 'all lies'.

Before the twins' McCowan court case, though, I'd had one somewhat odd yet memorable conversation with Ronnie, which gave me an inkling of how he believed that he and Reg had the power to get away with virtually anything.

It was one of those rare chats when you could see he was in a good mood and, of course, he wasn't always around when I turned up – by then, he was leading a somewhat separate life from Reg, what with having his own place in

Clapton, at Cedra Court, though the flat wasn't far away and he'd pop in to see his mum all the time.

According to Ronnie that day, their success in 'business' wasn't just through their contacts, their mixing with influential people. Their true power came from their genetic heritage: part Irish, part Jewish, part Romany.

The conversation started when I'd been trying to tell him about my Irish dad, who'd been a professional dancer in Ireland, one of the reasons I was so drawn to the idea of modelling and acting.

'Oh, we've got Irish blood, that's where our temper comes from,' said Ron. 'And we've got Jewish blood, that's why we're good businessmen – and we're gonna end up with an empire.'

And the Romany blood? 'That's why we can know when things are gonna happen,' he said, referring to each twin's often uncanny psychic ability to know what the other one was doing. Or what people were really thinking.

'We always know when people are lying to us. And then there's trouble.'

I already knew that Ronnie didn't tell lies – his mother had told me that repeatedly.

So he certainly believed the daft bit about 'an empire', though by then, of course, they'd long established a group of henchmen around them at all times – their Firm, as it was dubbed – who would go out and do whatever was necessary at the twins' behest.

I also knew by then that the twins were obsessed

with gangster movies. Ron even dressed in the image of Al Capone, the slick-backed hair, the luxurious pure cashmere coat, his own barber coming round to the house regularly. Ron's real heroes, he revealed to me that day, were men like Lawrence of Arabia, Gordon of Khartoum. Leaders of men, ever ready to go into battle. That was how Ron perceived himself. In the most grandiose terms.

'That's why they call me The Colonel,' he said and then he laughed his sinister laugh.

It was a fantasy world, fuelled by what he'd read and images he'd seen. I believe fantasy is fine if the mind is balanced, sane. But Ron's illness, tragically, could blur the line between fantasy and reality – to disastrous effect.

Such chats aside, I was well aware by then that I trod a fine line conversation-wise with everyone in Vallance Road. I might have wanted to know more, ask questions. But I knew when to stop. So when the topic of Reggie's marriage came up, I kept my opinions well under wraps.

I could see all the pitfalls of the marriage. Reggie was strong-willed but Ronnie, you could see, was never going to let up with his influence over his twin. Frances knew that Ron didn't like her, she'd said as much to Violet.

Violet, as usual, had assured her that Ron often behaved strangely but he was a caring person at heart. Frances remained unconvinced.

But it wasn't just Ronnie who bothered me. The twins, I knew, were out every single night in clubs and bars with their men hanging around them all the time.

How could that be a background for domestic happiness? Reggie was already leaving Frances with his mum when his 'business' demanded that he should be with his twin. And Frances was an extremely nervous girl. Could a girl like that handle such pressure and the reality of her situation? I wasn't so sure.

Then again, with what I'd learned about Reggie I knew that he'd never have wanted to marry a different kind of girl, no matter how gorgeous. Frances was young, beautiful, untouched and, importantly for him, from the East End. That counted for everything, as did her lack of independence.

He'd once said to me: 'Why do you go to work if you're married, anyway?'

'Me, I want to be independent, Reg. I want nice clothes like the ones I wear on the catwalk, and I want to run my little Mini. My husband doesn't earn enough for all that.'

Reg looked at me with that quizzical stare and said nothing more.

He obviously couldn't understand why my husband 'let' me go out to work.

I'd been doing Vi's hair for four years now, so I knew I'd get an invite to the wedding. I also knew there was no way that I could go. Some of the guests were bound to be from North London and might recognise me.

Perhaps, I schemed, as I drove back home after leaving Vi, I could just go to the reception and mingle in the party. That wouldn't be as risky as being there, in broad daylight, in the church. But that, I saw in the next couple of weeks, was a daft plan. You went to a wedding with your husband. Or you didn't go at all. I couldn't have it both ways and not have Patrick find out.

By this time, I'd started to cautiously introduce the subject of knowing the Kray family into conversation with my husband, mainly because I figured that I was approaching a time when my secret hairdo sessions at Vallance Road and my outings with the Krays would come out – and it would be better if it all came from me.

I'd started almost at the beginning by mentioning meeting Charlie at a pub charity night. My husband's brothers knew and liked Charlie so I felt like it was the safest introduction.

Patrick didn't seem too pleased at the news that I'd met Charlie but we didn't have an argument or anything. I was happy to leave it there. Even I knew when it was time to stop.

On the morning of the wedding that April, I went to do Violet's hair. As soon as I walked in, I could tell the house was abuzz with pre-wedding nerves. The mynah bird that Ron had recently installed in the kitchen was chirping away in its cage. Ron had already taught it a few words, one of which was 'bollocks'. But it had also picked up on another one of his favourite phrases.

' 'E ain't going nowhere,' chirped the bird, again and again, a strange sort of anthem for a joyful event like a wedding day.

Naturally, as I got to work, I was all ears to hear about The Dress. It was all lace and satin, Vi said. 'Bet she wears her hair up,' I said, carefully removing the curlers from Vi's hair, ready for the big brush-out.

The groom, immaculate as always in his smart hand-made suit, was nervously pacing round the kitchen. He was worried that they'd forgotten something, that sort of thing. No, Violet assured him. Everything was organised perfectly. All would go according to plan. But it was Ronnie, of course, who was determined to heighten the pre-wedding tension that hung around the little kitchen.

'Wot's 'e want to get married for?' he said as Reg nervously went upstairs to check something for the umpteenth time. He'd said this the last time I was there – it was obviously his rallying cry.

Despite Violet's admonishment not to upset his twin, Ronnie persisted.

'I'm not goin',' he snapped suddenly, in the way he did sometimes with a totally unnerving statement that came from nowhere.

Violet said nothing but her face fell. It was time to tread on eggshells.

This was beginning to sound bad.

Then Ron too vanished upstairs. If there was a

bust-up now with the twins upstairs, what would happen? And how could Reggie get married without his 'other half', as it were, beside him? I was starting to feel a bit nervous.

With one eye on the publicity that the wedding would bring, Reggie had already told all the journalists outside, immediately after the McCowan court case, that he and Frances were marrying. So it had to be a big event. David Bailey, an East End boy already famous as the top photographer of Swinging London, would do the wedding photos. It would be his gift to the twins, whom he'd already photographed for the *Sunday Times*. All the newspaper cameras would be clicking away. A last-minute cancellation was unthinkable.

For once, I just wanted to finish Vi's hair and get away from Vallance Road. I didn't want to be there if the two of them kicked off, thanks very much. So, my work done, I rushed out, promising Vi I'd try to get to the reception later, knowing full well I wouldn't dare do it.

A couple of days later I found my husband in our kitchen, staring at one of the photos of the wedding in the *Express*. There'd been heaps of photos in all the papers. Predictably, Frances looked stunning, purity and beauty incarnate. The twins looked as groomed and polished as ever. It had been, as Reg had wanted, 'the East End wedding of the year'.

'I could have gone to that wedding,' I piped up, unable to resist the chance to enlighten my spouse.

'What? How come?' He lowered the paper suddenly.

'I was invited. By Charlie Kray. Remember I told you I met him that day?'

'Good job you didn't go,' came the short reply.

'Why?'

'There were a lot of horrible guys there,' he said, turning to the sports pages.

That meant the subject was closed. I was REALLY glad I'd stuck to my decision not to go.

But I was never a girl to give up. He hadn't reacted that badly so far, I reasoned.

'Charlie Kray said I can go round and do his mum's hair 'cos she can't go to the hairdresser's any more,' I said one evening a few days later as we finished our evening meal; the usual potatoes for him and me.

That was my domestic routine. Six nights a week I had to cook Patrick fourteen potatoes, boiled, mash, roast if I had time, to go with our pork chops or meat pie (made by my mum) and cabbage. On Sundays we went to my mum's for a roast. Patrick's potatoes had become a bit of an in-joke, though his brothers were the same. The glamour world I was now dipping into was a nice break from this humdrum existence, rushing home from work, running down the Caledonian Road from the Tube station to be in by six to start peeling the potatoes.

Patrick shoved his plate away, one small potato still uneaten. That lonely potato told me I'd pushed my luck.

'I TOLD YOU WHAT NOEL AND CHRIS SAID!

DON'T GET INVOLVED WITH THEM, THEY'RE ALWAYS IN TROUBLE!'

OK, Maureen. Just shut up, I told myself.

But there it was, hanging in the air. He knew. So a few weeks later I just blurted it out that I'd actually been to the house in Vallance Road.

My story was that I'd been in Bethnal Green on my day off and I'd popped round to give Mrs Kray some flowers, say hello, introduce myself as a friend of Charlie – and, of course, as a mobile hairdresser. I hinted that that was the real reason – to get more hairdressing work.

'So she just invited me in,' I said innocently.

'Were THEY there?' Patrick demanded.

'No,' I said, dead casual. 'Just Mrs Kray. It's just a little house, nothing posh. And she's just like my mum, a really nice woman,' I added in an attempt to cajole him into thinking there was no harm in any of this.

Naturally, it didn't wash.

'Whadya wanna make yourself busy for? You've been TOLD to keep away from 'em. I don' even know why you're goin' over the East End!'

Patrick knew full well how much I loved street markets, browsing round the stalls for bargains. That, I assured him, was what drew me to the area. 'They've got some really good stalls there,' I added.

The phone rang, distracting him, so the conversation ended there. In his mind, I was pretty sure he really thought I'd obey him and stay away.

But he was so wrong. Finally, my secret was sort of out. I knew he'd forbid me to befriend the family. But how could I cut off my friendship with Violet Kray? I was a working wife, after all. I remained determined, one way or another, to make it clear to him that I was doing Violet's hair for her.

In the end, of course, all I did was create more grief for myself.

I'd popped round to her again, I told Patrick after work one night, offered to do her hair. Then she insisted on paying me.

Again, I got the 'I TOLD YOU NOT TO GO! WHY ARE YOU GOING THERE?' treatment.

But I wasn't giving in.

Violet Kray, I told him again, was a lovely lady. All I was doing there was washing and setting her hair.

On and on the row went, him insisting that 'we' didn't get involved with the Krays, me insisting that me doing her hair didn't 'involve' him – or his family.

The truth was, the Flanagan boys all knew the people around the Krays, people like 'Mad' Teddy Smith who'd been arrested with the twins over the McCowan affair and had mysteriously vanished the year after. They all knew each other. So what was the big deal about me doing hair? I did loads of people's hair, didn't I?

'Yeah, but they're not Krays. They're dangerous people.'

Oh-oh. The volume of the voice was going up. I knew

the signals. If I didn't go inside and look after the fourteen-potatoes dinner, things could turn ugly. So I stopped.

I wasn't frightened of Patrick, his brothers or any of them. He was right, in a way. The Krays *were* dangerous, even though it suited me not to fully acknowledge this, arguing to myself that they were always polite and friendly to me. And yes, I was already 'involved' with them, not in the sense that the Flanagans meant – of wrongdoing or criminal behaviour – I was involved because I got on with them, the family liked me, they'd all drawn me in: each one of them, the old man included, had a strange kind of personal charisma.

The twins, I knew, liked my friendship with Mrs Kray too. They now expected me to keep going round to see her, keep her company. I suppose what it boiled down to was that I'd developed a form of loyalty to the family, especially to Violet.

Loyalty is a funny thing. It can easily be misguided, of course. It was, at the time, also a kind of loyalty that was keeping me in my marriage, a marriage I should really have left after the first couple of years.

I'd admitted all this to myself after the one and only time Patrick and I ever went on holiday together to Rimini, Italy with my oldest friend and her husband. Lovely weather, hotel, food, the first time I'd eaten proper Italian. Patrick hated it, especially the Italian men giving me the eye. My bikini was wrong, the dresses were too short. One night it came very close to blows in a restaurant. A ruined

My first professional modelling assignment. I loved walking the catwalk. Modelling was my calling.

The three brothers outside their house in Vallance Road.

Above: Kray twins: so nearly professional boxers.

Right: One of my many charity nights. Collecting money from three famous faces, Geoff Hurst, Bobby Moore and Terry Venables. 1979 in a Leytonstone pub.

A rare smile from Ronnie Kray. He must have been having a good night. With his cousin Ronnie Hart and a good friend Johnny.

Me at No 10 seeing Mrs Thatcher on her first week as Prime Minister.

Charlie and I in the garden of 'The Guvnors' pub in East London.

'Flanagan. Ron and I together in spirit. Back as one. God Bless. Your friend Reg Kray (1996).'

BROADMOOR HOSPITAL
Crowthorne Berks RG11 7EG
Station : Crowthorne (Southern Region)
Telephone: Crowthorne (0344) 773111

Mrs. Flanagan,
52 Penshurst Road,
LONDON, E9.

Your reference

Our reference 7333

Date 29th August 1984

Dear Mrs. Flanagan,

Thank you for your letter of the 24th August 1984.

There is little I can do about Reggie's visits but I
have written to the Home Office seeking further
information from them.

Yours sincerely,

D. Tidmarsh

Dr. D. Tidmarsh,
Consultant Psychiatrist.

BUCKINGHAM PALACE

The Private Secretary is
commanded by Her Majesty The Queen
to acknowledge the receipt of
Mrs Maureen Flanagan
letter and to state that it has been
transmitted to the *Home Office.*

24ᵗʰ *June, 1984*

BROADMOOR HOSPITAL
Crowthorne Berks RG11 7EG
Telephone: Crowthorne (0344) 773111

Medical Director: John R. Hamilton M.D., F.R.C.Psych., D.P.M.

12 July 1984

Miss M Flanagan
52 Penshurst Road
LONDON E9

Dear Miss Flanagan

Thank you for your letter of 10 July concerning the
visiting arrangements between Ronnie and Reggie. I
have passed your letter on to Ronnie's Consultant,
Dr Tidmarsh, to deal with.

Yours sincerely

John Hamilton

John R Hamilton
Medical Director and
Consultant Forensic Psychiatrist

Inspired by Violet, I never
stopped campaigning for
the boys.

POSTCARD REVEALS KRAY'S UNREQUITED LOVE

The card (inset, top right) sent to Ronnie Kray by twin brother Reg (pictured, inset, above), which reveals Ron's plan to marry page three model Maureen Flanagan at the height of her career (pictured)

'She don't, Ron Ron!'

By ELSE KVIST

A CHRISTMAS card sent by Ronnie Kray to his twin Reg has reawakened a 20-year-old story of unrequited love.

For Ronnie urged his brother to ask former Page Three model Maureen Flanagan to marry him.

The handwritten card, containing the message: "Reg it would do you a lot of good to marry" followed by what appeared to be the name 'Flanagan', was sold for £250 as part of a mammoth auction of Krays memorabilia.

Former model Flanagan, now 68, was not surprised and she would "probably" have married the notorious gangster had he not been in prison. She said: "Reggie proposed to me three times – but I replied: 'You are not brave enough to marry me.' The first time was in 1980 when I was 40. Then two years later he sent his brother Charlie to my home to propose on his behalf.

"One year later, as I entered the prison, the inmates were singing Here Comes the Bride and he went down on one knee."

The brothers were both jailed for murder in 1969. Flanagan knew the twins from the age of 21, when she was their mother's hairdresser. She later featured in the Benny Hill Show and Monty Python.

"I have no doubt the card refers to me," said Flanagan.

She explained she had "great affection" for Reggie but that she did not want to marry someone who was in prison.

She added: "I had been married twice and wanted to keep my independence. I also had my young son to think of."

Flanagan, who now runs a charity shop in Hackney, said: "If they had let him out earlier then I probably would have married him. We would have made a great team."

Somehow the press got hold of Reg's many proposals. So they printed the story!

Right: My 50th birthday party was a lavish affair. Charlie and I perfected this pose over the many years of our friendship.

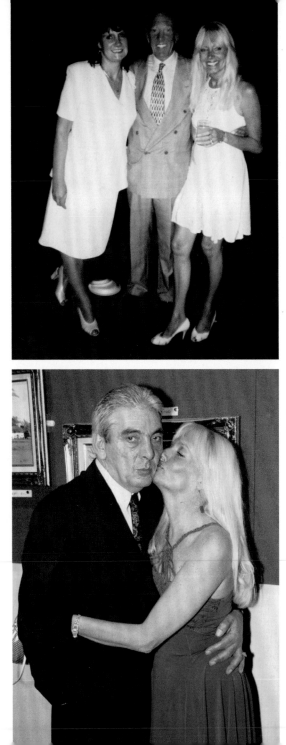

Charlie and I with his neighbour. This photo was taken two days before his arrest in July 1996.

Right: We held Ron's wake in his favourite pub. Charlie and I with Ray Winstone on the right.

Tony Lambrianou at the opening of his play.

Right: Waiting for Charlie Kray's hearse to arrive. Ready with my book of instructions from Reggie.

Overleaf: Ronnie Kray's funeral procession going over the Bow flyover. I kept my promise to be with the boys until the end.

holiday. One day, I vowed to myself at the time, I'll come back here, without him.

By then, I'd seriously considered moving out. But I suppose part of me was loyal and another part of me thought, well, maybe I'll conceive by some miracle. But the baby didn't come.

I did have a wonderfully understanding mother-in-law, something else I'd discuss with Mrs Kray. My mother-in-law had had thirteen children: seven sons, four daughters and two that died.

Mrs Kray, for her part, was always sympathetic about my marriage. She firmly believed that a baby would sort things out between us. But I was now starting to realise that a baby might heal the relationship, but it would bring changes I didn't really want. No more work, for instance. No more daytime working in the West End. When I thought hard about it, I didn't want to lose all that.

By now I'd left C&A and was working at a fashion house called Dolly Day in Margaret Street, just off Oxford Street. I started out as a house model but I later moved up as a sales manageress, selling wholesale to the buyers, many of whom I already knew from my other jobs.

It was a great job, the biggest wholesale-fashion show-room in the West End, on the ground floor of the same building as the big movie distributor, Columbia Pictures.

One day, that spring, I'd gone to a hairdressing exhibition with Diana. There we were in our Dolly Day gear; effectively we were modelling clothes at the exhibition – little white Courreges boots, white and silver minidresses – when a photographer approached us and started snapping away. He too asked if I was a model.

'Well, I do catwalk,' I said and we exchanged addresses because I wanted the pictures he'd taken.

Sure enough, when he sent me the photos he also gave me the name of a modelling agency in Soho, run by a man called Jeff Shane and his wife. I rang and made an appointment to see Jeff.

'You're wasted on the catwalk,' Jeff told me, after going through the photos. 'I'll take you on, get you lots of work. With your height and measurements you could do glamour shots – you're very photogenic.'

Well, that sounded great, didn't it? Jeff explained that he organised models for all sorts of events, including appearances in BBC-TV shows. But then he told me about the auditions for work. They could take minutes. Or hours. You couldn't go along and expect to be in and out.

How could I ever manage that, working full-time with a jealous husband, going round to Vallance Road afternoons and sometimes evenings? I already had all my time mapped out. So I left it. I'd told my sister Iris about it. She loved the photos, thought it was a fabulous idea. But at that point I couldn't see how I could manage it.

As for Reggie's marriage, Mrs Kray showed me the Bailey wedding photos not long afterwards. The newspaper photos were good but these pictures revealed just how gorgeous the bride was in her long beautiful dress, her hair piled high. Yet no one looked particularly happy about it all. Frances did smile, a bit. But the groom and his twin didn't look like they were having a rollicking time, Reggie didn't look anything like a man in love. They were like smartly dressed shop dummies, uncomfortable-looking, quite remote and very peculiar too.

In those summer months after the wedding, Frances didn't seem to be around at all at Vallance Road.

When I asked Mrs Kray one day, she simply said, 'I've only seen her twice. It's that family of hers. They don't like Reggie.'

They were a married couple now, it didn't make sense to me. Why should it matter so much whether they liked him?

The next time I did Vi's hair I learned that Frances and Reg had moved to a flat in Cedra Court. Their flat, apparently, was directly underneath Ronnie's. Yet after that I heard nothing more.

Of course I didn't have a clue what had gone down between the couple until a long time afterwards. And even then, it was difficult to know exactly what had happened because there were always different rumours going round and I couldn't keep asking Violet whether what so-and-so had said was true. But the gist of it was that Frances went back to live with her parents that autumn. After the wedding, there'd been a lot of to-ing and fro-ing but in the end she'd left Reggie. The marriage was over. The lavish wedding had been an expensive bit of publicity. It seems they hadn't even been together for six months.

Violet, naturally, felt sorry for Reg.

'Her family have turned her against him. Now they won't even let him in the front door of the house. He's her husband. In my day, that wouldn't have been right. You had to stay with your husband and look after him.'

Reg had also told his mum that Frances didn't like her husband out at all hours with his twin.

She could never have won in competition with Ronnie, I thought to myself.

Charlie, when I next saw him at Vallance Road, only reinforced my view of the situation.

'I can just imagine her life with him,' he sighed. 'He's never there. The only place he'd take her is to the clubs. She wants to be with him on her own. And she can't ever be with him on her own. Wherever they go, he's known. It's not a normal life for a young girl. I like her, she's a lovely little thing. But Ronnie . . .' He tailed off. He knew me well enough now that I could fill in the gaps. I understood all too well what Ronnie was like, wanting his twin with him at all times.

And so, almost without me realising it, by the end of 1965 the atmosphere at Vallance Road had changed. It shouldn't have been that way. The Kray family was growing: that same year, Charlie's wife Dolly gave birth to a little girl called Nancy, a sister for young Gary. Violet mentioned the new baby, and I'd seen how much she loved her grandson when he was at the house. But as the nights drew in and Christmas approached, I started to realise that this was not a happy home. Trouble was brewing.

For a start, Violet always looked slightly worried when I went round. When I asked her one day what was wrong, it was all about Ronnie. She kept saying: 'Ron's getting worse.' She was worried about his medication. It didn't seem to be working any more.

The next time I went round, I learned that her lively sociability was now under threat.

'People don't want to talk to me when I'm out. There's all kinds of stories going round about Ron. I don't listen to 'em. I just know how 'e is to me.'

I'd noticed something else too that made me wonder about the family. Charlie had told me early on that the twins earned a lot of money in their clubs. Yet in that house there was not a scrap of any evidence of this.

I'd been in and out of the Kray home for over five years now. But I never saw any sign of change. No new furniture, carpets, gleaming new mirrors or cabinets, not even fresh wallpaper. Everything was exactly the same. It remained spick and span. The carefully ironed shirts still hung there, waiting for their masters. But that was it. At one point, Charlie told me the twins had bought their mum a racehorse. At the time, he said Violet had turned to him and confided: 'I'd rather they'd bought me a new carpet.'

That new carpet never arrived. The twins would buy their mum big bunches of flowers and there were two tellys. One upstairs and a little one downstairs for her which, she told me, she only watched if there was no one around.

Whether they'd blown all the money or whether the stories Charlie told me had exaggerated their success, I would never know.

Yet it was a permanent mystery to me that the twins – who loved their mum so much – never troubled themselves to fork out for her to refurnish or brighten their surroundings. Maybe they just didn't want anyone coming into their house to decorate it. It could have been that. They certainly knew how to go about doing up their clubs to draw the punters in, I thought to myself.

Charlie Senior remained, as ever, a ghost rarely glimpsed. Superficially, nothing had changed very much. Reggie had been a married man briefly, but that was all over.

I was right.

Underneath it all and unbeknown to everyone, the lives of the family at No. 178 Vallance Road were starting to unravel. External forces were conspiring to destroy Ronnie's fantasy 'empire' and bring chaos, death and heartbreak in their wake.

The champagne years, if you could call them that, were slowly but inexorably drawing to a close for the Kray family . . .

Chapter 8

The wannabe model

Through the early months of 1966 I carried on working at Dolly Day. Yet Jeff Shane, now my agent, turned out to be very persistent. Determined to get me started in modelling work, he organised some test shots of me. I'd managed to wangle a half-day off work and I posed for the shots in a studio just before Christmas.

The results were some great 'Swinging Sixties' fashion shots, all thigh-high stretch boots, velvet trousers, white-fringed trouser suits, the 'look' of the era, similar to the up-to-the-minute outfits on display in the Dolly Day showroom. Mrs Kray was thrilled to bits early in the New Year when I took some of the photos round to Vallance Road to show her.

'Oo, Maureen, you look better than them girls on the telly,' she chirped.

Jeff, of course, had promptly sent out the test shots to ad agencies, magazines, papers, all and sundry. He called me afterwards, saying he was getting a lot of interest in my photos. I could definitely get work as a model if I started going on those auditions. In modelling, even then, you had to go on audition after audition, wait until you got a job, then there'd be more auditions, waiting – it all took ages before you could earn a little bit of money. The one thing you needed was free time to make yourself available at the drop of a hat. How could I find the time?

'Come and see us,' Jeff said. I muttered something vague but I didn't go in the end. Iris, my sister, was my sole source of encouragement. She believed in me one hundred per cent, and knew I could do it. She wasn't keen on Patrick. In fact, she often said I should get away from him. She'd seen for herself how possessive he was at parties, the minute he thought anyone paid me too much attention.

Each time I saw Violet now she seemed a fraction more troubled, a bit more careworn than the time before. The cheerful woman singing to the radio at the top of her voice was no more. It was as if she was under pressure, carrying a heavy load.

One day it all came out in a rush. It was about Ronnie. He'd had to move out of the flat in Cedra Court, he was that bad. He needed Vi to keep an eye on him, to try to control his terrible unpredictable rages and black moods. Reggie, she said, had instigated the move, telling her: 'Ron's blowing up over nothing, mum. That medication needs to be changed.'

'And Reggie's bad too, always going round Frances's parents' house, trying to get her to talk to 'im.' Vi couldn't find the words to finish what she was saying.

Reggie, in fact, was running back and forth to Frances's parents' house in Hoxton almost every night. The parents refused to have him in the house. So he would stand there on the narrow pavement until Frances opened her bedroom window and talked to him. Worried about all this and increasingly nervous about his twin's worrying and scary behaviour, Reggie too was on a permanent knife edge.

In February, Violet told me that the twins' screaming matches were getting worse. At the time, I'd only seen glimpses of them now and again. A couple of times I'd heard them screaming at each other upstairs. Vi didn't look embarrassed when this happened: she'd just look at me as if to say, 'This is what it's like now, Maureen.'

One day, Ron was briefly in the kitchen when I arrived. He was morose, withdrawn and, though I didn't understand it then, on the very edge of a breakdown. He was a very sick man. Even the combined efforts of his twin and his mum couldn't help him, couldn't calm him down any more, or save him from himself.

At one point, Violet informed me, they'd got Ron to a private doctor who'd changed his medication.

'We think it'll calm 'im down now,' she told me.

But she was wrong. What no one fully realised was this: a frenzied madness was building up in Ronnie Kray. A good psychiatrist who had an understanding of his illness would have recommended that he go into a psychiatric hospital, of course. But that wasn't going to happen. Not to a Kray.

Neither Violet nor I knew anything about the death lists that Ronnie was now drawing up, the people he was vowing to eliminate because, his fantasies told him, it was kill or be killed. His paranoia was taking over.

Then, one night in March, the madness overwhelmed him. Ronnie marched into the Blind Beggar pub and shot George Cornell in full view of everyone in the bar. At the time there was no real logic to the killing: only persistent rumour. Many claimed that Cornell had been overheard calling Ron 'a fat poof' and someone had run back to Ron and told him. In Ron's fantasy world, Cornell was poised to kill him. So he had to strike first. And, in doing so, seal his reputation as a big-time criminal. A cold-blooded killer.

The reality was, of course, that this was a murder committed by someone suffering from severe mental illness. The drugs to calm Ron down and keep his mood stable clearly weren't working. Ron was deranged, off his head completely. He'd crossed the line between wild fantasy and reality – a terrible place for anyone to be.

So much of the worst was kept a secret, from us all. Only Reg knew the truth of Ron's illness. Even the men around them, their 'Firm', had to cope with it on a day-to-day basis somehow, do whatever the twins ordered them to do.

But at the end of the day, they'd go off home, put it behind them briefly. They didn't live with it 24/7.

Vi witnessed so many of Ron's rages and tantrums now that he was under the same roof again. Reg had been right to move him back. But she didn't know about the guns Ron had hidden under the floorboards at Vallance Road, his secret stash of weapons from which he'd removed the Mauser automatic before setting off on his deadly mission to the Blind Beggar. We didn't have a clue about what had gone down that night.

Around the time of the murder I'd read newspaper reports that there'd been a shooting in the East End and a man called George Cornell, a big man, a South London villain, had died. But there were no further details. The rumours were true, it seemed.

And because a number of people had seen it happen in front of their eyes, the stories were already flying round the East End pubs and the tiny terraced houses of the area that mad Ron Kray had walked into the Blind Beggar and shot Cornell dead. No one talked about it in those terms where I lived. Or mentioned the Krays in connection with it. Well, not to me, at least.

The terrible stories going round Bethnal Green about the shooting of Cornell were never going to reach Violet Kray either. No one would have dared to tell her that. For sure, she seemed increasingly worried now whenever I did her hair. After it happened Ron was nowhere to be seen, of course, because Reggie had organised somewhere for him to lie low until all the fuss about the shooting died down. He'd told his mum that he was looking after Ron, and that she shouldn't worry. Of course, Vi was worrying more than ever because she wasn't around to help him.

The police managed to pull the twins in for an identity parade, which was a waste of police time: none of the Beggar's customers that night would be picking out anyone whose name was Kray. Reggie had made sure that everyone in the area understood what would happen to any witness who spoke up to the law. The power of their rule by fear was absolute then.

But it must have been so scary for Violet, already worried to bits about Ron's tantrums and rages, not knowing what was happening to her son. She must have known it was something really bad that was keeping him out of sight. But she never talked about that side of it to me. And I didn't ask. I imagine she told herself he'd had a terrible fight with someone, that was why he was staying God knew where. Only a handful of the twins' close associates knew then how they ran their lives away from Vallance Road, their 'safe houses', the places where they could lie low, keep changes of clothing. Vi was in the dark about so much of their lives because that was the way her sons all wanted it. They protected her and she protected them.

Every time I asked if she'd heard from Ron, she'd say: 'Reggie and Charlie go to see him, he'll be back here soon.'

Once, when Reg was in the kitchen when I turned up, he didn't say very much to me. But the minute Vi was out of the room he shook his head sadly, saying: 'Mum misses Ron. It's making her ill, being without him.'

To me, it seemed very strange indeed that Ronnie had suddenly disappeared. He'd had dozens of fights, everyone knew that. But he didn't run away to hide. That wasn't really his style.

We were completely in the dark, yet so much that was bad took place during that year. Charlie knew some of it, but he wasn't going to upset his mother with what he did know. The full story of Cornell's murder would come out in the courtroom of the Old Bailey a few years later.

But only a long time after the event did it become known that a few days after George Cornell was shot, Reggie's estranged wife Frances went to a local solicitor and legally changed her name from Kray back to her maiden name of Shea. Virtually everyone in the East End had heard the story of the killing in the Blind Beggar. So Reggie couldn't stop the rumours and the whispers about the shocking night in the pub reaching his estranged wife – and the Shea family.

It was all quite bizarre. Vi said Reg told her about his nightly talks to Frances through the window of her bedroom. Sometimes he'd go round to give her money, shoving an envelope through the letter box.

'Oh, Reg sees that she's all right,' Mrs Kray would say. 'He loves her. Why is she treating him like this?'

I could see a number of reasons why. The Shea family's worst fears for their daughter must have been realised when George Cornell died. What I also didn't know, at the time, was that Frances was really suffering and already in deep depression. Around June 1966 she wound up in the psychiatric ward at the Hackney Hospital for three months.

Throughout my visits to the house that summer, it was hard to lift Mrs Kray's spirits. She seemed so subdued and distracted by her problems.

I could cheer her up a little bit. Celebrity stories always enthralled her so I told her about meeting Sean Connery and Ursula Andress one day when they came into our reception area at Dolly Day. Me and another girl ran out and introduced ourselves. 'We work in here.'

I told Vi the story of how a somewhat bemused Sean Connery got accosted by two miniskirted blondes.

'Come into our showroom and see us!' we yelled after him as he turned to leave. Alas, he didn't but just meeting the fabulous-looking man who played James Bond was, to me, a feather in my cap. It wasn't the sort of thing that happened to anyone I knew, apart from the Krays.

It was Mrs Kray who first told me about Frances being in the Hackney Hospital.

'It's depression,' she said. 'She's bin on tablets. I know what that's all about 'cos of Ronnie,' she added sadly.

That World Cup summer of 1966 was good for me, provided I didn't think too hard about the state of my marriage. I earned a decent commission on my sales at Dolly Day and a lot of my earnings went on my Mini. I was always changing it – red, white, black – it became a sort of trademark for me. I'd spend the rest on clothes. It all kind of made up for my often dull home life, a routine that never varied. Eat dinner and watch TV. On Monday nights I'd go round to my mum. On weekends we might go to a pub or a party locally. I longed to tell my mother how bad things were at home but I was never going to tell her the truth – that I wanted out.

The nights out with the Krays were more or less over too, of course, with Ronnie in and out of hiding and Reggie as flat and downcast as his mum. Even Charlie seemed to have lost much of his sparkle when he'd pop in to say hello.

Each time I'd ask Vi about Frances I got the same response, even after she came out of Hackney Hospital.

'She's not well. Very depressed.'

I did see Frances once at Vallance Road. She must have popped round there – Reggie was nowhere to be seen. She didn't say much. But she looked so different from the outstandingly pretty girl I'd first met in the kitchen a few years before. She looked pale, thinner, like the life had drained out of her completely.

Then, towards autumn, I was told by Mrs Kray that Frances had tried to commit suicide at home. She'd taken pills but her dad had found her in the nick of time.

Even then, though, Violet wouldn't have it.

'Oh, she made a mistake. She took the wrong pills,' she argued.

She'd been in a psychiatric ward – something few of us knew much about then, I might add – she'd been so depressed, she'd tried killing herself. This girl was in deep, deep trouble.

As for Reg, he had enough on his plate with his twin, let alone trying to help his ex-wife whose family hated him so intensely that they wouldn't even let him through the front door. Love, it seemed, wasn't enough if you married into the Kray family.

If there was one bright distraction at Vallance Road for Vi, it was her grandson, Gary. I never saw his mum Dolly at the house, though I had briefly met her once or twice. Sometimes his dad would drop him off and Gary would sleep over at Vallance Road. As the only grandchild until Nancy came along, everyone in the family had always made a great fuss of him, including the twins. Gary was a good kid by now, growing and full of sweetness. Vi would spoil him to bits.

'When's farve comin'?' he'd say. He was so attached to his dad, he was his shadow. His dad was always 'farve', even when he'd grown up.

One of the things I'd discovered through Jeff Shane was that if you wanted to try to get any film or TV work, you needed to be a member of the actors' union, Equity.

How, I wondered, did you actually get an Equity card? My brothers-in-law had Equity cards because they'd had small roles (as hard men, naturally) in a couple of movies.

But how could I ask them? Diana didn't know, either. In fact, no one I knew had any idea how to get hold of one.

I should have known, of course, that the one person I knew who knew how to get an Equity card was Ronnie Kray.

Late one afternoon in November, he wandered into the kitchen unexpectedly as I was about to go home. It looked like he'd been sleeping, he looked untidy, unshaven, not at all like the Ronnie you usually saw. He plonked himself down in the chair as Vi immediately leapt up to make his tea, fuss around him.

'Bin doin' that modellin' stuff?' He peered at me with that intense stare. 'Mum told me about the photos.'

'Yes, I'm thinking about going on auditions. But someone says you have to have an Equity card if you want to do film or TV work,' I told him. 'No Equity card, no telly, nothing.'

'Nah, it's easy. Go to the Equity office. There's a man called Brannigan who runs it. Tell Brannigan Ronnie sent you,' he said, stubbing out his umpteenth fag before automatically lighting the next with a very flash silver Ronson lighter.

It was worth a try, anyway. No one else had been much help.

Two days later I did exactly what he told me to do.

Brannigan said yes, he'd get the card off to me. Within a week, I had the precious Equity card. But the next time I went round to Vallance Road, hoping to tell him the good news, Ron was nowhere to be seen.

Neither Violet nor I knew that for many months ahead Ronnie would again be hiding out in a flat in North London. And it was around this time that a man called Frank Mitchell, a friend of the twins, imprisoned in Dartmoor for life (for robbery with violence) would, thanks to the connivance of the twins, be dramatically sprung to freedom – only to be slain, on the twins' order, on Christmas Eve 1966: a crazy publicity stunt that Ron had dreamed up and that went tragically wrong.

Like everyone else, I found out about it all much later, when the twins' 'reign of terror' finally caught up with them.

It had to be one of the craziest ideas ever.

Ron had known Mitchell for over ten years, when they'd met in Wandsworth Prison. Since then, the twins had visited him and written to him regularly.

To Mitchell, a huge giant of a man who had spent most of his life behind bars – he'd been detained in Dartmoor during Her Majesty's Pleasure (i.e. indefinitely) – the twins were demigods. He wore their loyalty like a badge.

Ron's idea stemmed from the fact that business, for the twins, started to go downhill after the killing of Cornell. Crime is crime but murder, even in those circles, was something else. Clubs they'd been 'minding' for years for big money had dropped them. Reputational damage, as they call it nowadays.

Public sympathy, reasoned Ron, would restore their fortunes. So they'd help Frank Mitchell make an escape from Dartmoor. Then they'd take him into hiding.

While in hiding, they'd help him write letters to the press, explaining the injustice of his case, promising that he would surrender to the authorities in exchange for a review of his case. Or even for release. Once this happened, amid the huge amounts of publicity generated, all credit would be given to the Kray Twins, benevolent benefactors of the underdog, restoring their fortunes as 'businessmen'.

It has to be said that only a madman could dream up such a stunt.

The story of how Frank Mitchell, or 'The Mad Axeman' as the papers dubbed him (because Mitchell had threatened an elderly couple with a felling axe while on the run from a hospital for the criminally insane), had sensationally escaped from Dartmoor prison and was on the run certainly did make huge headlines in the papers that December of 1966.

It was one of those stories you couldn't miss, sort of 'Madman on the Run', scaring the life out of everyone. Of course, none of the papers mentioned who might have helped Mitchell escape.

At a Saturday-night party a week before Christmas Eve, I overheard my brothers-in-law discussing the escape.

'It was definitely something to do with the Krays,' I heard Noel say.

I didn't want to hear it. I jumped up from the sofa and started dancing furiously, taking Iris, who'd been perched next to me, up with me.

Ironically, someone had just put on one of my favourite sounds: 'Keep On Running' by the Spencer Davis Group.

Little did any of us know as I partied away, determined to enjoy the music and the moment, that Noel was right. The man on the run, Frank Mitchell, wouldn't be hiding for long.

The plan went horribly wrong. The escape itself went well but once he'd been driven to a hiding place in East London, Mitchell, guarded by the Kray's henchmen, became impossible to control. The big man felt trapped. Edgy. When were they going to let him go? His captors even brought in a girl, Lisa, a hostess that Reggie knew, to try to calm Mitchell down. But even sex didn't seem to help.

Ronnie, for his part, went nowhere near his friend because his depressions and paranoia had taken over – and he was in hiding from the authorities too.

Then Mitchell managed to snatch a gun from one of his minders. He threatened them. Unless they let him out, he said, he'd go round to Vallance Road and use the gun on the twins' parents. This, of course, was immediately relayed to the twins.

The twins made a decision. Reggie visited Mitchell in

his hiding place. He promised his friend they'd get him out for Christmas Day.

So on the night of Christmas Eve, Reggie's minder, Albert Donoghue, persuaded Mitchell to accompany him into his van, where 'Reggie's friends' were waiting to take him down to a farm in Kent.

Then, once inside the van, Frank Mitchell was slain in a hail of bullets by two men, Freddie Foreman and Alfie Gerrard. Foreman, later acquitted of the crime, eventually admitted that Frank Mitchell's body had been trussed up and dumped into the Channel afterwards. He had done it, he claimed on TV decades afterwards, as 'a favour to the Krays'. They were protected by the 'double jeopardy' card of the law which meant that he couldn't be charged with the same crime twice.

The twins had ordered the killing of Mitchell but they too were never convicted for this complicated crime. In court, in 1969, they admitted to helping him escape and harbouring him, yet his body was never found. Many years later, Reggie would admit that springing Mitchell from prison was one of their biggest mistakes.

So although I didn't know a thing about it, that Christmas of 1966, the same year that George Cornell died, the twins' time as free men was starting to run dangerously low. The authorities were now increasingly determined to ensnare the Krays. The East End remained consistently silent after George Cornell's murder. And it would all stay that way. But not for much longer.

So there weren't many happy Christmases left for the family to celebrate at Vallance Road.

By New Year, I'd made a big decision. I would start going to those auditions. I had my half-day off from Dolly Day during the week and I could use that – Patrick would be at work, anyway. Mrs Kray said she didn't mind if I didn't come every single week, she'd fit in with me.

It was, of course, a very slow beginning. It took ages to get any modelling or bit-part work: month after month of turning up with a lot of other girls, waiting to be called, walking around to show them you had the looks, the shape for what they wanted.

One day the agency sent me off to Pinewood Film Studios. Nine of us had to line up for a group scene in a film. It was a bit of a cattle market: you carried a card with your name and number to identify you. Then, clad in your silver skirt, little cropped top and high white heels, you had to turn round and go back again. Did they like you? You hadn't a clue. Next!

I gave one of the other girls a lift back to London, chattering excitedly about what an opportunity it would be to get a bit part in a movie.

'You'll never hear a thing about it afterwards,' the girl warned me.

She was right, of course. Naively, I'd fully expected a call. Not long after, Jeff enlightened me.

'You'll go on dozens of those before you get your first job, Maureen. Don't worry. You'll work.'

So I kept trying, though it was touch and go, fitting in the auditions. By now, of course, the genie was out of the bottle and I'd had to tell my husband about the auditions, which made him worse. Even if I was just going out with girlfriends on Friday nights, I'd have to sneak my outfit out of the flat, into my car and change into it at my girlfriend's place. There were a lot of crocheted see-through dresses then. If Patrick saw such outfits, he wouldn't let me out of the door. The more daring my outfits got, the more subterfuge I had to deploy to keep the peace.

Around this time, Noel and I decided to take a stall at Hoxton market on Saturdays. He already had a fruit-and-veg stall so it made sense for us to join forces. I knew exactly what the girls wanted to wear. Fridays after work we'd go to the wholesalers to buy the dresses, skirts and two-pieces to sell for thirty-five shillings. We split the profit fifty-fifty, small money, but we usually sold everything on the three little rails. The stuff just flew off the rails.

Time was passing by so quickly. Then in June 1967 the first bombshell came, with a late-night phone call from Charlie. Luckily Patrick happened to be out that evening.

'Maureen, it's Frances,' he said without waiting for me to speak. 'She's gone.'

'Gone where?' I said, not understanding.

Silence.

'Frances is dead, Maureen. Some sort of accident. With pills. Reg is going potty.' I could hear Charlie's voice cracking.

This was devastating news for everyone. We all knew how much Reg doted on Frances. Only recently, Mrs Kray had told me that he still hoped to win her back.

She'd gone to live with her brother Frank who had a flat near Islington. Apparently Reggie had persuaded Frances to go with him on a holiday to Ibiza, a sort of second honeymoon. They'd even gone to the travel agent's to get the tickets the day before. But that night she'd taken a huge overdose of phenobarbitone tablets. Her brother took her in a cup of tea the next morning when he went off to work. He'd thought she was still asleep. But he came back at midday – and found her dead. I didn't know that she'd tried to kill herself a second time at her parents' home earlier that year, but that her dad had again found her in the nick of time. Mrs Kray didn't know about it, either.

I thought it best if I kept away for a bit. 'Tell Violet I'll come to see her next week,' I told Charlie. They wouldn't want outsiders hanging around the house after such a terrible shock for everyone. As close as I was to the Krays, family was family. I sent flowers to the funeral and kept my ear out for all kinds of gossip flying around about what had happened. The inquest made it clear – Frances had killed herself.

One day, Patrick asked me, out of the blue: 'Did you

ever meet Frances?' I mumbled something about 'never saw her' and realised that he still believed I'd just been popping into Vallance Road on the odd occasion to do Vi's hair.

When I did turn up the week after Frances's suicide, I found Mrs Kray all alone. I didn't quite know what to say to her. What do you say when a young, beautiful woman has married into a family and then killed herself?

I said the usual consoling phrases, but you could see that Violet was in quite a state. Then, to my surprise, she started crying. In all the years I had known Violet, I had never seen her cry. She seemed truly cut up about the whole affair. I cuddled her, comforted her for a bit until she'd stopped and then I started making us a cup of tea. I half-expected her to start talking to me about Frances, about how sad it all was for everyone, especially Frances's family. How awful had it been for her brother to find his sister dead in his home?

Yet Vi's tears were for her son alone and that made me even sadder for the poor girl who took her own life.

'My Reggie's a broken man. We all loved her. But I knew she couldn't be a wife. She couldn't cook. She couldn't even make a cup of tea properly. Or wash a shirt. You saw her, Maureen. She should never have married him. My Reggie needs a girl to look after him. Like I've always done.'

It was quite astonishing. A girl had died by her own hand. She'd had to deal with a difficult marriage, one she wasn't mentally mature enough or ready for. It had broken down in just a few months. It couldn't have been easy for her or her family.

Nothing in the world would let Violet point any finger of blame at her son. She was grieving, for sure. But it was all for Reggie. Every bit of it.

Frances's parents had lost their much-loved daughter for good. Her brother had gone through the horror of it happening under his roof. How wretched they must have felt. But it was as if they didn't exist.

'Where's Reg now?' I wondered.

'Drunk somewhere. 'E's always drunk these days,' Violet replied, somewhat angrily.

There was more. Charlie had been round that day to tell her, although she'd tried to ignore the letters that had been coming through the letter box for ages.

178 Vallance Road, the house they'd rented for nearly thirty years, was going to be demolished, along with all the other houses in the street. Violet, her sister May and other family members would all be offered new homes to rent not far away. Or, if they wished, they could leave the East End altogether, with its grimy associations, for a place in the suburbs.

Vi's entire world, all she'd ever known, was crumbling.

'Maureen, I don't wanna move. I feel safe 'ere, with my boys. I don't think I want to be around any more.'

I didn't quite get this comment. She was so distraught.

I busied myself with the cups, thinking all the while: what does she mean, not wanting to be here? Was she suicidal too, wishing herself dead and buried?

By the time I'd put the tea in front of her she'd gone really quiet. Very un-Vi.

'How about I do your hair, Vi, make you feel a bit better?'

'No, Maureen. Thanks. I don't feel like it. I don't feel like doin' anythin' now. How'm I gonna be, leavin' this place? We can't go and live in one of them country places, we like it round 'ere. Me, me sister, me family, we know everyone round 'ere – and they know us.

'They made us go to the country in the war. But we came back, fast as we could, didn't we? We said sod 'Itler, we wanna be in the East End. It's our 'ome.'

I tried to lift her mood. I told her, in some detail, about my mum's friends who'd recently been moved to a brand new maisonette in Harlow.

'All mod cons, Vi. Proper heating and everything. And lovely gardens.'

Silence.

Then a small outburst.

'And where's my Ronnie? I don't even know where 'e is. Reg keeps saying "Don't worry, mum." But I do. I do.'

It was all too much for Violet. One son weeping for his dead wife when he wasn't blind drunk and the other one God knew where. Let alone having to think about the move.

'Maybe they'll offer you a new place round here, Vi,' I said brightly.

There was always a chance, I thought.

'Somewhere you can live with the boys but still be near Bethnal Green.'

Amazingly, just the mention of being back with the boys seemed to perk her up.

Violet nodded. Yes, that might happen. 'Come next week, Maureen, and I might 'ave some good news,' she said, ushering me to the front door.

It was Charlie who hinted to me about the mayhem that was about to ensue. I'd gone to Bethnal Green to buy some material and bumped into him. We went into Pellicci's for coffee. He seemed very tense and angry, which was quite unusual. Yes, Vi was OK now, but the move had unsettled everyone. He wasn't like the usual Charlie, he seemed very tense and angry. In the end, I had to ask him what was wrong.

'Those two brothers of mine will be the death of us all, Maureen. And it's our mum I feel sorry for. She's done everythin' for 'em and they still expect her to run around for 'em, comin' in at all hours, wakin' 'er up. And now 'e's pissed off.'

When Charlie said ''im' or ''e' he always meant Ronnie. But he clammed up after that, and changed the subject.

Long afterwards I realised that Violet, on that day, must have already had a strong feeling that everything was ending. All of it – the glamour, the celebrity parties, the nights out with her at the centre of the twins' glittering universe – it was all crumbling away. Along with the houses in Vallance Road.

A couple of weeks later, I rang and insisted I should take her out after doing her hair. 'You need to get out of the house, Vi,' I told her.

We drove down to Whitechapel Waste, opposite the big hospital. The idea was to have a cup of tea in a café, do a bit of shopping off the stalls.

I thought it was working. We bought some fruit, some flowers and she seemed to have cheered up quite a bit.

Until we bumped into two old ladies she knew.

' 'Allo, Vi,' one said. Obviously, she expected Vi to stop and chat.

Vi pulled me along, not wanting to stop. They looked stunned – it was totally out of character for Vi.

'Don't you like those two?' I asked her as we made our way along Whitechapel Road.

'Oh,' she said, with some disgust. 'All they'll keep asking about is poor Frances. What about my poor Reggie?'

I was gobsmacked. This was the first time I'd ever seen Vi so unsympathetic, so uncaring. No blame for Reg, how he hadn't been able to tear himself away from his twin or attempt to lead something like a normal life with the woman he loved. No.

Frances had chosen suicide over life with her son. But Violet didn't think it had anything to do with him! I suppose that was the first time it dawned on me that no

165

matter what happened, the twins' mother would always defend them, protect them with her love. Right to the very end.

Part Two

Chapter 9

A prediction

Reggie looked dreadful: gaunt, dead-eyed and tortured. He'd lost heaps of weight in a matter of weeks. You couldn't talk to him at all. He just took his tea from his mum and disappeared upstairs. A broken man.

'I've never seen 'im drink so much, Maureen,' Vi whispered as I was rinsing her hair.

Vi still wasn't doing anything much apart from worrying about the twins and the dreaded move. She seemed apprehensive, reluctant to even go out of the house again. Our little outing hadn't made much difference. It was as if she couldn't face the world outside the relative safety of the home she was about to lose. I'd hoped she'd pick up within a month or two. But I was wrong. Frances's suicide turned out to be a turning point in all their lives: a tragedy, and a catalyst for what was to follow.

With Reggie so torn up and Ronnie, out of hiding, constantly goading him, nudging him towards mayhem, all the grief and hidden guilt that had been torturing Reggie

169

erupted in a terrifying climax that autumn. Less than two years after Frances's death, the story would all come out in the courtroom: how the twins had Jack 'The Hat' McVitie lured from the Regency Club in Stoke Newington to a 'party' in a flat belonging to a girl called Blonde Carole in nearby Evering Road. And how a drunken Reg, taunted mercilessly by his twin, had wound up stabbing McVitie to death in a grisly, meaningless slaying.

None of it would ever make sense. Reggie, so the story went, had apparently been upset with McVitie, yet the idea that he wanted to murder him was ridiculous. More like give him a good hiding, yes. And why do something like that in front of a roomful of witnesses? Reg was the cool, calculating one. He had stopped Ronnie from doing many awful things in the past. Yes, Reg too had done his share – the story was that he'd shot Albert Donoghue in the leg, yet afterwards Donoghue went to work for him. But the killing of Jack 'The Hat', with the police already out to nail the twins, was a botched crime, an orgy of blood and violence that would destroy many lives.

There was no sign of Jack McVitie's body. In the end, there were statements from witnesses that convicted the twins and members of the Firm for his murder. Yet it wasn't until 2000 when Freddie Foreman, who'd agreed to take the body away for disposal, openly admitted that he had dumped McVitie's butchered remains at sea. As he'd done with Frank Mitchell's bullet-ridden body.

The eldest Flanagan brothers used to frequent the Regency Club quite a lot. They'd told me and Patrick about the stories that were then circulating at the club, that the Krays had been involved in something terrible. Yet, because there was no corpse, it was all sheer rumour and speculation.

But as the stories from the Regency died down, I actually saw for myself, yet again, how terrifying Ronnie's rages could be.

I'd not long arrived at the house when suddenly there came some very loud, frightening shouting from upstairs. Violet's face went white. She got up and walked to the bottom of the stairs. Was she half-expecting this explosion from Ronnie?

'If you can't do what I ask, FUCK OFF, ALL OF YOU!'

Violet started shouting for Ronnie to come down, with me standing behind her.

Then we heard a huge thump and Ronnie Bender came tumbling down the stairs. He quickly got up, obviously shaken, and came into the kitchen.

'It's all right, Vi, it's OK,' he said, not wanting to get her involved.

Then Ron emerged.

'What, mum?' he said, struggling to calm down but not really succeeding. His face was ugly, totally contorted. His breathing was rapid.

'Ron, you've got to calm down! 'Ave you taken your medicine?'

Not a word from Ron. He just turned round and went back inside.

Down in the kitchen, Ronnie Bender went to the tap, gulped down one glass of water, then ran himself a second one. He was a big, burly bloke who could handle himself in any situation. But you could see he was seriously twitchy.

'What's upset him, Ronnie?' Violet wanted to know. 'Who's he bin shouting at?'

'All of us,' came the reply.

'Is 'e shoutin' at Reg?' their mum demanded.

'Nah. Don' matter. 'E'll be all right in a minute.'

Then Reg appeared in the kitchen. His gaunt face was like thunder.

Vi wouldn't let up. 'WHAT is goin' on up there? Ron sounds terrible today.'

Reg merely put both hands to his head, like he thought it might explode.

'I dunno wot we're gonna do with 'im, mum,' he wailed, frustrated.

Then, from upstairs, more terrible screaming.

'REGGIE! GET THOSE TWO OUT OF 'ERE BEFORE I KILL 'EM!'

Quick as a flash, two men bounded down the stairs and out the front door, opened by Reg. Then it all went quiet.

I'd seen behaviour like this before, all control gone.

But this was still very ugly. Violet remained bewildered, uncomprehending.

'Oh, why are they annoying 'im?' she moaned.

It was still 'Why are they picking on my boy?' Just like it had been in the playground but I could tell this was very different.

Back in the kitchen, Reg put his arm round his mother, trying to soothe her. They were united, as ever, in struggling to deal with all this.

'I've seen as bad,' I piped up, hoping to ease the tension. Reggie looked at me with his intense Kray stare. Why could I never keep my big mouth shut?

'I don't think so, Maureen,' he said, quietly turning away and walking back upstairs.

Everything was changing very fast for all of us by early 1968. Our one weekend market stall had become two and I was beginning, albeit slowly, to see results for my fledgling modelling career. Violet didn't seem concerned when I told her I might not be able to do her hair as regularly as before. She was far too preoccupied with her other problems.

I'd started to earn small amounts of money for things like bikini shots in the *Daily Mirror*, posing on Hampstead Heath. Only an hour's money, £12 an hour. But once the photo appeared in the paper, it was a mini-breakthrough. The bookings from the agency were still only a trickle – the odd fashion shot for *Woman's Own*, that sort of thing

– but it was encouraging enough for me to believe that I was on my way.

I kept doing the cattle calls but I longed for film or TV parts, and there was quite a bit of promotion work selling programmes at movie premieres, things like that. Patrick didn't like it one bit. But by now he knew better than to try and stop me.

I got on well with the other girls I worked with, though somehow I always ended up as the hairdresser, the organised girl who always had something in my bag, something or other that the girls had forgotten.

It was a bit of an eye-opener, this modelling game. Some of the girls, I realised, weren't remotely professional. Chipped nails, dirty hair, dirty feet. Pretty girls who'd just tumble out of bed with their boyfriend, throw something on and turn up at the job. Once they were made up, they looked sensational. But they'd frequently turn up late. Or they were just trouble. Many of them didn't even realise that it is the photographer that creates the magic, calls the shots. I just took it all in and learned the basic rules: be pleasant, always be on time, don't make a fuss or create problems, get on with everyone. A recipe for success in many fields, not just modelling.

As for the Krays, Vallance Road was now about to be demolished.

Vi eventually said that the family had been allocated a brand new flat. On the ninth floor of a big new multi-storey tower block, Braithwaite House, near Old Street Tube.

One of the Family

Lots of these huge tower blocks, built by local councils, were going up around London in the 1960s. Many people hated them, some with justification. Later that same year, a newly built tower block, Ronan Point, in Newham, East London would collapse with three people killed, thanks to a gas explosion on the eighteenth floor.

But Vi's fears about moving were not concerned with safety – though being up on the ninth floor, high above London, was a strange prospect for a woman who had only lived in a cramped little terraced house for much of her life. Her distress was mainly focused on leaving the only world she'd ever known, Bethnal Green and the East End.

In fact, the new flat was only a couple of miles away, a short bus ride. But it might as well have been on the moon as far as she was concerned.

'Me and the old man don' wanna go, Maureen, but we gotta go,' she told me early in that year, just before the houses were finally demolished.

That day, the last time I did her hair at the house, was tinged with sadness for me too. I did feel desperately sorry for her. No one in her family saw the move as anything other than a disaster.

To an outsider it would have looked like they were ungrateful, leaving a rotten slum for better living conditions. Yet their emotional attachment to their fast-disappearing world was fierce, partly because they were all so close to each other, had come through the worst together – and managed to survive.

What with all the confusion about moving, we weren't sure when I'd see Vi next. But I arranged with her that Charlie would ring me, keep me posted.

Heaven knows how they managed it, but the twins had gone out and purchased a big Victorian house in the country. The Brooks was located in Bildeston, near Sudbury in Suffolk. The plan was that the twins would use Braithwaite House as their base and relax at The Brooks on weekends. Charlie Senior and Violet would live down in Suffolk in a lodge adjoining The Brooks, 'the pink house' as Charlie called it.

The purpose of this plan, of course, was not really to do with Violet's convenience. The Brooks was a place the twins hoped to 'retire' to one day, so that they could play country squire –something they loved doing. Now she'd be stuck out there in the country with the old man, living only for the boys' visits on weekends. Why, I wondered, when the upheaval of leaving Vallance Road was so upsetting for her, send her to a strange place in the country?

But things were moving too fast for me to keep up with all their news for not long after my twenty-seventh birthday, I took the plunge and left Dolly Day. A nine-to-five job didn't work for me any more. I wasn't making much money modelling but the Saturday stalls made up the difference and, while the modelling was still stop-and-start, I needed the freedom.

My little portfolio now boasted a couple of photos in the *Mirror* and Jeff was starting to get more bookings for glamour shoots for stockings, boots, magazine work.

Charlie kept me in the loop about Vi. He'd been down to see her, told me the house was lovely with beautiful grounds. Predictably, she didn't like any of it. He felt she was too isolated there.

Around Easter, I finally got to see Vi at the Kray's new flat in Braithwaite House. I arranged to meet Charlie there; Vi was coming up to London to see her family.

At first, when I walked in, she seemed quite bright and breezy. But it became obvious that she felt lonely down in Suffolk. Cut off from everything she knew. Old Charlie, of course, was in the same boat. He couldn't walk out the front door and go round the corner to the familiar pubs and haunts of the East End. If he wanted to do that, he'd have the long drive up there. And down there, of course, Violet couldn't be the doting mother. Away from the twins, she had little to do but fret about them.

'Oh Maureen, I do miss 'em. I'm a cockney girl. I belong in the East End,' Violet wailed.

I looked over at Charlie, her loving son who lived close by. Without his mum seeing, he raised his eyes to the ceiling. He was second-best to the twins yet again.

Number 12 Braithwaite House didn't really impress me. It wasn't a very attractive tower block. For a start, the building had a horrible little dingy lift, quite small and dark. The flat itself wasn't especially welcoming, though it was carpeted and newly painted.

The hallway led to a lounge area and a separate kitchen, complete with a brand new cooker and fridge. The twins had obviously done all this. From the kitchen you could see Old Street below, with all the buses and taxis, and the lounge, it has to be said, had great views, all over the City.

The twins, I thought, could sit there like lords, surveying their fantasy empire from high above. But their mum had lost the warmth and reassurance of the familiar sights and sounds she'd left behind. All their old furniture had been moved in, the cream mock-leather suite with the square arms, the maroon felt cushions, all Vi's 1930s mirrors. Even the ducks on the wall were there. The flat had a brand new bathroom and toilet too: Vi had only ever known the chilly, damp outdoor loo in that horrible back yard.

But even with all these modern amenities, the place felt sterile, and cold. It had none of the cosy homeliness of Vallance Road. This felt like a place where you came in, went to sleep, got up, washed and went out again. A bachelor pad, not a family home.

Which is what it was: the twins' bolt-hole after a night roaming the clubs. A bedroom for Ronnie to take his boys back to and one for Reg to bring home a hostess if he wanted to. Charlie had told me that Reg had already brought his new girl, Carol, to meet Violet down in Suffolk. She was happy for him, she said. But her main concern remained Ron and his medication.

That day she didn't want me to wash her hair but I did

a tidy-up anyway, a backcomb and spray. Then she went into the kitchen to make the tea.

As soon as she left the room Charlie spoke. 'Don't tell mum, but I think something big is blowing up,' he said quietly. He'd heard that the police were really on to his brothers. A detective called Leonard 'Nipper' Read (ironically the nickname was because he was a police boxing champion) was determinedly on their trail.

'And it's all of their own making, Maureen,' Charlie confided.

'We could 'ave 'ad the best clubs, the best casinos. We didn't 'ave to touch prostitution, drugs, anythin' like that. We 'ad everythin'. But 'im. 'E always wanted more.'

I knew he was referring to Ronnie but I still didn't quite understand what Charlie meant. I had heard the odd rumour about the police asking questions about the Krays all over London, not just around the East End, but at that point Charlie was getting something of a warning: there really was a serious and determined plan to bring down the twins and their Firm once and for all.

The twins, of course, had their spies all over the place. That was how they operated. But the people who ran back and forth to them with stories usually traded information for personal gain.

Ronnie's boyfriends, for instance, were dubbed 'little spies' by Charlie because some of them hung around Ronnie because of his generosity: he'd buy them Savile Row suits, Turnbull and Asser ties, expensive watches

– that was Ronnie's way. They'd repay him with sex, of course, and snippets of gossip. Yet what Charlie had heard wasn't a trade-off. It was the truth.

That day, Charlie left me there with Vi for a while. After they'd gone, she started crying. She didn't want to go back to Suffolk. She wanted to be where the twins were.

I tried to point out the positives. 'Aren't you better off in the country, Vi? You don't see the boys anyway, they're always out at night, waking you up when they come in.'

'Yes, but I've 'ad that for years,' she countered, dabbing her eyes with an embroidered hanky. 'I'm not better off down there with 'im. All I've got to look forward to is weekends when the boys come to visit me.'

I knew that even this wasn't true. Charlie had already told me they didn't go every weekend. Still, I tried to make her laugh.

'Vi, you must be glad you don't have to do the shirts any more.'

But she didn't even smile.

'I don't care. I'd do an 'undred shirts a day. I just wanna be with them.'

As I left, I promised I'd try to see her next time she came up from the country. It was such an unhappy situation. All Vi wanted was to be with her twins. For ever. She'd have happily lived with them at Braithwaite House.

It was just as well she was ignorant about so much

involving her sons. For within a year she'd be separated from them in a way that she'd never imagined. For good.

About a month after my visit to Braithwaite House, Charlie rang to say he wanted to meet in Pellicci's, our usual haunt.

The place was packed when I got there. It was so noisy that you could hardly hear yourself speak. Charlie got straight to the point. He looked unusually strained and very worried.

''Ave your brothers-in-law in North London 'eard anything about us, Maureen?'

I told him what I'd heard, the rumours about the police going round the clubs, asking questions about the twins. That was it, really.

Charlie looked a bit relieved. If I did hear anything more, would I please let him know straight away?

'Sure. But you've done nothing wrong, Charlie.'

'Yeah, but when it all comes on top, I'll 'ave to pick up the pieces,' he warned me.

Now I was starting to see how serious it all was. The twins had been arrested before, charged, then acquitted. Yet I'd never seen Charlie like this, genuinely eaten up with worry. Only later, when I ran through it all in my mind, did I suddenly remember something.

One evening, before I'd visited Braithwaite House, I'd gone into the Old Horns pub in Bethnal Green to talk to someone about a charity night that was being planned.

It was early and Albert Donoghue, Reggie's minder, was standing at the bar.

I liked Albert. Of all the twins' Firm members I'd met at Vallance Road he was always polite, friendly. The questions poured out.

Did I want a drink? Had I seen the twins?

'No, I haven't seen any of them,' I told him.

'That fuckin' Ronnie is *mad*,' Albert said. 'He 'as me 'ere, there, everywhere. Never a thank-you for it.'

Then he promptly apologised for swearing.

This criticism of the twins was very unusual. Whoever heard any of the twins' men talking like this? Disgruntled and unhappy – this wasn't how it was in the Firm.

Normally, the men danced round them. They existed to carry out the twins' every whim.

Albert seemed perfectly sober. But you could see he was very angry. And he was speaking out in what was more or less regarded as a Kray pub, one of their haunts. He knew full well that had anyone overheard him they'd have run back to the twins or even to one of their cohorts with this snippet of conversation, and all hell would have been let loose, especially with Ronnie. Yet Albert didn't seem to care at all.

It was in May 1968 that the news broke. I was at home with Patrick when there it was, in the paper. All three Kray brothers arrested in a dawn swoop at their mother's council flat at Braithwaite House. Helping with enquiries relating to offences including conspiracy to murder, fraud, demanding money with menaces and assault. The largest police operation of its kind ever to be carried out by Scotland Yard.

'Huh. Bound to happen,' said Patrick with smug satisfaction.

I didn't say a word. My thoughts went instantly to Violet. The twins had been arrested before, they knew the ropes, how to get the top lawyers, and they were good at looking out for themselves. But what about their mother? And why had Charlie been arrested too?

Charlie knew, I said to myself. Whoever had been talking to him knew it was going to happen.

With all three arrested who could I call? Charlie's marriage was rocky and he was seeing a lovely girl called Diana, who worked in promotions. Luckily, I had her number. Diana confirmed the news: all three had been arrested and more, the hangers-on, the Firm, all of them. Charlie had managed to get someone to call Di and tell her he was OK. They'd been taken to Brixton Prison. Violet and Old Charlie, she said, were being brought up from the country to stay in Braithwaite House, so they could get to Brixton every day.

Diana sounded terrible. Shocked beyond belief, as you would be when you adored your boyfriend and hadn't a clue about why he'd been arrested. I too was stunned by it all.

'Di, if you can ring me when you find out anything, that'd be good,' I told her. 'If I get any news, I'll call you.'

But as I put the phone down, I knew it would be better if I just stuck to taking any calls from Di that came through. It all sounded so serious, so I knew I'd best keep away from them until things calmed down.

Of course, they didn't calm down. This was the beginning of the end. Though the dramatic dawn arrest had been meticulously planned by 'Nipper' Read and his team, it still carried high risks: the major witnesses the police needed to convict the twins had not yet revealed everything they knew.

Without these dramatic revelations which would smash the wall of fear that surrounded the twins, they could have wound up with just a short sentence. Yet the police were secretly striking deals with many from the criminal community: immunity from prosecution in return for everything they knew about the Kray Twins' crimes.

The night before the arrest, police had been readying their net, covertly observing the twins as they went about their usual routine: visiting The Old Horns pub with the Firm till closing time, then going, as usual, to the Astor where they remained until five a.m. before being driven back to Braithwaite House.

Nipper's plan was a perfectly synchronised arrest, with teams of police storming into homes at different addresses. Twenty-six names, including the twins and Charlie, were on the list of wanted men.

Nipper Read was armed when he and his team smashed in the front door at Braithwaite House at six a.m. and made a dive for the twins who were both asleep in their rooms, Reggie with his girlfriend, Ronnie with his latest young man. Yet no weapon was needed. Neither twin put up any resistance. All Ron is reputed to have said when Nipper put the handcuffs on him was:

'All right, Mr Read. I'll come quietly. But I've got to 'ave me pills.'

Just as the Krays' world was coming apart, my marriage too was coming undone at the seams. The modelling work was picking up steadily and over the years, with a lot of hard work, I managed to get tiny bit parts in BBC-TV shows. I'd tell Patrick where I'd be going, of course. But that made things worse, because I'd often be home late.

The rows got worse. His jealousy and suspicion, all unjustified, were driving us both mad. He'd even start making excuses, saying we had to be somewhere at a specific time, so I couldn't go on jobs: 'We've got to be at my mum's place at five o'clock,' that sort of thing. When I'd tell him I couldn't make it, he'd explode:

'WHAT ON EARTH ARE YOU DOING FOR TWELVE HOURS AT THE BBC?'

He couldn't understand it and didn't want to understand. Why couldn't he be married to a woman who did a NORMAL job? That was all I heard.

By the autumn, the full horror of what the Krays were reputed to have done started to be revealed. When I read the newspaper reports of the long Bow Street committal hearings about the murders of McVitie and Cornell, I couldn't quite take it in. It just didn't seem real to have it all printed in the papers like that, for the world to see and read.

How evil it all sounded. Two people I'd been out with socially, in their home regularly, treated like one of their family. That the twins were capable of so much evil and violence was shattering.

I was so shocked that I even asked Patrick if he thought it was all true. He did, and so did his brothers.

'We said they were scum,' he growled.

Yet the contrast between what I'd seen of them and what the police and the media were saying they'd done was so extreme: yes, I knew they had tempers and were fighters, and I had seen the fear that Ronnie could generate in one of his tantrums.

But I'd never seen anything else. They never even swore in front of women. Murderers who were polite and respectful, gentle and kind to their mother. Could the same people be so evil? And why was Charlie involved in all this? I knew for sure that Charlie wasn't interested in violence, wasn't the same kind of man as his brothers. Were the newspaper stories lies? I knew things could be exaggerated. And how, I wondered, would Violet cope with all this?

Then Diana called me, saying that Vi wanted to see me. She and the old man had settled into Braithwaite

House. The big house in Suffolk was up for sale.

I stalled. 'I'll call you back, Di. I've got to check a few things,' I told her.

I was apprehensive about staying involved now – who wouldn't be? I'd been warned by Patrick to not get involved. Now I had to decide: was I involved or not? What had started so innocently as a pleasant afternoon doing a nice, kind woman's hair had turned into a horror show involving the police and accusations of murder and extreme violence.

I tossed and turned all night, deciding what to do. Stay away, Maureen, my rational side warned me. It's not your family, is it?

Then I started to realise that whatever the truth was, it was Violet who needed a trusted friend. And we were good friends, we'd confided in each other. She had her family, certainly, all true East Enders, they'd be close, supportive, no matter what. But why should I abandon or ignore her now that things had got so much worse for all of them? She'll be a broken woman, I told myself. She's done nothing wrong. Turning my back on her, or making excuses not to stay in touch just didn't feel right. There were plenty of other people who would do that but I wasn't one of them. Whatever the twins had done, their mother was innocent of any crime. Now what would her life be like? No, I reasoned, Violet Kray didn't deserve to be shunned.

A week later I rang Diana and told her that I'd be going

to see Vi. I'd be bringing a friend with me. Jackie Docker was twenty, very pretty, an identical twin, in fact.

Vi knew her and her father Johnny, who was an ex-boxer.

Jackie was keen on the idea of modelling so I'd helped her and her twin Lorraine get some pictures done.

So there we were at Braithwaite House with a big bunch of flowers. Vi didn't look outwardly different, still neat and tidy. I thought to myself, it's going to be OK.

Once we'd settled down with the tea and biscuits to chat, she let go. She sobbed her heart out for ages.

'They're saying they murdered people, Maureen, but I know my boys. They're kind and helpful to everyone.'

Then we heard Violet's mantra, repeated throughout her life.

'It's all lies, they've made it all up. They've picked on them because they've been successful.'

I'd read all the newspaper reports very carefully. No, I thought, they didn't harm the little old ladies they'd buy Guinness for in the pub. Or the kids they paid for to go to the Repton Boys Club for boxing training. These people and their families were the recipients of their generosity, always had been. Yet if the newspaper reports were all true, it was the villains, those in their immediate circle, who'd been their victims.

'It might not be true, Vi,' said Jackie, quietly. What else could you say right now?

Vi had gone to the Bow Street committal hearings with

all her family. They'd supported her through it, listened to all the awful things that the twins were supposed to have done.

'They don't believe a word of it, all those things they're saying.'

'But what about Charlie?' I asked her. 'He's not being charged with murder, is he?'

'No, but they'll find something else to charge him with,' said Vi. 'They're out to get all my boys, aren't they?'

As we talked I realised that Vi had done a good job convincing herself that despite the murder charges there was another acquittal ahead. The twins would have primed the rest of the family to tell her that.

But a blind man could tell you it was all far too serious for that. She must be clinging to that because she can't cope with the idea of the twins going down for years, I thought to myself. What was her life without them?

I didn't have my hairdressing bag with me, so I just tidied her hair up, made her look a bit more presentable. Then we chatted a bit about my work and the modelling jobs. Her family were coming round later, she said, so we hung around until early evening.

'If you want anything at all, Vi, just tell Diana,' I said as we hugged goodbye.

Vi had never rung me at home, of course, because of my husband. I'd best stick to Diana as my intermediary for now, I thought. With the boys on remand, Vi was being driven to see them regularly, taking them food that she'd cooked at home. As long as she could still do things for them, she could carry on. The best of mums doing everything she could for the worst of children, her twin sons.

Funnily enough, despite the Bow Street reports, quite a lot of people still seemed to believe that the case against the Krays was one that would collapse because it was mostly untrue.

Some people had only known them, as I had, as polite and generous. As for their history of court appearances, being in prison was no big deal in the East End. It was part of the landscape, had always been that way. People went in and came out all the time, didn't they? The police in that part of the world weren't trusted at all. Most of them were 'bent', living off the fat of the land thanks to the many bribes they took, the average East Ender would tell you. It seemed that Vi was not alone in wanting to believe it was 'all lies'.

Despite the 'm' word.

Thanks to Diana, I managed to do Vi's hair a couple of times before the end of the year. Jackie came with me each time. The second time, Jackie mentioned that she could read palms: would Vi like her to have a look at her hand?

Vi nodded with some enthusiasm. Why not, I thought? It's a small distraction and Vi could do with some good news. After studying Vi's hand for a few minutes, Jackie announced that Mrs Kray would lead a long life. At the time she was fifty-eight. In those days, a 'long' life was anything over seventy. Then Jackie made another prediction which did, uncannily, prove partially true.

'The twins're going to be in a film after they come out of prison,' said Jackie.

Violet, of course, perked up. 'That'll be something nice to tell the twins when they get out. Ooo, they'll like that, Jackie,' she trilled.

That was an understatement. The twins had always been movie mad.

And their mum truly believed that they could do anything they wished. They'd met lots of movie stars, hadn't they? They certainly looked as good as them, the smartest blokes in the East End. Why shouldn't they be up there on the silver screen too?

So by the time I'd finished Vi's hair and we climbed into that horrible lift, Jackie and I went home feeling quite pleased with ourselves. We'd done Vi some good. Or rather, we'd given her some hope . . .

Chapter 10

Life means life

It was Diana who now became my main link with the Kray family. She managed to see Charlie in Brixton whenever she could, then she'd phone me with reports. Charlie was excessively downbeat about their fate.

'I knew this would happen,' he kept telling her. But he said Ronnie was totally delusional about the severity of the situation.

'You ought to 'ear 'im in the mornings, Di,' he'd told her. 'Like 'e was getting up and getting ready to go to 'is club. Everything done for 'im, bossing 'em all about, dictating what 'e wants to eat.'

Ronnie, it seemed, didn't understand that the commands and orders he dished out to everyone on the outside didn't necessarily apply on the inside. He couldn't just snap his fingers and have whatever he wanted when he wanted it. Despite his older brother's entreaties to keep quiet, calm down, stop ordering people around, Ronnie just carried on as usual: an over-indulged child for whom reality was a foreign country.

I had to laugh, though, when Diana repeated some of Ronnie's antics. Apparently he was busy telling some of the other prisoners that when he came out he'd be employing them! This one could be his driver, that one could work at his club – or their sons or daughters could work there too. He was a one-man Job Centre in there.

Obviously, he didn't believe anyone would dare speak out against the twins, despite the gravity of the murder charges. As far as Ronnie was concerned, the entire exercise was an inconvenience, a blip: everything would continue as it had before. Fear of the mighty Kray reputation would ensure silence from anyone who might consider grassing them up.

Ron didn't get it that those days were history. Some people were now willing to cooperate, give evidence against the twins. The police had done their homework. This time, they'd made sure that people were going to stand up in court and tell the truth about the twins. Charlie would have understood that after Ronnie Hart's chilling confession at Bow Street Magistrates Court in October about how he had seen Reggie stab Jack McVitie to death while his twin held McVitie from behind, saying 'Kill him, Reg.' The wall of silence around the Krays' 'empire' was now poised to come tumbling down.

As for Reggie, Di said Charlie had described him 'like a coiled python, waiting to strike. He's going to flip,'

Charlie told his girlfriend. 'People are more wary of him than they are of Ronnie.'

I couldn't help but feel sorry for Violet. What a dreadful Christmas it was for her with the big Old Bailey trial hanging over all their heads. Dubbed 'the trial of the century', it was scheduled for January 1969. Gary was staying with Vi at Braithwaite House, some small comfort for her, though it would have been impossible to take her mind off the big trial ahead. I wondered if Gary and his little sister Nancy, who'd watched as their dad had been carted off by the police, had been told that her was away 'painting the queen's house'. That's what they used to tell kids in North London when someone went to prison. 'When dad finishes painting the house, he'll be home,' they'd tell the kids.

Strangely enough, both Vi and I would come to regard that Christmas as one of the worst we'd known. Secretly I had to acknowledge to myself that this was surely the last Christmas I would spend with Patrick as his wife. After that, it was just a matter of timing.

Just after New Year, as we watched the TV news reports of the start of the Old Bailey trial on 7 January, I had to admit that Patrick was right, for once, when he passed judgement on it all.

'They're all going away,' he said that day. A week or so later, my brother-in-law Noel popped round to our flat, echoing Patrick.

'Not looking good for them,' I heard.

The rumour around North London was that the police had done deals with various 'naughty' people who were guilty of other crimes. They'd been promised immunity from prosecution if they'd grass on the Krays. This was all turning out to be true.

Of course, with the twins still denying everything, including the murder of McVitie, some people in the East End continued to wonder if they really had been set up by the police.

Yet as the Old Bailey trial went on – it lasted for over eight weeks – it became clear to everyone except Ronnie and his mum that this was going to be the end of the Kray Twins' reign over London. On the outside, at least.

Violet didn't go to the court all the time. It would have been too exhausting for her to go every single day. She and Old Charlie turned up looking their best for the cameras, spruced up East End-style. Later Vi told me that Old Charlie became quite pally with the father of the two Lambrianou brothers, Chris and Tony, who were in the dock as part of the twins' entourage, accessories to the murder of McVitie. Mr Lambrianou spoke very broken English. Yet the two men seemed to share an odd camaraderie.

Afterwards Violet told me Old Charlie wasn't outwardly upset by the downfall of his sons and the hugely publicised trial. She confided that she thought he was 'good' in being the supportive husband, accompanying her to court 'seeing as how he didn't like the twins or what they did'.

Well, he wasn't going to change his view now, was he? Though the twins would have gone mad if he hadn't been at the side of 'Our Mother'.

At the time, it was the longest-ever trial in British history, with noisy police vans leaving the court, racing through London's streets Chicago-style, on the TV news every night.

How Ronnie will love all that, I thought. The twins insisted that the press should be present throughout. Every word said in court would be written down and reported. They wanted it that way. To them, the exposure sealed their celebrity, rather than shaming them as criminals brought to justice.

Being filmed in that police van night after night spelled glory to the twins. That, for them, was what counted: that the world knew that they were the country's meanest bastards, the most notorious criminal duo. Top villains, just like in their favourite movies.

Charlie told me that it was Ronnie who was always the morale-booster during the trial, as the twins, Charlie and the other men in the dock travelled to and from court in the police van.

'No one,' Ronnie told them, 'is allowed to be miserable. Or whinge. Whassamarrer with you? It's a nice day out there,' he'd tell them. 'The sun's out.'

Here was Ronnie's fantasy world writ large: even in this situation he could be the general or the commander rallying the men before battle. No moaning about how long it was all taking or the way the case was going. The man on permanent medication for a mental disorder, whose illness had sent him into a spiral of madness resulting in murder, turned out to be the supportive leader of his brothers and their cronies. He was still making jokes about his nemesis, Nipper Read.

'Wonder when 'e's gonna take that awful tie off?' he'd wisecrack.

I went to Braithwaite House to do Vi's hair a few times during the long trial. She was determined to keep up appearances – 'like they've always seen me'. She told me little bits about the court, though it seemed she had only a hazy appreciation of the judicial process, believing what the boys and her family had told her: that it was all a stitch-up and the boys would get off.

She told me about the day Reggie went crazy in court and screamed that the police were 'scum' for daring to turn up at Frances's funeral. (At the time, in fact, Ronnie was in hiding and the police were there because they were looking for him.) Violet said that the judge, Melford Stevenson, seemed permanently bad-tempered.

'That man always glares at me,' she told me. But she'd still managed to throw a cheerful wink at the boys.

Court hours made it difficult for me to find time away from work. I couldn't be there for most of it. I did manage to get to the Number One Court at the Old Bailey once, though, and the place was packed to the rafters.

It happened to be the day when the barmaid at the Blind Beggar gave her evidence. She looked really nervous – and who wouldn't be? For the first ten minutes, I wondered where it would go. Then, without warning, we all saw her look across the courtroom at Ronnie, as impassive and stony-faced as ever, and she seemed to change.

Ronnie had denied even being in the pub, saying that Cornell was a friend of his. Yet, all of a sudden, the barmaid found her courage. She knew all too well that what she was going to say would be momentous. She didn't falter: the court heard that it was definitely Ronnie Kray who had shot George Cornell.

At that point, a voice came out of the crowded courtroom.

'Liar.'

She wasn't perturbed or afraid any more of Kray retribution against her or her family. She felt safe. Even right in front of the men in the dock.

A series of former trusted friends gave evidence against the twins. In a way, I always felt it was the women's evidence that carried the day. Jack McVitie's wife wound up telling the court they were 'murdering bastards' who had killed her husband. The evidence of Blonde Carole, the girl who had been living in the flat where McVitie met his end, was equally compelling.

She told the court that she'd been given money to clear up her house: the blood-drenched carpet where he'd lain butchered, the 'lost' eiderdown his body had been wrapped in had been hers. Her kids were in the house that night. How terrified she was by what had happened in her own home. Until then there'd been nothing but denial. There was no party, the court heard. Carole's evidence smashed the denials to smithereens.

That day I saw Billy Exley give evidence against the twins too. He arrived in a wheelchair; he'd had two heart attacks. He'd provided a safe house for the twins at one point. In court, he told how Ronnie had gone to see him after the Cornell killing. When Billy wanted to know what happened, he told the court that Ronnie said: 'I've shot Cornell.' There were gasps all round.

In the end, it was no surprise that a verdict of guilty was passed on the twins for the killings of Cornell and McVitie. Sentencing came a day later. (The twins and the other men were later acquitted for Frank Mitchell's murder, due to lack of evidence at the time.)

I didn't go to the sentencing. Nor did Violet, as the boys didn't want her there on sentencing day. But we were all in for a big shock.

'REIGN OF TERROR ENDS, 30 years at least for the twins' was the headline on the front page of the *East London Advertiser* on Friday, 7 March.

Life imprisonment but no less than thirty years for the twins and ten years for Charlie for helping to dispose of McVitie's body.

Violet heard the twins' sentence on the radio at home. She told me how she wasn't sure if the announcer on the radio had said 'three years' and how she had to wait until someone turned up at the flat to finally tell her the truth.

It was the most devastating news of her life.

The twins had fully expected a life sentence for a guilty verdict, which could have meant fifteen years. Naturally, I wanted to go round and comfort Vi but there was little I could do for her at that point.

My working life had gone crazy: after New Year, the modelling work started pouring in. It meant travelling all over the country, flying up to Scotland for just a few hours' work. There wasn't time to stop and think – about anything. I just went for it.

That spring, I was offered a two-day modelling job in Birmingham. It meant overnighting in a hotel, something I'd never done before but a sure sign that my career was on the up.

'No,' thundered Patrick. I couldn't go.

'I'll lose money and my agent if I don't,' I pleaded.

By then, Patrick had lost his job. For the last eighteen months or so we were dependent on my money to keep us going. Yet he still insisted I couldn't go. I told him defiantly that I WAS going.

The next morning, I started pulling everything I'd need out of the bedroom cupboard: shoes, boots, outfits. I needed to get organised for the shoot the next day.

Patrick came into the bedroom and threw my precious

portfolio of photos and cuttings at me. Then he started to try to rip up some of my outfits.

'YOU ARE NOT GOING!' he yelled at me before storming out of the house and sauntering off to play cards with his friends in Holloway Road.

That evening I made the dinner, as usual. Then he asked me if I was going to Birmingham. Just as I had done on my nights out with Vi, I told him that I'd be going with another model friend, who was also married, and that I'd pick her up first before we drove up to Birmingham.

'OK,' he said grudgingly. 'But call me from the hotel.'

Off I went, my first ever night away from him in nine years.

I had a brilliant forty-eight hours. The shoot was hard work, hour after hour of posing for the camera, but who cared? I was doing what I wanted to do. And the trip itself gave me so much confidence: at twenty-nine, I was old for a model. But I didn't look it or feel it.

A short breathing space can often get things into perspective. By the time I got back, a decision had been made. My marriage was a prison. I'd found independence, and a way of life I relished. There was no lingering guilt about the lies I'd told Patrick. If I didn't go for it soon I knew I'd spend the rest of my life regretting it.

I didn't get to Braithwaite House again until early that summer. Jackie Docker was happy to come with me, to try to help cheer Vi up. Things were so different now for Vi, I needed that familiar face: extra support for Vi – and me, if I'm honest.

In the lift, I warned my friend: 'Don't mention the sentence unless she does.'

We had to tread carefully, after all.

Mrs Kray was alone in the flat. 'The boys are going to appeal,' she told us as soon as we'd settled on the sofa. 'Ronnie's told the Old Man, "If Reggie says 'e didn't do the McVitie murder – 'e was there, but 'e didn't do it – it would just be down to me."'

This sounded typically Ronnie. Get Reg off the hook and take the blame for everything, more gangster fame for Ron.

'Reg won't go for that,' Charlie Senior had told his wife.

He was spot on there. Apparently Reggie's defence lawyer, John Platts-Mills, had told Reggie that he could plead diminished responsibility for grief over the loss of his wife and the dominance of his twin. Of course, it never happened. No matter what was said, Reggie wouldn't let his other half take the blame alone. The bond between them was far too strong.

Yet whatever her husband said, we soon realised that Violet preferred to cling to the slender hope that there would be a successful appeal – and that one of her twins would be coming home soon.

Charlie, of course, would get out at some point – in the end he served seven years – but just the thought that Reg, at least, might be around soon was something to help keep Vi going. Almost anything less than thirty years was something to hope for. After all, she was nearly sixty. Fifteen years away? Well, she might be around but certainly not for another thirty years.

Vi didn't show, outwardly, any sign of distress. She was her usual self, neat and clean in her kitchen gear, pinny and slippers. She was in the mood for chatting so to switch things away from her dreadful situation I told her about my decision to leave Patrick.

'I've got no babies, Vi, and if I have to leave my nice flat with just a suitcase, that's what I'm going to do,' I told her simply.

I didn't expect to hear what came next.

'I should've gone years ago, Maureen. And taken the boys with me,' said Violet sadly. 'Don't stay there if you're not happy. Go and do your modelling work and enjoy your life,' she finished.

This was the first time Violet ever admitted to me that her marriage was so unhappy that she believed she should have left her husband.

She'd had plenty of time to think, of course. Maybe she was blaming herself in some way for the way things had turned out, done the 'what-if' thing and comforted herself that it might all have been so different if she'd got away from her husband when she was younger.

'Where will you go to? Your mum's?' Vi asked.

'No. He'd only come to get me there,' I told her. Vi was from an older generation and in her day, of course, women had little alternative but to run back to their parents' home. And all too often, if they did, after a couple of days the husband would come round and they'd go back.

I was determined that wouldn't happen to me. I didn't know yet where I'd go but I was working on it.

I didn't understand it all then but I was on the cusp of freedom at just the right time. My marriage had lasted more than nine years but in those days everything around us was changing, whichever way you looked. Women now had the contraceptive pill, the abortion laws had changed, and there were more opportunities for women to work and have financial independence.

Even the divorce laws, so hard on women before, with private detectives hanging around the streets or hotels, trying to 'prove' adultery, were about to change. The stigma surrounding divorce was about to dissolve. It would be much easier now for me to divorce Patrick even if he was dead set against it.

Yet for Violet the word 'freedom' must have had a terrible resonance. Whatever she hoped for, it looked as though her twins might never experience freedom again. They'd managed to keep their worst crimes, their violent secrets away from their mum's eyes and ears through the years in Vallance Road.

But now they could no longer protect her from their truth. They'd been charged and convicted and were being locked up for life. Violet, the most loving and caring of mothers, could now only look forward to being a prison visitor. In a way, she'd be serving that life sentence with them. But she wouldn't look at it that way, I realised. She'd just keep hoping that somehow it would all change.

The authorities split the boys up not long after the sentencing. Reg was sent to Parkhurst on the Isle of Wight while Ron went to Durham. Charlie went to Chelmsford, Essex, initially. Me and Jackie popped in to see Vi on the spur of the moment, one afternoon that summer. We took her a nice Victoria sponge cake to go with the pink roses Jackie had chosen. It was Charlie Senior who opened the front door.

'Yes?' he snapped, as unwelcoming as only he could be, glaring at me as if he'd never seen me before. He didn't look like he wanted to let us in and he looked really angry too.

Then Violet appeared, tea towel in hand. She looked upset and flustered. I'd have put money on the fact that they'd been rowing when we knocked. Of course, she was happy to see us.

I swear you could have cut the atmosphere inside that flat with a knife. As soon as she brought the tea tray in for us and sat down, she burst into tears. I hugged her, tried to comfort her, but it was of no use. She was in a state.

'The lies,' she said. 'All the lies people told in court. Who's gonna look after my Ronnie? How will he get his medicine?'

She knew very little of the prison system, especially in

relation to Category 'A' imprisonment, the high-security prison status of all her sons.

Then Charlie Senior appeared and plonked himself down in the armchair. He obviously wanted in on this conversation.

I did my best to explain.

'Vi, any prison has to send a doctor if someone takes a bad turn. They'll know what tablets Ron's on, they'll make sure he takes them every day.'

My words fell on deaf ears.

'I'm going to the Home Office,' she said defiantly. 'I can't have my Ron in prison. I want him in a hospital,' she insisted.

'Vi, he *can't* go into a hospital unless he's taken ill in the prison—' I started to say.

Then Charlie Senior joined in.

'I KEEP TELLIN' 'ER THAT, I TELL 'ER THAT EVERY BLEEDIN' DAY!' he shouted. But Vi, stubborn, wouldn't listen to either of us. Her idea of getting Ron into hospital had taken over her thinking.

That afternoon we were there for ages. She told us how she had visited Charlie in Chelmsford and Reggie in Parkhurst. Her family had gone with her. But she hadn't yet visited Ron up in Durham. We tried our best to make her understand what she could and couldn't expect from the prison system. But Vi couldn't or wouldn't take it in.

'Who's this "Hat" man they're supposed to have killed? And why've they put Charlie in prison for ten years for helping get rid of someone – everyone says there's no body. How can they sentence him for getting rid of it?'

She had a point. Charlie's ten-year sentence was patently unfair – everyone knew he hadn't been there at the time. But Charlie's misfortune was to be the twins' brother. I couldn't explain this to Vi properly. She still believed that everyone who had stood up in court and given evidence against the twins was lying and that the twins were innocent. Round and round it went, with the conversation returning to the one topic that was obsessing Vi: getting Ron out of prison and into hospital. In fact, it would be another decade before Ron would be sent permanently to Broadmoor, a hospital for the criminally insane.

But Vi's insistence that hospital was better than prison for Ron was about her believing that in a hospital she'd be able to visit him all the time, sit by his bedside and be his loving mum, at his beck and call as usual. It didn't occur to her that this was a man serving a life sentence of thirty years for murder.

At one point I thought I was getting through to her, making her realise it wasn't as simple as she believed. Charlie Senior interrupted me at one stage as I went through it all again with her, point by point.

'I told 'er all this when the case was goin' on. I spoke to the lawyers and barristers. Everyone knew there was no way they wasn't gettin' a long sentence. You won't be able to get either of 'em out from where they've bin put. Not for *years!*'

'Oh shut up, you!' Violet bit back. 'Leave us to talk. Maybe Maureen'll help me write to the Home Office,' she said.

That at least was something productive we could do to help the poor woman. Charlie stomped off for his coat, slamming the front door behind him. Jackie had been a secretary at one point, so the three of us sat there composing the letter.

It said: 'Please can you consider taking my son Ron out of Durham Prison and put him into a hospital where I can look after him? No one can look after him like me. He has never been apart from me or his twin for very long.'

We sat there, crossing out lines, rewording it as best we could until it seemed readable. Of course Jackie and I knew it was hopeless: to the Home Office it was just yet another letter from a mother. They must have received thousands.

But with the draft of the letter finished by Jackie for Violet to painstakingly copy later, Vi seemed a bit brighter. She'd show it to her niece Rita, her sister May's daughter, she said. She'd probably take someone from her family with her to the Home Office. But not her husband: 'He's been wasting my time, him,' she said.

The funny thing was that in years to come I would realise that the old man had got it wrong.

In a way, you could say that Vi knew better than the authorities. Ron had been certified back in the 1950s as a paranoid schizophrenic, and it might have been better for him had he gone to Broadmoor straight away.

Violet's efforts were not entirely in vain, especially when Ron finally went to Broadmoor and the doctors there were happy to talk – and listen – to her. A mother's appeal, in certain circumstances, can hold sway sometimes. I'd known Mrs Flanagan do that in court when one of her sons faced a suspended prison sentence.

But Mrs Flanagan was a realistic woman. Violet couldn't accept the truth of the situation, that the twins had been handed life sentences because they had killed people and run rings around the law for far too long. The authorities would now be making all the decisions.

Violet then announced another plan.

'I'm going to Durham and I'm gonna talk to the Governor,' she told us. 'There's certain things Ron can't eat,' she stated.

By then, Jackie and I were raising eyebrows at each other, wearying of Vi's dogged determination to be all things to her son in his hour of need. Reg, funnily enough, wasn't mentioned. Violet was consumed by her love and need to be Ron's mother.

What made it that much more difficult for her to comprehend, of course, was the fact that when they'd been locked up on remand the rules were totally different.

On remand meant she could still do things for them as usual – deliver food to the prison, bring clean shirts to the court each day (the twins still insisted on that). Even if, for some reason, Vi couldn't do it one day, someone else would step in for her.

Charlie Kray later told me that frequently, when they were on remand, she'd bring them so much food that there'd be too much. So one of the other accused men would sit down and tuck in to a cooked dinner, prepared by Violet's loving hand.

But there was no cooking, washing or ironing available for the mum of Category A high-security prisoners. Violet's main role in life had been taken away from her.

A role she desperately wanted back.

I started being more of a politician, throwing in words of hope, knowing full well that they were no more than platitudes, hot air if you will.

'Maybe they'll find some other evidence, Vi,' I ventured.

She liked that idea.

'My career is on the up,' I told her, moving the conversation on for a change. Vi said that she'd been thrilled to see my photo in the paper the other day.

'See, Maureen, the boys always said about the modelling, didn't they?'

There was truth there but it was one of those times when no matter how hard you tried to shift the conversation away from the twins, everything went back to them.

It was frustrating, but you couldn't be too harsh on her. For all her troubles, Violet was as proud and supportive of my increasingly glamorous-sounding modelling career as if she'd been my own mum. Glamour, lovely clothes, parading around in them, being photographed were food and drink to her in many ways, because of the life the boys had led for years.

That glamour was now lost to her. But she still had this surrogate 'daughter' who was part of that life. At least she could enjoy a fraction of the sparkle, the glitter. By proxy, as it were.

'She won't have any luck, Jack,' I told Jackie as we climbed into my Mini. 'They're never going to put him in hospital unless he's really ill.'

We'd done our best. But all the kindness and friendship in the world wouldn't shake Violet Kray's belief in her son's innocence – and in Ron's desperate need for his mum. It would stay that way for a long, long time.

I managed to pop round again a couple of months later and do her hair. Then I suggested a little trip back to Bethnal Green.

Of course everyone recognised her and asked after the boys.

'I'm visiting,' she told the man on the fruit stall. 'But there's not gonna be any appeal.'

In Pellicci's café it was as if a Royal had popped in for a cuppa. Neville, the proprietor, charged out of the kitchen and enveloped Vi in a bear hug, and his wife cuddled her, Italian style. They made a huge fuss of her. Here, at least, nothing had changed.

We tucked into our meat pie with mash and cabbage,

washed down with tea. I was so glad I'd thought of it. An everyday trip to an Italian café – but it meant so much to Violet. Briefly, she got her old identity back.

Then she called Neville over.

'I want to take the boys home-cooked food, some nice apple pies. They'd like that, wouldn't they?'

Neville had run this East End café for years. He was well versed in prison rules. No, he told her gently, she couldn't do that.

'But what can I take, Neville?'

'Violet, you can't take anything. They just want to see their mum.'

On the way back to Braithwaite House, I realised that Neville at least had got through. The penny had dropped.

'Next time I go to see Reg I'm takin' an apple pie and I'll give it to the guards. They can't say no if I say it's for them or their family, can they?'

She was right. Over time, prison staff at Durham and Parkhurst got used to Violet Kray cheerfully handing them a freshly baked apple pie or a few mince pies on her visits. They didn't refuse and everyone was happy. In Violet's mind, the staff would be nicer to her boys because they couldn't refuse their mum's home cooking.

That November, the inevitable happened. After a massive row with Patrick one night, I waited till he had gone out in the morning to his card game.

One of the Family

Just go, Maureen, you've waited long enough, I told myself. Start packing.

First I phoned my sister-in-law to come round in her Mini, told her my plan and, together we piled all my possessions into the two little cars.

There was so much stuff in there, I don't know how we managed even to see to drive. I'd only taken my own things. I knew that taking any household items or furniture would cause more grief than it was worth.

We drove off to Knightsbridge to my model friend Diana's place. She had a room in a large flat owned by a record producer she knew. She'd told me weeks back that I could stay at her place until I sorted everything out. Somehow we managed to get all the clothes, boots, shoes, hats and make-up into her room, though it was a bit of a tight squeeze.

It was far from ideal. But I was out, a free woman at last. I had no intention of relenting.

Patrick might rant, rave, say what he liked.

I was never going back to him.

Chapter 11

The dawn cleaner

I'd left my marriage but there wasn't even going to be time to talk to Vi about her worries or what I'd done.

For within a couple of weeks I was sharing a huge apartment in a skyscraper just off Fifth Avenue in the heart of New York with a group of other models.

We had been flown there for three weeks to promote British fashion in the big Manhattan department stores like Macy's. It was the era of hot pants, little white Courreges boots and Mary Quant sack dresses and there we were, right in the middle of the most exciting city in the world, being treated like movie stars.

What a difference from running home from the Tube station to peel fourteen potatoes, eh?

We were just models but the New Yorkers, crazy about everything they'd heard about Swinging London, loved us to bits. We were invited everywhere: ritzy nightclubs, parties, swanky bars, all manner of smart restaurants. We'd never known anything like it – most of us had never even been abroad before. The men queued up to talk to us, chat us up, hear our 'cute' British accents.

One night, in a bar, one of the other models, a bit tipsy, told a guy that she'd been dating Beatle Paul McCartney (we all knew she was lying, but who cared?) and it was unbelievable: the guy promptly proposed to her on the spot! I'd never had such a good time as I did that year in New York.

I flew back, full of confidence, just before Christmas and spent it with my mum. She thoroughly approved of me leaving Patrick. He'd been round to see her several times, looking for me. I didn't want to see him but eventually he spotted my car and caught me at my mum's.

We wound up going for a drink with Stephen, the husband of the sister-in-law who'd helped me move. Patrick wanted me back but there and then I gave him the truth: I was going to a solicitor and I wanted a divorce.

'You'll never get a divorce from me,' he huffed and slunk off to drown his sorrows. Early in 1970, I sat in the solicitor's office. I didn't mention the violence – I didn't have to. The no-fault divorce was now law. Thousands of people like me could now set themselves free from outdated laws and unhappy lives. Patrick held off from signing the papers for as long as he could. But, in the end, he had to face up to the inevitable if he wanted to move on in his own life.

I saw Vi days after I got back. Amazingly, she was quite cheerful. She positively lapped up my stories about New

York, particularly about the handsome American men who had been wooing us. Of course, she reminded me, she'd met many Americans with the boys. To Vi, from a generation where uniformed free-spending American servicemen based in London spelled wartime glamour, 'the Yanks' (dubbed 'oversexed and over here' because of their huge pulling power) were the ultimate catch. Yes, she said, I deserved a better life, now I'd left stay-at-home Patrick.

'Didn't you find a nice millionaire, Maureen?' she said. 'You could go and live there – and get into proper films.'

She was much livelier, more positive, than I'd seen her for ages. She'd visited both twins a couple of times by then. Yet she still didn't get it about the regulations.

'I asked them what they wanted for Christmas and they said: "Not allowed, mum."'

No more silk socks and Harrods underwear for the twins. Prison-regulation gear must have been a shock to the system, especially for Ron. Still, it was wonderful to see Vi cheerful, chatting about all sorts of things as I did her hair.

But her optimism didn't last. That March, the authorities decided to move the boys. Ron was shifted from Durham to Parkhurst, Reg was moved from Parkhurst to Leicester. By the time I saw Vi again, she'd been up to Leicester to see Reg. It was, she said, a better place than Parkhurst, but she was baffled by the authorities' decision to move them again. Why couldn't they move them both to the same place?

'They'd be a help to each other,' she wailed.

It didn't add up at all. By then, I'd been writing to Reg. Ron wasn't much of a letter writer and I thought I'd get a bit of sense out of Reg. Anyway, I wanted to tell him I was seeing Vi – I was sure he'd tell Ron in a letter, too.

In those early days of their sentence, the twins wrote to each other in code, a sort of backslang, where you took the first letter off a word. I could never do it or understand it. But they used the code to communicate with each other: it made them feel they'd created some form of privacy, I guess. The letters they wrote to their mum were odd, too: written on a slant, all down one side of the page in their very odd spidery writing.

Typical of Reg, I got a reply straight away, thanking me for seeing Violet.

Would I please keep up the visits to Braithwaite House? I'd told him about our visit to Pellicci's.

'What lovely people they are,' he wrote. 'We were always treated well there. The food's dreadful here.'

I wanted to visit, of course. I'd have gone with Violet, taken her to the prison. But as high-security prisoners, only immediate family could visit the twins.

Reg, of course, was worrying himself sick over Ron. 'I know what he is when he loses his temper and now I'm not there,' he wrote.

I think at that point he was more worried about Ron than he was about himself.

In the early years, they were not even permitted to visit each other. Which was very tough for them.

Yet in a curious way, in an emotional sense, not that much had changed for Reg or Violet. They'd spent years worrying themselves sick about Ron's illness, believing that as long as they were around they could protect him from himself. Now the twins were locked up, neither could be on hand at any time to help him. In that regard, their worst fears had been realised.

Yet Violet still couldn't accept why they were locked up. It seemed there was no way she'd let herself accept that they'd killed people. As a result, she vented her frustration on all the people that 'told lies' in court, all the men who had given evidence against them. She railed against what she saw as the injustice of this.

'Those people used to come to my house, drink tea in my kitchen, tell me all about their families,' she'd recall.

In the end they'd been disloyal, had saved themselves, I thought. But why didn't Violet get it? By the time Nipper Read and his men had got to work on the Krays' associates they were bound to turn against them.

Yet in the Kray family, delusion reigned. The twins had believed no one would dare turn against them and their mother couldn't believe what they'd done. I longed to say: 'Violet, they DID kill those people.' But I didn't.

One good example of this was when our talk turned

to the barmaid in the Blind Beggar pub. Her evidence in court had been so compelling that it had helped to send them down but poor Vi insisted to me, time and again, that the woman had been lying.

'Vi, she *saw* Ron walk into the pub and shoot the man,' I pleaded.

'No,' Violet insisted. 'She was told to say that.'

I had to give credit to Charlie Senior who, from what Vi told me, was frequently trying to push her to face up to the truth. But all that did was increase her rejection of everything he stood for.

'Don't believe all the lies, mum,' Ron would tell her, knowing full well that Reg and Charlie had been drilled to say exactly the same.

Vi hated Parkhurst. She said it was so cold and forbidding, a truly depressing place. The only good thing about it, I gathered, was that she managed to make friends with the staff, knew a couple of prison officers by name, chatted to them about their lives, their families.

'They don't talk to other families like they do to me,' she told me and it was true. Vi had amazing charm and could easily win people over. There was no guile in it. She was genuinely interested in others.

But the journey to Parkhurst was awful for her. Durham had been bad enough, over 250 miles away, and in those days, the journey took five hours each way by train. It was extremely exhausting, especially for someone of Vi's age who'd hardly left her own patch. Yet Parkhurst, in a sense, was worse, because it meant an initial three-hour train ride to Portsmouth Harbour and then you could only reach the Isle of Wight itself by ferry.

Of course, she had to go in all weathers and it always meant a very early start because the visits started at two p.m. She'd always have someone with her from her family but sometimes winds or storms meant the ferry that they'd hoped to catch was cancelled. So they'd be stuck there, waiting. On one occasion, she told me, they'd got to Portsmouth Harbour and all the ferries were cancelled until it was too late to visit. So they'd had to turn back. In bad weather, they'd have to brave a really hazardous crossing, the ferry bobbing up and down, the passengers below weaving from side to side if they attempted to get up. A freezing cold journey to an equally freezing cold prison.

'I 'ate that crossing, Maureen,' she'd tell me, wincing at the memory. 'I always 'ave to take an extra cardigan or something 'cos it's *always* cold, even in the summer. My stomach don't like it, either, specially when it gets really choppy. One time, May looked at me face and said: "Vi, you've gone a nasty shade of green."

' "You don't look too good either, May," I said. But we was never sick or anythin' like that.'

Even after the ghastly ferry ride, it wasn't over. If they were early, they'd go to a pub close by for lunch, then they'd have to take a taxi to the prison.

By then, Violet had had a reply to her letter to the Home

Office about moving Ron to a hospital. A nicely worded refusal, of course. But she kept on hammering away at the authorities, writing letters, insisting that her Ron should be moved. At one stage she went to Durham Prison and spoke to the Governor there. He'd told her it wasn't up to him and then the penny dropped. She'd be better off focusing all her efforts on the Home Office. They were the ones who called the shots. She decided she was going to write to them instead. Letters to and from the Home Office became a major part of Vi's life from that point on. She would campaign on behalf of her twins for the rest of her life.

Meanwhile, I was enjoying my new life. 1970 turned out to be a busy year for me, lots of photographic shoots and even a small sketch for TV – on *Monty Python's Flying Circus*, which was such a big comedy hit on BBC-TV in the early 1970s. Violet understood the occasional long gaps between my visits. And my family all knew about and understood my friendship with the Krays now. But at that point in time, it was really Violet and Charlie that I regarded as good friends: had you asked me about whether I saw the twins the same way, I might have hesitated. Remember, I knew what they could be like: the interrogations, the need to pick your brains all the time. If you did visit either or both of them, they'd expect you to come back and see them again. But since they were all Category A prisoners initially, visiting wasn't an option.

The twins were human yo-yos as far as the authorities

were concerned. Early in 1971 Reg was transferred back to Parkhurst and the twins were finally together. Violet, of course, was convinced it was because of her letters to the Home Office: she'd gone there in person and had even lobbied the Prime Minister, Edward Heath.

But, as it turned out, the decision to reunite the twins at Parkhurst was a practical one: Ron had attacked another prisoner, had hit him over the head with a bottle. He'd attacked another inmate a few days before that. Having his twin around might help calm Ron down, the authorities believed.

I wrote to Reg frequently. He was an informative letter writer. He'd ask questions too, whereas Ron's replies were short, just complaints about the food and the conditions in the prison.

Ron desperately wanted to see his old friends – he missed them. For Reg, this didn't matter so much. He was more interested in what was new, whether it was your private life, your clothes, or just where you'd been.

Reg always wanted to move ahead. Ron wanted the past: the old boxers, the club people. It really upset him in Parkhurst that he couldn't have that contact.

With both twins in the same place, Vi and I slipped into a routine again. I'd go round to do her hair every fortnight. By that time, I'd moved into a friend's place in the East End. If I happened to be working one week, we'd just leave it till the next.

I kept it to myself but I was a bit apprehensive about the

authorities' decision to put the twins together. It sounded good. But it didn't necessarily mean they'd be in the same place for the next twenty or thirty years, did it? The main thing was, it made life simpler for Vi. She took them photos of the family – these were permitted in their cells. But there was little else she could take for them on her visits.

To Violet, her boys were 'settled'. She didn't know that, in fact, Ronnie started many fights which Reggie had to calm down. At one point, Ron had a row with an officer about his medication and hit him in the face. As a result, he got two months' solitary confinement and a diet of bread and water. There were also fights involving both twins where they were charged with malicious wounding. It was a bad time for them – even though they were together.

Braithwaite House, alas, never became friendly territory for Vi. She didn't like the local shops around Old Street: she missed Bethnal Green and Whitechapel, the market stalls, the cheerful banter of the stallholders she'd known for most of her life.

Naturally, the other people in the block knew all about the dawn raid in 1968 when the front door to Flat 12 had been kicked in. Everyone knew who lived there now. Vi would have liked to chat away to her neighbours as she'd always done. But it didn't happen. She'd often get into the lift with someone on the same floor and down they'd go, in total, freezing silence.

'No one wants to talk to me,' she told me one day. 'And

anyway, even if they did, they might start running the boys down.'

What it all added up to was semi-isolation: going to the shops, getting back into the lift and up to the flat. Living with the one man she didn't want as company. She saw her family, they'd come round, of course. But that was it.

In 1972 my divorce finally came through. That same year I'd posed topless as one of the early Page 3 girls in the *Sun* newspaper. I didn't hesitate when my agent asked me if I'd do it: no longer married, I didn't have to answer to anyone and my family, the people who mattered, were supportive rather than shocked. The paper wanted my age for the caption and dropped a decade, saying I was twenty-one! But the Page 3 work, though brief, resulted in as much work as I could handle. I'd also done a few more BBC-TV sketches: three more *Monty Pythons* and even a stint with Dave Allen on the *Dave Allen at Large* TV show.

By that time I was using the name 'Flanagan' as my modelling name.

At the divorce, my ex had asked that I should not be permitted to use it. But the judge ruled in my favour. Since that time, friends have always called me Flanagan, or 'Flan'.

The Krays were delighted with all this, knowing I'd been on the telly. Even Ron, when I wrote and told him, replied properly.

'Told you you should be doing this,' he wrote. True, I thought, but how Ronnie Kray loved being right.

One of the Family

Now and then I'd chat to Charlie's Diana on the phone. She was writing to Charlie but keeping her distance, living up north, busy with her work as usual. Things might change when he got out, but she wasn't sure. My letters to Charlie were always received gratefully. But every letter came back with the same response.

'I knew this was where I'd end up, giving up these years of my life because my surname is Kray.' That was always his line.

'Yes, but you've got something to look forward to,' I'd reply. 'You won't do ten, you'll probably do six. Your brothers can't look forward to that. So keep your chin up.'

I knew Charlie wouldn't make it harder for himself in prison. He'd make friends. He wouldn't go round using the Kray name, bashing people up. No one would be trying to fight Charlie.

In all my conversations with Vi, I'd frequently remind her that if he only did six years, at least she'd have one son nearby. She'd nod. We both knew that it wasn't the son she wanted.

Charlie Senior had stopped going on the visits to the twins regularly – he preferred just to see Charlie. Much to Vi's relief. She didn't like going with him, anyway. At that stage, the regulations gave her only one visit a month to Parkhurst. From what I could glean from Vi and from Reg's letters, her visits helped Ron, made him feel a bit better. Yet his twin felt quite guilty at seeing his mum having to travel all that way, especially if there was a bad ferry-crossing sometimes. Ronnie needed that knowledge that here was his mum, treating him like a little boy. How it always was.

There were, even from those early years, always 'to do' lists for Vi to bring back from visiting the twins. These were lists of people the twins wanted to keep in touch with, keeping the myth of their gangster power alive, if you like. But there was a method to it: these were also people that they could ask for 'favours' or who could give lifts to their mum when she visited Charlie. They didn't like the idea of her going on the train if she could be driven there.

As time went on, it started to dawn on me that money was a bit of a problem for Vi.

She didn't say it in so many words and I figured a few old friends gave her a bit of money to help out. Charlie Senior still did a bit of buying and selling so there was something coming in. But life was harder for Vi. Despite all the daft stories about the millions that the Kray Twins were supposed to have stashed away, the family were no better off than the average East Ender. So much for the hype.

Early in 1973 Violet got some good news. Charlie was no longer a Category A prisoner and was being moved much closer, to Maidstone Prison in Kent. She was going to see him very soon. I could go there with her.

I'd visited a prison once before when I was married. In the early days I'd gone to see Noel Flanagan in Pentonville so I knew prisons were awful places, cold, drab, lots of checks, bits of paper to produce, grim waiting rooms.

Vi hadn't told Charlie I was coming. Charlie, of course, had loved my Page 3 news – he'd been showing them the newspaper in the prison. 'This is our close friend,' he'd tell everyone proudly.

We went to Maidstone with Checker Berry, an old family friend of the Krays. Maidstone wasn't anything like as forbidding as Pentonville. It was much better. The staff seemed friendlier: the minute we went in and showed our VOs (visiting orders) the men at the door greeted Vi, new to the place, as an old friend.

This was a much more cheerful set-up, inasmuch as it could be. In the crowded little visiting room we ordered tea and waited. The room was full, kids running everywhere. Then the door opened and about a dozen men were let in. I'd last seen Charlie as I had always known him: tanned, immaculately shod, smart-suited. His tan meant a lot to Charlie. The worst thing you could do to him was not allow him anywhere near a sun bed.

So my first thought as he came towards us was: 'Oh my God, Charlie's WHITE!'

How he must have hated that.

White or not, he was still handsome blue-eyed Charlie with the lovely smile.

'So pleased to see you now you're famous,' he quipped.

'Not as famous as you,' I teased back.

'Aaargh, more like infamous us three.'

Soon we were laughing away with Charlie as we'd always done.

He told us that the minute he'd got there he'd applied for a job. 'Working in the gardens, mum,' he told Vi, pleased as Punch.

'No escaping!' I warned him. 'Or it's back to square one.'

'Nah, now I'm on the road home.'

I half-expected him to give his mum lots of hugs and kisses when we turned up but there was nothing beyond the initial cheek-peck. I remembered something about the three Kray sons I'd often noticed at Vallance Road: none of them were particularly demonstrative towards Violet. They adored her. But they were not touchy-feely sons. Not in any way.

The woman they loved best of all never got anything other than a quick hug or a peck on the cheek. Even in prison.

Maybe it was them, maybe they were just men of their time. Nowadays you see men putting their arms around each other, kissing each other on the cheek – even villains do that now when they greet each other. But not the Kray boys.

Charlie wanted to know all about *Monty Python*, my life outside. But we kept straying back to the twins. Did he write?

'Yeah but they don't wanna talk about what went on,' Charlie half-whispered to me, so Vi couldn't hear. He reminded me, as he would many times in the future, that it had been him who had warned the twins that their so-called loyal henchmen would be the ones to turn against them.

'Everything I told them came true, Maureen,' he said quietly.

Violet, of course, wanted to hear about the prison conditions. Were they treating him OK?

Charlie assured her that he was fine, that this was different to prison life on the island.

'And now you won't have to go so far to see me, you'll get a lift here.'

'Well, it's really broke me, all the travelling' Violet said somewhat unexpectedly. 'I've had to go and get a little job working at the Blue Coat Boy in Bishopsgate.'

We both stared at her, too stunned to talk. I don't know which one of us was more surprised. Violet working in a pub? When and how could this have happened? Without any of us knowing?

'Wot you doin' there, mum?' Charlie said, frowning, clenching his teeth, a sure sign that he was worried.

'Oh, I go in early to do the cleaning.'

Charlie looked aghast.

'Don't do it any more, mum. You can't do all that and the visitin' too.'

Yet Violet was resolute. She could be unbelievably stubborn at times. 'Charlie, I 'ave to do it. All those journeys cost a lot of money.'

Violet and I frequently confided in each other. Yet she'd kept this secret from me. It was bizarre. Here was this woman in her sixties doing early-morning cleaning jobs to pay the fares to see her sons in prison. Sons whose reputation had soared off the back of their success running casinos and nightclubs. The Krays still had millions, so the stories went. It didn't add up. I simply couldn't believe it.

She'd known the glamorous life – fur coats, nightclubs, movie stars. And now she was cleaning out a dirty East End pub at five a.m.

It just wasn't right.

But there were more family stories. In the beginning, Charlie's wife Dolly had been to see him with Gary and little Nancy.

'But now she don't want to come any more. So I can't see the kids. I've been away from them for long enough. But now I'm in a better place, and I still can't see them.'

Vi promised she'd go to see Dolly, try to talk her round.

Then Charlie perked up, asked me more about the modelling, the telly, shared a few laughs with Checker. Despite Vi's sudden revelations he was on quite a high when we left. I guess he figured that he'd solve it for Violet somehow.

On the way home, I decided to say something.

'Vi, this work you're doing, starting at five a.m. every day, then coming home to go to the prisons. It's too much for you.'

But Violet, as I'd suspected, wasn't having any of it.

'I've got to do it, Maureen. I need the money so's I can see the boys.'

'But don't you get lifts?' I pleaded.

'I don't like to ask,' she said.

'But what about all the twins' old friends? Won't they give you a lift?'

'All their so-called friends that worked with them are in prison, Maureen,' came the answer.

Checker was driving, so he could hear every word.

'Don't worry, Vi, I'll bring you in two weeks' time,' he promised her. And he did.

I never really got to the bottom of why Violet took that cleaning job. Charlie Senior, with all his faults, had always given her housekeeping money for bills and food. Maybe she just didn't want to ask him for anything else, it could have been that. But he'd have known she was getting up at the crack of dawn and going out, surely? So why didn't he stop her? It baffled me.

Then I remembered that Violet had told me that Charlie Senior had gone with her to Parkhurst to see Ronnie but it had turned into a bad visit.

The old man had said something derogatory about Violet which Ron didn't like. He got very angry and the visit had to end quickly. Maybe that was it. Perhaps Charlie just resented handing over any cash to Vi to help fund her visits. I knew, from Violet, that he still stuck to his same old routine: he was always out drinking, his big love in life was the nearest saloon bar. Now, of course, he could hold court in the pub and tell everyone exactly what he thought about his notorious twins . . .

Someone once mentioned an old wife's tale: everything in life goes in threes.

In my case, it was true. I had won my freedom, my exciting modelling career was going better than I'd ever dreamed and then bang!, in the summer of 1973 I fell madly in love.

It was at a charity night in a pub called The Alex, in Victoria Park. I was there selling raffle tickets to raise money for handicapped kids in Tower Hamlets. At the bar I spotted this guy, surrounded by people. Everyone was laughing their heads off.

'Who's that guy making everyone laugh?' I asked a girlfriend.

'Oh, that's my cousin Terry,' she said.

Terry was short – five foot, four inches – and dark-haired. The complete opposite of the six-footers with blond hair that I usually went for.

Yet the minute I was introduced to him, his personality overshadowed everything. One hour in Terry's company and I knew he was one of the funniest, liveliest, most entertaining people I'd ever met: a wonderful, warm, vibrant individual. Mr Charisma.

At closing time he said: 'I'll walk you home.'

And that was the start. I knew straight away that

this man was for me – it was like a thunderbolt in my life. A great personality and a businessman to boot.

Terry was an East Ender born and bred. Within three weeks we went off on holiday to Spain where Terry had a flat in the centre of Benidorm. We had a fabulous time. When we got back we had to decide: should I move in with Terry at Gloucester Terrace, north-west London, or would he move in with me in the East End? The East End won. By then, I'd fallen in love with the East End as well as with the man. Life was getting better all the time.

As for Vi, she was determinedly keeping up her routine: cleaning the pub, visiting the boys whenever the rules permitted, constantly petitioning the authorities. The twins had only served a few years of their sentence but Vi wasn't the only one to campaign: as time passed there were frequent petitions from people in the East End to reduce the twins' sentence. Eventually I too was involved in the various campaigns. You could say we were all being a bit naive. Or misguided. But no one knew about or understood at the time the authorities' desire to keep the Kray Twins locked up for life.

Terry had a totally different attitude than my ex to my friendship with the Kray family. He was the least jealous person I'd ever known. He never worried about other men or me being tempted, he knew me well enough to understand that I would never stray. I felt the same way about him. We could go for a night out and I could chat to a hundred people and it wouldn't bother Terry – he'd be talking to the other hundred people in the room, anyway. Together we were quite dynamic.

He was right for me in other ways too. In March 1974, I went on a modelling job for the *Sunday Mirror* on West Wittering beach in West Sussex, near Chichester.

West Wittering jobs, I might add, were a model's nightmare. The area itself was often deserted but the place in winter was usually freezing and, of course, for glamour shots you had to get in and out of the water, which I hate.

That day I'd walked into the water to waist depth while the photographer clicked away. By the time I got home, I felt ill. I stayed in bed feeling dreadful and a few days later my doctor said he thought it could be pneumonia. I needed an X-ray of my back. So off I went to the hospital.

I had no idea what was coming.

'That's a baby,' they told me that afternoon, pointing to the X-ray.

'Rubbish,' I told them. 'I haven't missed a period. It's just a bad chill from the cold. Can I see another doctor?' I waited, somewhat irritated. I was sure they'd got it wrong, I knew it.

Half an hour later another doctor came in and confirmed it: I was five months pregnant. I was in total shock. OK, there'd been no contraception. But by then I'd given up on ever getting pregnant again. I was thirty-three. I'd had no sickness, no soreness in my breasts, not a single symptom that women were meant to have. Terry too was initially shocked; he already had two boys from his first marriage.

But that night we were happily celebrating our surprising news.

'Maybe it's the girl you've always wanted, Flan,' Terry said.

Much to my surprise, Terry got it wrong. I gave birth in Islington to our son, JJ, on 17 July. He arrived two weeks early.

A couple of years previously, I'd done a short stint on the Benny Hill show, being chased by Benny with a net. Me and some of the other girls who'd been in the show became quite friendly with Benny. He'd invite us over to his flat in Queen's Gate on Friday nights, when we'd all sit around eating fish and chips. (We had to take our own because he was quite mean, was Benny, though he did provide a couple of bottles of cheap plonk.)

Imagine my amazement, the day after the baby arrived, to see my friend Cherie Gilham, accompanied by Benny at the bedside. All Benny wanted to know was the baby's name.

I'd been so convinced I'd be having a girl that I hadn't even thought of a name.

'Call him Jeremy,' said Benny helpfully.

That sounded good. James was my dad's second name. So Jeremy James it'd be. Which the nurses immediately shortened to 'JJ' for the little bracelet on his wrist.

Terry turned up later on and immediately said that he didn't like Jeremy as a name. He thought it sounded 'too poofy and theatrical' so it was James Jeremy when I finally registered it.

Yet our gorgeous little son was to remain JJ right from the start. He still is.

JJ was two months old when I finally got to see Violet. There I was at the flat, handing over my completely bald, beautiful blue-eyed son for Violet to cuddle, one proud mum to another.

It was a big moment for both of us.

'What's that funny name you've got?' she enquired, taking JJ into the living room to admire him, chuckling and cooing at him whenever she got a smile – JJ was a very smiley baby.

'Well, I've got something for you, Maureen,' she said, handing JJ back and bustling off into the bedroom.

I fully expected she'd got me a little gift for JJ.

Violet handed me a beautiful old-fashioned necklace, a real antique. It had a white gold chain and was shaped like a teardrop with a small diamond on either side and one in the middle. A truly beautiful piece of jewellery.

I didn't want to take it but she insisted.

'My Ronnie gave it to me but I want you to have it. You've been good to the boys and me, we all love you. It's from all of us,' she said, handing me a piece of tissue paper to wrap it in.

*

One of the Family

I've still got that necklace, one of my most treasured possessions. At the time I couldn't understand why she'd given *me* a gift and not something for JJ.

But of course, I realised much later that she wanted to use JJ's arrival on the scene as a way of showing me how much she valued our friendship – and how thrilled she was for me that now, finally, I had my own baby to love and cuddle. Motherhood was everything to Vi. I'd come to it now by sheer good fortune. We already had a bond, Vi and I. But JJ's arrival put the seal on it. For good.

Chapter 12

The inmate in the expensive suit

Life was on an undreamed-of upturn for me with my beautiful new baby. For Vi, too, things improved a little bit that autumn: Charlie was going to be allowed out for a three-day home visit, a sure sign that his sentence was coming to an end within a year or so.

'This is the first one,' Vi told me triumphantly. 'Now we've just got to keep asking for the other two to come home.'

Vi organised a surprise party for Charlie in the Blue Coat Boy where she worked, a proper East End knees-up with lots of his old friends and neighbours to welcome him back.

It turned out to be a fabulous night for everyone. Half the East End crowded into the Bishopsgate pub to welcome Charlie back into the fold. Violet got seriously dolled up. Out came the precious white mink stole and the diamante earrings. Even Charlie Senior put on his best suit and a happy party face.

One of the Family

Charlie had been told they were going for 'a few drinks'. But as he walked up the stairs into the bar and spotted all the familiar faces waiting for him, brandishing the first bucket of bubbly, he was visibly overwhelmed. For a minute I thought he might cry, but he kept it together.

He looked fabulous: a new suit and, would you believe, a suntan out of a bottle! Somehow he'd wangled the fake tan. He was quite a bit thinner than he'd been. But that was a minor detail, really. A noisy cheer rose from the crowd waiting to greet him as he stepped into the throng.

'Not long now, Charlie,' I chirped, giving him the biggest of hugs. Of course, with JJ at home I couldn't linger. But it was enough just to see Charlie having a whale of a time, surrounded by people he knew well. The expression on Vi's face, after all the tears she'd shed, was quite wonderful to behold. There she was, for that night at least, still the proudest mum in the East End, surrounded by Kray well-wishers.

By the beginning of 1975 I was working again. By sheer good fortune I hadn't put on any weight at all during my pregnancy. So when the phone rang with JJ's mum's first post-baby booking, I didn't hesitate. JJ was, I admit, a very good baby, no trouble at all, and Terry and I were such a well-drilled team that we knew we could fit things around JJ. All it took was organisation – and I've always been good at that.

Vi carried on with the cleaning job, dividing her time between visits to Maidstone and the five-hour train/

ferry/taxi trek to Parkhurst. But then came a massive blow: the authorities had decided to put both twins into a psychiatric section at Parkhurst. She was gobsmacked. Where oh where was the sense of this?

We didn't know why this happened at the time. I kept writing to the twins and they'd write back. But they said very little. A long time later I learned, via Charlie, that all they were doing was having fights. Younger men were always trying to wind them up, make a name for themselves in the prison by saying 'I fought one of the twins and won' – that sort of thing.

Obviously, the wardens had to look away sometimes. But sometimes, Charlie learned, it would be a warden who would wind Ron up on purpose. Essentially, it was non-stop violence. So the powers that be figured that the only way to contain it was to have them together. In a psychiatric wing in the prison hospital.

Charlie was now out of prison for good. There was a lot of publicity at the time and often, when I look at those newspaper photos of Vi looking up adoringly at her oldest son, I wonder what really went on in her mind then.

Was she secretly wishing that it was her Ron, the son who needed her most of all, sitting there with her? Ron's illness made him, to her, a hundred times more vulnerable. Is that what it was? Do you love a seriously sick or handicapped child more because they need you, their mother, so much? I never tried to talk to Vi about all this. Her tears and her worried face whenever the next disaster struck with Ron were enough. I knew how much she loved him. More questions wouldn't help.

Charlie went back to Dolly, to see the kids, but things weren't improved. He'd learned that after his conviction for the McVitie case, the prosecution's main witness, Ronnie Hart, had made a statement under oath saying he had lied about Charlie's involvement in the crime. Charlie was seriously considering taking his case to the Court of Human Rights in Strasbourg at one point. But he was now a free man and decided against it.

What mattered to him was repairing what was left of his old life and the first step was finding his Diana. He eventually tracked her down in Leicester. They fell in love all over again and Charlie got divorced. Vi, of course, was just happy he was a free man. The whole Court of Human Rights thing would have been over her head anyway.

That year, Terry and I decided to get married. JJ was coming up to nursery stage and we'd been together close to three years. He'd been asking me for about a year. But I kept stalling: things were great, why tempt fate? I asked myself.

Then I made up my mind. I borrowed a lovely ring from a jeweller I knew in Hatton Garden and proposed to Terry in a pub on Valentine's Night at Rules in Covent Garden.

Terry was overjoyed.

'I've got the ring,' I told him.

'How much?' said Terry warily.

'Haven't paid for it. It's just borrowed. But you have to pay for it tomorrow!'

A week later I went to see Vi, bursting to tell her my good news. I could see straight away she was very shaken up about something. I kept quiet while I washed her hair, then, when it was all done, I asked her what was going on.

It was Ron. She'd gone to see him with Charlie but it turned out Ron had had a really bad fight a few days before. He'd been badly bashed up. For reasons of their own, the wardens had insisted that the visit should take place in Ron's cell.

That was awful for Vi. She'd never had to visit him in a cell.

This one was filthy. It stank. Charlie had been in Parkhurst but even he was shocked at the state of the cell.

Ron was dishevelled, his shirt was torn – he looked a complete mess.

Vi couldn't help herself. She burst into tears.

'Don't cry, mum,' Ron told her. 'Don't worry, there'll be another day when I'll win. They're all cowards.'

'My boy, sitting in that filth,' Vi sobbed as she told me the story.

Apparently he'd been complaining about the food.

'He said it was disgusting, wasn't fit for pigs,' Vi wept, dabbing her eyes with her hanky.

In the 1970s, prison food could be really awful. Ron probably threw it at them, provoking a serious beating. It sounds awful but that was how Ron had lived his life, in furious combat.

Now Vi saw the stark, ugly face of the consequences of the life that Ron had lived and how destructive his illness could be. I could see how much it affected her. To cheer her up, I told her all about my proposal. Yet when I left she was still very subdued and flat. It would take a while, I figured, for her to get over this.

Now he was out, Charlie had at least managed to convince Vi to give up the pub job. He wasn't going to go in the pub knowing his mum was cleaning it out – it just wasn't on, he told her. Now she only had the Parkhurst visits once every three weeks – all she was allowed – life was a bit easier for her. So she gave in. The good thing was, now she could go with Charlie. The old man didn't have to be involved at all.

Terry and I got married that September at Caxton Hall, Westminster. Back then it was the traditional registry-office choice of stars and celebrities. I wore a green outfit with pearls in my ears. JJ was dressed in green too. Ben Jones, my favourite Fleet Street photographer and a really good friend, gave me away.

By then we'd bought a house in Bow and Terry opened a cash-and-carry business in the East End, selling wines and spirits to pubs and clubs. I didn't have to work now, but I still did when the phone rang. I was still in demand.

As for Vi, the boys were in a shocking state. Her letters

to the Home Office were going off all the time: 'Please move my son. He's the worst I've ever seen him.'

She wasn't exaggerating. Ron was more or less out of control. Even having his twin there made no difference. If anything, the situation made Reggie worse. He was permanently on edge. Each day he'd wake up and his first thought would be: 'What's he going to do today?' or 'What will someone else do to him today?' Reg, naturally, would end up fighting the people who'd start on Ronnie. As ever, he was still picking up the pieces after his twin.

By 1979, Terry, JJ and I had moved to Chigwell in Essex. I didn't want to leave the East End but Terry was earning big money – he saw it as the next step up to go to the area where the Bobby Moores of the world had gone to live. It was the time when areas of Essex 'went posh' as far as East Enders with money to spend were concerned.

So there we were in this lovely house with little JJ at private school. I didn't work very much then, just now and again, short photographic jobs that didn't interfere with my domestic routine. I certainly didn't want this marriage to go the same way as my first one.

Violet was a bit perturbed when I told her we were moving.

'Ooh, will you still see me, Maureen? You said you didn't like the country.' She was half-joking. I could tell she wasn't sure about this development.

I assured her it made no difference. I'd drive up. As

long as I was back home to pick up JJ, that was all that mattered.

The same year we moved, I got a call from Charlie. He wanted me to hear the good news straight away. Ron was being moved to a high-security prison hospital for patients with psychiatric problems. A place called Broadmoor, in Crowthorne, Berkshire.

'He can have his own room and his own clothes,' an excited Vi told me when I went round. 'And he can have TWO visits every day!'

This was truly incredible news for Violet. If, for some reason, she couldn't go, there were plenty of people who wanted to visit Ron and hadn't been able to because of the regulations. Let alone the people he didn't know who now wrote to him and Reg all the time.

Vi went with Charlie a couple of times. Then I went with them. I didn't know what to expect: what would a hospital for the criminally insane be like? I was curious to go. But given all the stories of what had happened to the twins in Parkhurst, I was still a tad apprehensive.

I needn't have worried. Broadmoor might look sinister from the outside but everything changed once you were in there.

A cheerful person was on the reception desk with a big visitors' book. There was no visiting order needed, no identity check. You just said who you were and signed in. Visits were permitted for two hours in the mornings and two hours in the afternoons. So if someone had lots of visitors, it made for a much fuller day than the ordinary prison regime permitted.

I was amazed to walk into a great big visiting hall with big windows, sun streaming through, cheerful staff greeting Violet, shaking Charlie's hand. The hall was dotted with several tables with four chairs. It was a big area but all the tables were already taken by visitors.

Everyone, I realised, was already sitting there with the person they were visiting.

Except us. We sat down and waited. Five, ten minutes passed. Where was Ron? I asked Charlie.

'Oh, 'im. He's getting ready.' Charlie laughed.

Sure enough, the keys jangled as the big door was unlocked. And in strode a sergeant major, thumping his way towards us across the floor, the sound echoing in the grand room with all the tables turning to look at him.

A few people nudged each other.

'That's him! That's Ronnie Kray,' I overheard people gasping, incredulously.

It really was quite a sight to behold. All the other patients were in their own clothes but most were casually dressed. Some were quite scruffy: unkempt, old shirts, tatty jumpers.

This patient, however, looked quite different. Imagine a very successful Harley Street specialist and you get the idea: a beautifully tailored navy pinstripe suit. A white silk shirt and a beautiful plain dark silk tie. Double cufflinks, black highly polished brogues, a ruby and gold tie pin, a white silk hanky in the breast pocket.

What an entrance. What presence. A movie star sauntering onto the set. Enter Ronnie Kray. Gangster, killer and schizophrenic. A man so notorious that he and his twin received more fan mail than had ever been known within the British prison system. The first British celebrity gangsters.

Ron had aged a bit since I last saw him nearly a decade back. But he was very calm, controlled, even. ('That's the medication working,' I thought to myself.)

Ron kissed his mum on the cheek, shook hands with his brother and gave me a peck on the cheek too.

'See. Told you you should be a model. We've got all your pictures. Everyone knew you at Parkhurst,' he told me, beaming.

It was astonishing. Despite all the stories from Vi and Charlie, all her tears, here was the same old Ron, but a far more relaxed version.

When he'd been a free man he'd made it his business to hang out with well-known people, anyone who could remotely be called famous. In Parkhurst, he'd been puffed up about knowing me. Not about knowing Maureen the hairdresser who did his mum's hair all the time and had become a close friend for Violet, you understand. He'd conveniently forgotten all that.

Now I was in newspapers and had been on the telly I'd become, like all those celebrities in his glittering club years, currency. He'd shamelessly used their fame in photos to enhance his own celebrity. Now it was my turn. From Lord Robert Boothby to Flan, Page 3 girl. To Ron, it meant the same thing. Exposure (if you'll excuse the pun).

I didn't quite get it at that point but Ron had already decided what my modelling was worth: contacts, newspapers, Fleet Street. He'd already mapped it all out in his mind.

'So do we call you Flanagan now?' he queried, obviously having studied the captions.

'Yes. No more Maureen,' I told him. 'Even when you write to me it's Flanagan.'

Ron looked at us all.

'Whadyawanna drink?'

At that moment, I had a powerful flashback. Déjà vu. We could have been sitting round a table at the Astor. Or in the Grave Maurice.

We could have tea, coffee, a cold drink, Ron told us. Even a non-alcoholic lager called Barbican, if we desired.

'I've got some lovely cakes all ready for you,' Ron told us. Then he motioned to a young man hovering nearby, nervously clutching a tray.

'Pot of tea, pot of coffee and bring those cakes, they're already in the kitchen,' he ordered.

Sure enough, the young man hurried back with everything just right: our drinks and three beautiful strawberry tarts made in the Broadmoor kitchen. To Ronnie Kray's specification.

'Ordered 'em this mornin',' Ron said proudly. Then he opened the ring of his can of Barbican as only Ron could. No pop when he lifted the ring. No fizz. Silently the can came open. It was a unique party trick. Everyone who came with me to Broadmoor in the future would say the same thing: they'd never seen anyone open a can like that.

He was still smoking Players incessantly. No rules around smoking then, of course. But I noticed he'd changed his way of smoking, holding the ciggy way down his fingers, Noël Coward-style. All that was missing was a holder.

I had to ask: 'Ronnie, why are you holding your cigarette like that?'

'I smoke this way now,' he replied airily.

'Well, don't blow it across here,' I retorted, waving the smoke out of my face. 'It'll give me wrinkles.'

Polite as ever, he blew the smoke out sideways, away from me.

'Wot does your 'usband say about Page 3?'

'Well, he's not like the first one, Ron. I'd never have done it with him, would I?'

Ron gave his usual half-snigger. Then he turned to his mum.

''Ow's the old man? Still moanin'?'

'Same. Goes out for a drink. Don't take any notice of 'im,' she reassured Ron.

Ron was obviously pleased to see me and Vi but he hardly spoke to Charlie.

The questions came to us all the time. Then, after about twenty minutes, he turned his attention to his brother.

'So. Wot are you doin'? All I keep 'earin' is you're in nightclubs,' he sneered. 'Did ya bring anythin' with you for us?'

Sure enough, Charlie had dutifully brought his brother a hundred Players. Visitors were allowed to bring things into Broadmoor. All you had to do was leave them in a special box for the person you were visiting.

But the Players were not good enough for Ron.

'Don't mean that,' he snapped. 'I mean money.'

Then he turned away, knowing full well what the answer would be.

'I've no money for you, Ron. I'm just about getting by myself.'

By then, Charlie was working with Diana in the promotions business. She'd managed to get him work at big events, like the Ideal Home Exhibition. He had to be there on a stand, twelve hours a day, chatting people up about whatever was being promoted. But mostly, once people knew who he was, he just stood around, signing autographs.

'The next time you come, bring some money,' snarled Ron.

Same old Ron: commands, expects. The attitude was always 'You're free, I'm not, so go fetch for us. We're family.'

Then he wanted to know what Charlie was getting for

Reg. Which was daft, because Reg couldn't have things handed to him the way you could at Broadmoor: the regulations were far too stringent.

'It's all right, Ron. Reg's got what he needs,' said Vi, anxious to placate, as usual.

But there were more orders, important matters that had to be dictated. Ron then turned his scary gaze onto me.

'I want you to bring a Fleet Street editor 'ere. I'm gonna give 'im a very good story.'

'Be better to bring a photographer and take a picture of you now,' I quipped back. 'You look like a film star, Ron.'

'No. Not pictures. I WANT AN EDITOR!' He shut me down.

Then I tried to explain what I'd learned about Fleet Street from Ben Jones.

Ron couldn't possibly get a Fleet Street editor down there. They were either in the office, in the pub, or out having long lunches at the Savoy Grill. First, you had to find a journalist to talk to you, then the journalist would go back to the editor if he thought it made a story. Sometimes there might be money involved for the story, so a price would have to be set first by the editor.

I knew that was what Ron was on about, of course, when he said 'give him a very good story'.

But it wasn't quite as simple as Ron believed. Nor did I know back then that if money did change hands for a story, the rules were that a newspaper could not pay a prison inmate direct. There were rules around everything once people were locked up. Though I later discovered that there were ways round the rules. Sometimes.

Ron was looking a bit miffed. With an ordinary person, you'd ignore it but with Ron you didn't want him to start getting more upset.

'Look, I've got a photographer friend who's got great contacts with the newspapers, so I'll talk to him,' I told him soothingly, like a mum to a child.

It worked.

'Leave it to you. But we gotta earn some money.'

Those were the words I would hear time and again. Ron was permanently seeking to 'earn' money. In the earlier years of their imprisonment, the twins became middlemen for non-stop fund-raising, taking a cut from whatever money was raised on the outside, in exactly the same way they'd run their various protection scams and schemes on the inside. 'We're the Kray Twins: you owe us.'

The way it worked with the fund-raising, people would be constantly writing to them to tell them that so-and-so had six months to live, so could they help raise some money?

Of course they could. Sick kids, the boxing club, old ladies who'd been mugged and written up in the papers, really poor kids with no toys – letter after letter would go out, mostly from Reggie, to all his friends on the outside to get them to turn up at these fund-raising events, usually in an East End pub. Reg would write to the publican, ask him to put on the food as a favour.

It all looked so good, the generous Kray Twins helping the needy – like they'd always done.

But, of course, they were demanding a percentage of whatever was collected. In those early years, that was the way they were earning. The schemes and scams to earn from T-shirts, books, films, security enterprises just got more sophisticated over time.

Because of the 'box' system at Broadmoor where visitors could leave gifts, envelopes stuffed with money were also popped into Ronnie's box. Friends, businessmen who were doing well, would happily contribute to enable the Kray Twins to retain this all-important element of their life, albeit on the inside.

The constant stream of visitors to Broadmoor, some donating generously, meant that Ron would keep up appearances in there in quite spectacular fashion.

At one stage, he got me to go and see his old tailor, Barry Scott.

'Can you go and see Ron?' I asked Barry.

'What for?' said Barry, somewhat cautiously.

'He wants a new suit,' I told him plainly.

'But . . . he's in Broadmoor,' came the answer.

'Wait till you see him, Barry, and you'll see what I mean.'

Sure enough, every year Barry would trot down to

Broadmoor to measure Ron up for his new 'Christmas suit'.

That first-ever visit stands out in memory because it was so obvious that the twins were determined to do whatever they could to keep everything running on the same track: ask, persuade, extort, get 'favours' from others. They could do this on the strength of their name alone. They couldn't physically harm anyone on the outside. But the reputation – 'Do it, 'cos it's the Krays' – was as powerful as ever.

As the three of us got to the car park that day, I turned round to Charlie.

'Nothing's changed, Charlie. Except the address. He treats the place like he's in the Astor, not a mental hospital. And he still *looks* like he's going to the Astor!'

Violet got the joke too. We all laughed.

'You won't change Ron,' said Charlie, shaking his head.

It was perfectly true. Ron was happy to be there. At one stage, there was talk of him being sent back to prison for the rest of his sentence. He played up a bit then: why would he want to go back to prison when he had all this? Reg was pleased about it from the word go: he knew Ron's illness would be treated properly. But after the move to Broadmoor, the twins would see very little of each other in the future. Just annual visits.

By the beginning of the 1980s, I was a happily married, somewhat over-protective mum, living in a lovely house in a leafy setting. There were no money worries: Terry, me and JJ holidayed abroad often and we'd just celebrated my fortieth birthday at my favourite restaurant, Rules, in Covent Garden where my husband presented me with a beautiful diamond brooch. Who said life begins at forty? For me, it was certainly getting better all the time.

Violet, I'd been pleased to see, had her much-loved grandson, Gary, now permanently living with her and Charlie Senior at Braithwaite House. Then in his early twenties, Gary remained a shy, vulnerable sort of lad, timid but loveable. He adored his nan. I couldn't help but laugh the first time I went round to see her after Gary had moved in. There were the neatly ironed shirts, all hanging up in the hallway, echoes of Vallance Road.

Not long after I turned forty, I noticed that Terry started to change. Monday was his collection day, when he went round to all his clients to get paid. Often, of course, it would mean drinking in the pub until closing time, which wouldn't have been a big problem.

But now he started coming home at four or five a.m., waking me up sometimes. Yet on the times when he did wake me up, I'd notice that he wasn't at all drunk. And, of course, he'd have driven home in his big Range Rover. I had no idea what was going on but I was going to find out.

I started asking him questions about all this. Oh, he'd say, he'd stopped drinking at midnight, then he'd go on to drinking clubs so he could still collect the money but he'd be drinking orange juice.

I didn't believe a word of it. Drinking men don't

switch to orange juice without raising several eyebrows, particularly East End men running a drinks business. I knew Terry was bored stiff in a pub without a drink, anyway. It was all a big mystery. I just couldn't figure it out.

Several months before this, I'd made an application to visit Reg in Parkhurst as a family friend. Violet had told me the authorities would now let him have a visit from a non-family member because he'd served ten years of his sentence. I had to apply to the Home Office and the process took several months but officially I could now go.

A man from the Home Office had come to Chigwell and had asked me lots of questions. A real grilling. But a week later I was cleared to visit.

I went with Charlie. Parkhurst was such a miserable, grey, Dickensian place in those days, housing some of Britain's most notorious criminals like Ian Brady and Peter Sutcliffe, the Yorkshire Ripper, at various times. (Today, it's just called HMP Isle of Wight and it houses Category B prisoners, so it's no longer a top-security prison.)

It was freezing that day. The ferry was cold, the prison even worse.

When Reg came into the visiting room I was shocked.

OK, I hadn't seen him for eleven years but his hair was turning grey and he was shorter and thinner, like he'd shrunk somehow.

Yet he bustled his way in, shaking hands with other families while he was en route to our table, being introduced to an awestruck mum or an uncle.

No expensive suit for this twin: a striped shirt and jeans. Still immaculate, mind you, though seeing a Kray Twin in jeans seemed odd: sartorially, of course, they belonged in the 1950s, long before everyone wore jeans.

Under his arm, Reggie carried a file. I'd gone there as a friend, to say how are you? But as far as Reg was concerned, there was more to it than that.

Just like Ron, he ignored his brother.

'Hmm. It's good you saw Ron,' he said after a while.

'See your mum all the time. And I take my son JJ to see her sometimes.'

'Married again, eh?' came the answer.

'Ah, but to an East Ender this time, Reg. Someone with a brain. Not jealous, either,' I added.

That was a laugh, given how possessive Reg could be. But he blithely ignored that. Try as I might to bring poor Charlie into our conversation, he might as well not have been there.

'Yes', Reg said. 'I've had a few fights and have been quite ill. I'm OK now.'

But Reg didn't really want the small talk. He opened the file, all businesslike.

'First of all, I want you to contact the Home Office. You've gotta write that I want to see Ron three times a year at Broadmoor.'

Charlie couldn't help himself. He sniggered as if to say 'you'll be lucky'.

'Why not?' snapped Reg. 'They've separated us but Broadmoor's not a prison. I should be allowed more than once a year,' he stated.

Then he turned back to me. 'Are you writing all this down? Look, I've brought paper for you so you can take a note,' he said, handing me a pen and paper from the file. 'Second, I need things. I want trainers, jeans, underwear, vests for the gym, socks, shaving stuff.'

I looked at him bleakly. I'd been told that you couldn't take anything into Parkhurst.

What Reg wanted was money to buy some of those things from the prison shop but the clothes he wanted had to come from shops he knew on the outside. Once I'd bought the clothes, the trainers, those things could be posted to Parkhurst. The office there would keep it all and then he could collect the things after the staff had opened the parcels and cleared them.

He knew, of course, that it wasn't my money that would buy these things.

My role was to get the money for Reg from certain people. Ask for it.

This, to me, was a favour too far. Asking for money in this way was akin, I believed, to begging.

I knew Terry wouldn't mind handing over fifty quid. He felt sorry for Reg. But he was my husband. Reg handed me a list of people, old friends and acquaintances. He was after people who he believed owed him 'favours'.

Charlie said nothing. But I could see that he too was in total disbelief at all this. Very few people had rushed to 'treat' him when he came out. No one wanted to give him a job. It was Diana who had rescued Charlie by getting that promotions work for him.

I sat there shocked at Reggie's effrontery. How – and why – would I go to these men and beg on behalf of Reggie Kray?

The twins were always alert to the slightest change in facial expression. He saw my incredulity.

'Look, these people can send stuff in to Ron, so why not me? When I think of all the things we did for people,' Reg said bitterly. 'It isn't much.'

'What things?' I wanted to scream.

Things like killing men for no good reason? Depriving women of their husbands? Taking protection money? Bashing people up?

The way the twins told themselves everyone 'owed' them was quite mind-boggling. Of course they were the Kray Twins. The whole world owed them.

Now he wanted me, their mum's friend, to go up to people and say:

'Excuse me, have you got twenty quid for poor old Reg, 'cos he wants new trainers?'

And they couldn't be any old trainers. They had to be

a specific brand. The twins were brand-savvy before the words even crept into everyday life.

I was sorely tempted to tell him to get stuffed. But I didn't. I reasoned that this was a one-off favour, something he'd had too much time to think about before the visit. Little did I know, this was the first of a series of similar 'favours'. On and on it would go, for years.

In future, of course, it wouldn't just be me. Other women would be happy to carry out the twins' bidding. I already knew that Reggie had a powerful charisma with women, I'd noted that in the old days, and even the prison gear and grey hair couldn't diminish that. And, of course, he'd always been the organising brain of the twins' enterprises, the schemer who knew how to get things done. When it came to organising things, Reggie could have organised a war, I'm sure of that. In another life, he'd have been a very successful businessman. Without breaking the law.

Over time, though, I learned that the best way was to treat all these 'favours' as a big joke.

'Hello, I'll be visiting the twins next week, have you anything you can give me for them?' I'd breeze to one of his cronies. There really was no other way.

But on this first-ever prison visit to Reg – and let's face it, I wasn't unaware of what the twins were like around favours and money – I was still pretty taken aback by all this.

I tried to wriggle out of it.

'I don't *know* most of these people – how can I go up to them?' I wailed.

'I'll tell you where to go and 'e'll go with you,' said Reg, flicking his finger in the direction of Charlie who was getting angry.

'Wot you talkin' about, Reg? I'm not askin' these people for money,' Charlie insisted, trying to talk some sense into him.

'No. You don't do nuthin' for us, do you?' Reg snarled back. 'Just go to nightclubs and live off our name. Why don't you go outside? I want to talk to Flanagan privately.' Just like that, he dismissed Charlie.

'Not comin' back,' said Charlie, fuming, as he got up.

'Don't!' came the reply, quick as flash.

It was shameful, in my opinion, the way the twins treated their older brother.

'We've come all this way, Reg, and you talk to your brother like this!' I had to say something.

'My brother's a playboy. Ron called 'im that and that's what 'e is.'

As far as Reg was concerned, what Charlie should have done when he came out of prison was start up a business and split the proceeds with them.

'We should be getting money off 'im every week.'

'Charlie's such a nice guy. Everyone in the East End likes him,' I argued.

''E's a ponce,' was the retort. (Which was a laugh, since someone in the criminal fraternity had openly described the twins, who always wanted a slice of someone else's action, as 'thieves' ponces'.)

Sure, it was ugly, their treatment of Charlie. He'd lost seven years of his life because of them, for not much more than being their brother. Another man would have never gone near them after he came out.

But those old East End values glued them all together. Loyalty, family and don't grass on anyone. No matter what you knew to be true.

I wasn't too sure I'd go to see Reggie again after that. I told Charlie as much as we travelled back.

'He said you should be sending them wages every week, Charlie!'

'They're still livin' in 1961, Flan,' was Charlie's response.

As usual, Charlie was right.

Chapter 13

My promise

Not long after my visit to Reg in Parkhurst, the authorities opted to move him yet again, this time to Long Lartin in Leicester. A shorter journey for Vi, but the bleakest of times for Reg.

But in early 1981 I had my own woes to deal with. My dear mum was diagnosed with bowel cancer. They operated quickly and, thankfully, she seemed to get better.

But then, that spring, everything came to a head at home. Terry's bad tempers, his late nights, his moods had turned him into a totally different man. I'd worked out for myself what was behind all this: it was the 'D' word.

Terry knew all too well my feelings on drugs. I couldn't stand them. Almost every model I knew in the 1960s and 1970s took LSD, purple hearts, smoked joints: drugs became part of the lifestyle.

Not for me. I never took anything, nor was I tempted to try. Vain and health-conscious I am, certainly. But I'd seen enough around me to know how destructive drugs can be. Especially cocaine, which had become the 1980s drug of choice for anyone with cash to flash.

I'd tried to get at the truth. I had confronted Terry a few times, asked him direct: was he taking drugs? Doing coke? He'd denied all knowledge, of course. But finally, after a blazing row when I told him I knew what he was up to and I wouldn't have that kind of thing anywhere near me or our son, he 'fessed up. He'd leave, he said. He told me that, financially, I shouldn't worry. He'd pay the mortgage and give me money. At the time I'd just started working part-time, a photographic saleswoman for Ben Jones, selling his work around Fleet Street.

I was shattered. I didn't want to lose him but Terry knew I meant every word. He made no attempt to promise me he'd change, he knew all too well I wouldn't be in any way swayed by promises. He just packed his bags and went to stay with a friend.

JJ, of course, was devastated, bewildered. One night I came downstairs and he'd vanished. Panicking, I ran from room to room until I found him hiding behind the sofa, a confused seven-year-old, crying his eyes out. He adored his dad.

'Is he coming back, mum?' he pleaded as I cuddled him. I had to be honest. Painful as it was for both of us.

'No, but you'll see him every Sunday, JJ,' I promised. That seemed to settle him a bit.

And so Sundays became the high point of JJ's week.

Terry would come over with his two boys from his first marriage, ages twelve and sixteen, and off they'd all go. It was great for JJ, they all adored each other. That, at least, kept JJ on some sort of level ground.

Vi, of course, was shocked when I told her, though she was as supportive as ever.

'You can't have that sort of thing around you and JJ, Maureen,' she said flatly. 'Why couldn't 'e just stop taking 'em?'

'He knows me, Vi,' I told her. 'Even if he swore blind he'd stop doing it there and then, Terry knew I wouldn't buy into that. He knew I wasn't even prepared to *risk* JJ's dad bringing those things into our home.'

Vi looked at me and tutted. But there was a hint of admiration in her voice. 'Most girls would've gone with a promise, I s'ppose. But you've got a strong head on you, I'll say that. You can make up your mind and stick to it. Can't say that for a lot of people.'

'Look, Vi, never mind about the others. It's not just about me, is it? JJ and me, we love Terry. But I want what's best for JJ and if that means his dad won't be living with us any more, that's what's gonna happen.'

I can talk tough but it was, just the same, a very bad time all round. While I struggled to adjust to life with a broken marriage, a broken heart and a son I desperately wanted to protect from all hurt, Vi's own troubles didn't let up. That autumn, Charlie visited Reg in Long Lartin. On his return he told his mum not to visit.

Reg had been in a disgusting state, dishevelled, scruffy and rambling.

Somewhat incoherently Reg had told Charlie he wanted to fight the officers – which wasn't the way he'd been at all in Parkhurst.

He also told Charlie of his fears that he was being poisoned which scared the life out of Charlie – Ronnie's problems had started with irrational fears back in the 1950s.

'They're trying to drive me mad,' a confused, distraught Reg told his brother.

Ronnie, of course, knew that something was going on. He could feel it. You could put those two in separate prisons at either ends of the Earth and they'd still have that telepathy.

I was sworn to secrecy by Charlie. Vi must not know all this. He'd told her that Reg had had a fight and been in hospital, that was all.

So Violet never knew the truth about Reg's stay in Long Lartin. Though I could see she was going through private agonies of wondering what was going on. One day she told me she wasn't sleeping properly because she was having terrible dreams.

'I keep dreaming the twins are trapped in this hole, trying to get out. But they never get out,' she told me.

That day, I realised that Vi had lost quite a lot of weight. Her *joie de vivre* and vitality seemed to be draining away, but after thirteen years of visiting prisons, it stood to reason that this would have some effect on a woman of seventy-one.

'Are you eating properly?' I asked.

'Can't be bothered with that,' came the reply. 'Too much stuff on my mind.'

Those nightmares were telling Violet a fearful truth. Because in Long Lartin, Reg tried to commit suicide on two occasions. The doctors put him on Largactil, a powerful drug used to treat schizophrenia, hoping to control his behaviour. A month later, Reg tried again, using a razor blade to slash his wrists.

Ron, on hearing this from Charlie, sprang into action. He got his solicitors to ask that Reg should be sent back to Parkhurst. There were very real fears that Reg too would be certified insane and sent permanently to Rampton, another institution for the criminally insane.

Thankfully, that didn't happen. In March 1982, Reg was moved back to Parkhurst. Around the same time, my mum, Nell, suddenly took a turn for the worse.

Me, Iris and Leo took it in turns to sit by her bed in the nursing home. On 2 April she asked Iris to get her some jellied eels. She couldn't even feed herself by then, but we left at teatime to pick up our children, then my brother Leo sat with her all night.

She died later in the early hours of 3 April .

It was dreadful. After mum's funeral, I took JJ away for a week to Spain to get away from it all and find some time to recuperate. When I finally got round to Braithwaite

House once more, I was ready to pour my heart out to Vi as usual.

Within thirty seconds of seeing Vi, it was painfully obvious that she was as ill as my beloved mum. She'd aged dreadfully in a very short time – she'd lost even more weight.

'I've got something to tell you,' she announced. 'All that weight I've lost, there's a reason. I've 'ad terrible stomach pains. The doctor's said it's cancer. My sister May knows. I've told everyone not to tell the twins.'

The week before, she'd gone to see Ron and he'd instantly been alerted to how drained and frail his mother looked.

'I'm just tired from all the travelling,' she'd assured him. Then she begged me, yet again, not to tell the twins.

'I'm so frightened what they might do in there and if they know something is wrong with me it might send them over the edge.'

My mum's operation, I reasoned, had at least given us another year with her.

'Can't they operate, Vi?' I was lost for words.

'Not yet. I've got to go back to Bart's for more tests.'

'Look, Bart's is a terrific hospital. They'll get you right,' I told her. There was very little else I could say. She went quiet after that. Then she looked at me and said: 'You won't say anything, will you, Maureen?'

'It's a secret until you say otherwise, Vi,' I promised her.

I went round there again a week later, in the evening.

Charlie Senior was hovering, even more stony-faced than usual. He knew. I needed to get him on his own, find out how bad she was. I needed to know if she was in pain, if she was getting up in the middle of the night. What was happening to her?

There wasn't a single word of complaint from Vi as I snipped away and gave her her usual hairdo. She didn't mention her illness. She just asked me about JJ, how my family were getting on. But there was a flatness about her, a passive acceptance of her lot that rang serious warning bells.

As I left, I asked Charlie to come down to the car with me. He understood immediately.

Silently, we got into the lift. Then, out on the street, I asked him point blank. What had the doctors said? Did she have much time left?

I have never ever forgotten the reply.

'Well,' he said. 'I don't think we'll see her this Christmas.'

No one had told the twins, he said. 'Only a few of us know.'

He looked terribly sad, I reflected, as I drove home slowly, my mind awhirl with what all this would mean to the Krays. Old Charlie would have a lot to cope with. And how would the twins react with their mum gone? For them, their father was no replacement for Violet. Would they even be allowed to go to her funeral? Couldn't see that happening. No, I thought. Brother Charlie would bear the brunt of most of it. As usual.

For several weeks, nothing much happened. She didn't go into hospital or anything. I heard no more about 'tests'. I did manage to coax her to come out with me in the car and drive to Bethnal Green, a visit to Pellicci's.

'Everything's the same,' she said, looking round the busy café, brightening, as always, at being on familiar ground. 'Just like the 1960s.'

A couple of weeks later, Charlie called to tell me that Vi had taken a turn for the worse and was in Bart's Hospital. Could I visit her tomorrow afternoon and stay till five when he could get there?

Jackie came with me. Seeing Violet, propped up in bed in the big ward, her hair a matted mess, as pale and wretched as I'd ever seen her, was a shock for both of us.

As you do, we pretended everything was normal. I tidied Vi's hair and Jackie kept up non-stop chat about trivial things, the way we do in hospital when it's glaringly obvious that the game is almost up and the person we love is perilously close to the end.

Then, unprompted, Violet asked me a question.

'Do you think about your mum now she's gone, Maureen?' she said wistfully.

'Every day, Vi,' I said and it was true: losing our mum had left a huge hole in her children's lives. Then she blurted out:

'Oh, I feel ever so sorry for Charlie. To think he went away all those years when he'd done nothin' wrong.'

'He went away because he was their brother.'

'Wasn't right. Wasn't right.'

It was so sad, I had to look away from her. I wasn't about to start blubbing. We'd never really discussed this aspect of Charlie's life. Now, of course, Vi was struggling to come to terms with it all.

I'd never used the word in connection with this family before, never even thought it.

But now there was only one word to describe it all: tragic.

We went back again two days later. Charlie was busy organising as many visitors as possible so there was someone at Violet's bedside constantly.

Cautiously, we made our way towards Violet's bed. Even in forty-eight hours she'd deteriorated. She looked so frail and thin, her skin pallid, her cheeks hollow. When she saw us, it was a struggle to summon her usual smile. All she could do was nod weakly.

I sat down and grabbed her hand. Jackie did the same on the other side. We were hanging on to her for dear life. But she was definitely leaving us.

'Eaten anything, Vi?' I whispered.

'Yes, I had breakfast. And guess what? I've given up smoking!' She tried a smile.

Violet wasn't a chain smoker, not even a pack-a-day person. She'd have one or two a day, just a puff. I murmured something reassuring. I surmised that she'd heard that, with cancer, you shouldn't smoke – though back then people still smoked themselves silly in pubs, trains and planes.

Then she revealed what was really going on in her mind.

'If I die, what's gonna happen to them two?'

There really was no answer to that but I tried.

'Look, the twins will still have visits – there's always people writing to them and visiting Ronnie.'

But she wasn't reassured.

'Promise me *you'll* still visit the boys, especially Reggie. Anyone can go and see Ronnie but Reggie can only have seven visits a month.'

Her grip on my hand tightened. Jackie was pretty close to tears, it was an effort to keep it together. Violet was weak and at death's door, but the twins' future, locked up for life, was the only thing that mattered to her. She didn't cry. She was just desperate to see her lifetime's work carried on. By another woman. Someone who knew her boys. Someone they all liked.

And so I smiled at her and made my promise to Violet Kray. It seemed an easy promise to keep. At that point, I believed I'd still be visiting them for a fixed period of time after she went, maybe a year or so. Beyond that, who knew what would happen? Life for all of us had been so upside down, I didn't care to think too much about what lay ahead.

'I had one of them dreams last night,' she said. 'I saw my little girl, Maureen.'

Jackie looked at me across the bed, as if to say 'Oh no, she's rambling.'

But she wasn't. Not really.

'The boys would've loved their sister.'

Then she closed her eyes. I thought she was nodding off but suddenly she opened her eyes again.

'Maureen, do you think the boys was as bad as people said they was? They were always so good to me.'

'Yes, Vi, they were really good to you,' I said. 'They loved you.'

'Maureen, I did the best I could. I could only love 'em.'

'What about all the times they took you out, when you met all those film stars?' I reminded her, desperate to get away from the topic of murder and violence.

It worked. The memories.

'Yes. I met George Raft. All those posh people came round our house. That Diana Dors came round to see us at Braithwaite House. They said it was the Government that put them away. But this time, they listened to me – they moved Reggie for me, didn't they?'

This was true. Whatever the real reasons behind the authorities' decision to move Reggie back to Parkhurst, the Kray family's entreaties had finally borne fruit.

She could take credit for that. Violet Kray's last curtain call.

She seemed to be drifting a bit. Then she stirred. There, by the bed, clutching a huge bunch of red roses was her grandson Gary, with his dad. Time for us to go.

Yet even as we kissed her goodbye, she didn't let up.

'You will keep your promise, Maureen, won't you?'

'I promise faithfully, Vi. But don't talk like that – we'll be back tomorrow.'

'Thanks for coming,' Charlie said, polite as ever as we made ready to walk away.

But Violet was determined to have her last word.

'Look at her,' she said to her son. 'She's just like your sister. One of the family.'

I knew what she meant. But I didn't say anything to Jackie as we left the hospital: I was too choked up.

'What was all that about the sister?' Jackie asked when we got into the car.

I tried ringing Charlie the next morning but there was no answer. I kept trying.

Late that afternoon he rang.

'Mum's gone,' he said, as devastated and stunned as any loving son could be.

They'd rung him with the news very early that morning. He'd already been to the hospital and he'd seen her, said his private goodbye to his lovely mum.

Now, of course, he had to go and see about The Other Two. He hoped they'd allow him to visit them. I did offer to go with him. But no, Charlie Senior would go, he said.

Violet had died on 4 August, 1982, just one day short of her seventy-third birthday. Jackie's prediction had been right: she did lead a long life.

One of the Family

She had had an aggressive form of stomach cancer, but who can say whether the thirteen years of travelling to and from the prisons and the worry, stress and exhaustion involved hadn't contributed to her illness?

Women like Violet – mothers, wives and girlfriends of those who pay their debt to society by being locked up for decades – are, in a way, innocent victims too of the crimes their loved ones commit. Often, their entire lives revolve around their visits, year in, year out. It's a terrible way to live.

Losing Violet so quickly, just months after my own mum had gone, stunned me. Having JJ helped, of course: children are the best antidote for grief, simply because you have no choice but to get on with everyday life with them. You can't take to your bed, pull up the duvet and wallow in your pain. Yet it was still a very strange, bleak time for me.

Vi's death was in all the papers, of course. But we never imagined that her funeral would turn into a major event. As it turned out, Reggie wasn't going to let Charlie or his dad have any say in the matter of his mum's funeral. Violet, whose entire life had revolved around living in the East End, would not be buried there. She'd be buried alongside Frances in the cemetery at Chingford Mount.

This, Reg had decided, would be the family burial plot where they would all eventually be laid to rest; he had purchased the plot when Frances died as a family ground.

I wrote to the twins, told them how I'd sat with Vi the day before.

'In her last days, her thoughts were still with her sons,' I wrote, struggling to find any words of comfort. I told them of the promise too. I'd be keeping it, I assured them.

The funeral came on 24 August. Jackie and I were totally unprepared for the huge crowds of people outside the church of St John's, what with the Rolls-Royces dropping off the mourners, the TV cameras recording the event. There was even a police helicopter circling above.

The twins were given permission to attend. The Home Office had told Charlie it was a high security risk and therefore meant a lot of expense. Charlie was relieved to hear that. Trouble at his mum's funeral was unthinkable.

We laid a lovely sheaf of pink carnations by the door of the church to add to what seemed like hundreds of wreaths (in fact, I later found out there were three hundred) and we just stood there, staring at the huge crowds, total strangers who didn't know Violet or the twins. The crowds lined the road to the church, inside the grounds, all waiting for a glimpse of the twins, the first public sighting of the notorious Kray Twins since the 1960s. Then the police cars and the funeral cortege started to draw up.

Ron got out of the car first: immaculate, bespectacled, hair sleeked back, handcuffed to a giant of a policeman, a man seven feet tall. As usual, Ron walked far too quickly, half-dragging the guy with him.

A cheer went up from the crowd the minute he appeared.

'God bless ya, Ron,' said a little old lady.

One of the Family

It was like a scene from Dickens. Then Reggie arrived, a coiled-up wire, alert, already looking round for familiar faces. Reg had arranged the funeral with Charlie. Or rather, Reg had told Charlie exactly what he wanted. But I don't think the twins had anticipated the crowds that had turned up to say goodbye to Vi. Nonetheless, he behaved regally, acknowledging his subjects, smiling at everyone. It was quite surreal.

In the church, Jackie and I were seated right behind platinum-locked Di Dors. Then the doors were closed. Only then were the boys brought in, handcuffed to their escorts, and marched to the front row of the church. Immediately behind them sat the twins' dad, Diana, Charlie and Gary. Everyone in the church started clapping.

I was shocked. Even the clergyman, Father Hetherington, looked a bit stunned. Essentially, the message was: 'We're East End people. You're here to say goodbye to your mum. And so are we.'

Jackie and I sat there, holding hands. We still hadn't come to terms with the idea that Violet was gone: it all seemed to have happened so quickly. The twins seemed impassive. They just sat there, watching their mum's coffin, staring straight ahead. Men of granite. No tears.

Through the service, my mind wandered off to all my times with Violet, her kindness, our long conversations, how she'd always smile with satisfaction when I'd show her the finished hairdo in the mirror, how being the twins' mum was her reason for living. It was, of course, a real worry, wondering how they'd react to losing her. But, judging by their performance today, they were holding up. They still had each other. Even far apart they could lock into each other's minds, feel each other's pain.

It was a brief service, less than half an hour. There was a very short poem and just two hymns. Apart from the clapping, there were no other incidents to mar this last farewell to Violet.

Father Hetherington, the twins' old friend, had known the family since the boys were children. Reg had obviously contacted him and asked him to conduct the service. He'd genuinely appreciated Violet's dedication to her boys.

'I had great regard, respect and affection for Mrs Kray,' he told the packed church. 'Among her qualities was loyalty, a loyalty to that which she held to be right, a loyalty to her family, whom she loved.'

Try as I might, I couldn't see the twins properly, just the backs of their heads. Only when the service ended and the coffin was ready to be carried out were they allowed to exchange the briefest of hugs with their family. Then the police marched them separately through the back entrance of the church, to be whisked away into vans back to their respective prisons. They wouldn't be permitted to watch their mother's burial at the nearby cemetery.

Outside, Jackie and I managed to exchange a quick hug and a few words with Charlie and Diana but now all I wanted was to get away. My mum's funeral still lingered with me. I was still trying to cope with it all.

One of the Family

'Come on, Jac, let's get out of here,' I told her as we left.
I couldn't handle the moment of Vi's burial, I knew that.
I was far too raw. I wouldn't have wanted to break down
in front of everyone.

I'd lost my marriage, my mum and now Violet was
gone. It was too much.

What I didn't know on that August day was that it was
going to get worse before it got better. Because I hadn't a
clue what had really been going on with Terry.

The first I knew of it was a knock on the door in
December, one Friday afternoon.

Two men stood there. They had a county court order
for repossession of the house.

The mortgage hadn't been paid for quite some time.
The Midland Bank were poised to repossess. Eviction,
they said, was due to take place in twenty-four hours.

I stood there, totally lost for words. Then JJ appeared
behind me, wanting to know what was going on.

'Is this your son?' one of the men said.

'Yes,' I said. 'I've just fetched him from school.'

The man started to soften. I was sure he could see I'd
known nothing at all about this.

'I suggest that over the weekend you take everything
belonging to you from the house and you leave. We'll be
back on Monday morning to repossess the place.'

And off he went, leaving me with my life in bits.

Terry, when I rang, informed me that he'd borrowed

£200,000 from the bank and used our house as collateral. He'd then got deeper into debt and stopped paying the mortgage. The bank had every right to repossess. He'd find me somewhere to live, he said. Over the weekend.

But I'd had enough. The following day, my new boyfriend Mitchell came over. I'd met him on a night out a few months before, a very handsome blond, blue-eyed twenty-one-year-old, as kind and helpful as he was good-looking. Mitchell helped me and JJ load all our clothes, toys, other possessions and furniture into a van I'd managed to borrow, and on Sunday morning we drove off towards Victoria Park, towards our new home, a big three-bedroomed flat, just a few doors down from where I'd lived when Terry and I had first met.

I'd rung Terry the day before. He had been living in the big three-bedder. But he was the one that could find himself another home, I told him. Me and JJ were moving into the three-bedder. Our son was not going to be homeless. Not even for a day.

What could Terry say? He'd blown it big-time and he knew I was right. Just before we'd arrived, he'd managed to pack his bags and move out. My family rallied round and helped us move in. I wanted to lie down and cry my eyes out. But I couldn't. It was better all round just to get on with it.

JJ would have to go to a school in Hackney after his lovely little private school in Chigwell. Fortunately, JJ is like me, he doesn't hold grudges or look back. So he too followed my lead. And got on with it.

As for the Krays, they too were trying to get on with it. Charlie had opened a business, a security and chauffeur service, with a friend in Whitechapel. For a while, it was quite successful. Gary stayed on with his granddad at Braithwaite House.

I managed to see the twins once, just before Christmas. Reggie seemed unchanged, organised – he'd bounced back from all his crazy depressions not long after moving back to Parkhurst. He seemed OK. He'd formed a good friendship with a younger guy called Steve Tully. Together they were planning to compile a book of cockney slang.

Ronnie, though, felt his mum's loss much more intensely. They kept him on heavy medication after the funeral and when I visited with a friend of his, Jack Leigh, we tried our best to raise his spirits.

'I don't know why I'm in here with all these mad people,' he demanded.

I answered, 'But Ronnie, you are mad!'

He laughed before adding, 'It's a good job you're a woman saying that,' and we all laughed together.

We took him a pork pie, some smoked salmon and some Puccini LPs – Ron loved Puccini. But that didn't work.

When I mentioned the smoked salmon all he said was: 'Are they in bagels?'

Well, no. So that had to change. From then on, you

had to buy Ron smoked salmon in bagels, purchased from Brick Lane.

'I think mum was ill for a long time and didn't tell us,' Ron told us, after a very long silence.

I didn't mention that the family had known about the cancer. What was the point?

The man was obviously in a bad way, unusually quiet. Sure enough, about halfway through visiting time, he just stood up. 'I've got to go, going back to my room.' Then he marched off.

In March 1983 Charlie rang me unexpectedly. That morning, Gary had found Charlie Senior lying at the foot of the stairs in the flat. He was gone, just seven months after Violet, ironically just two days before his seventy-fifth birthday.

'He couldn't live without her,' I thought to myself. For all that the marriage had been so difficult for Vi and he'd been a less than considerate spouse, he'd needed her just as much as the boys had. Would the boys be going to the funeral? I wondered.

In fact, they decided not to apply for permission to go. Charlie told me they'd said the old man had showed himself up at Vi's funeral.

At Violet's graveside, her husband had been behaving oddly – drinking, according to Charlie, stumbling around to the point where they thought he might tumble into Vi's grave.

'We tolerated him because of our mother,' the twins told Charlie. 'But we're not going to his funeral.'

Had they applied, they'd probably have been allowed to go. But their pride, their star billing at their mum's funeral had been jeopardised, in full view of their public. As far as they were concerned, their dad had shamed them.

To me, this was unfathomable. Sons who adored their mother but hated their father so much that they wouldn't pay him their last respects. I couldn't help but wonder which one had led on this decision. One certainly wouldn't have gone without the other.

Now I was back in the East End, trying to put the pieces of my life together.

I continued to work for Ben Jones on a commission-only basis. I still did a bit of modelling or promotions work if it came up and could be fitted in with school hours. I kept up the regular visits to the twins, once a month to Ronnie, once every two months to Reggie.

Of course, Vi would now be a frequent topic of conversation when I saw them. I still missed her, I told them, and indeed I missed the sheer homeliness of Violet, the warmth of her welcome, her concern for me and my life. The twins never ever talked about the past in terms of what they'd done to bring upon themselves their lifetime sentences. But they always loved to talk about their mum.

I made it an annual ritual to visit Vi's grave with flowers every Mothers' Day on their behalf. Just talking to Ron about that visit, how I'd tidy up the grave site, wipe the stone down, would please him.

I remember one time he stared into the distance, took a long pause and finally said, 'I believe we killed our mother, all that travelling to all the various prisons, and the worry, the stress. She never let us down, but we let her down.'

I was stunned by this. I mean it was the first time, I believe, he's admitted it to himself.

Reg, on the other hand, sometimes kept the talk about his mum quite brief because he had so many other things he wanted me to do for him.

They had very different approaches when it came to asking me to help them.

Ron would just ask, hope I'd remember. Reg wrote everything down – and I mean everything. A master of organisation, Reggie would tell it like he was dictating to a secretary. Ronnie, however, could be a bit more entertaining about it all.

One day, completely out of nowhere, Ronnie announced that he had a lady he wanted me to meet. 'Nice lady, bin visitin' me,' he told me.

My ears pricked up.

'What do you mean, "nice lady"?'

'She's got two children and she reminds me a lot of our mum.'

I got it immediately. Someone else to look after Ron. I knew it wasn't a romance. Ron had made himself far too busy with the young men he had as lovers in Broadmoor. At that point he had a steady boyfriend, a handsome young guy called Charlie who had, I learned from Ron, killed two men before winding up in Broadmoor.

There was nothing covert or hidden about the relationship. All the staff at Broadmoor knew about it. In fact, such was Ron's influence, he told me, that he'd wangled Charlie one of the best jobs for inmates in the hospital – serving the visitors with drinks, cakes or snacks in the visiting area. Having Charlie as a lover in the hospital in no way prevented Ron from seeking out another external relationship. With a woman.

'Yeah . . . well, I 'ave to 'ave someone lookin' after me, don't I?'

The woman had initially written to Reg and then visited him. Reg had approved and suggested she visit his twin. Charlie had met her too. Now, as an unofficial part of the family, I too needed to 'approve' her. Yet I had no idea that Ron was plotting marriage.

A couple of months later, I turned up at Broadmoor to meet Ronnie's new friend, Elaine. She was divorced, very pleasant, plump, well groomed, dark hair, olive skin. Definitely a mum. Not the glamour-girl type.

Ronnie introduced us. Then, completely out of the blue, he fixed Elaine with his unmistakable glare.

'Elaine,' he said. 'Are you gonna marry me or not?' A real-life Prince Charming.

Poor Elaine was totally flummoxed. To say she was taken aback was an understatement.

Then she looked at me. 'What do I *say*?' she mouthed.

'DON'T LOOK AT HER, look at me and answer me!' boomed Ron.

'Oh. Yes, Ron.'

Ron leaned over, rubbed the back of her hand.

'Good girl.'

'Where's Elaine's ring, then?' I wanted to know.

'Nah, she don't want a ring, do you, Elaine?'

Elaine, I could see, was far too nice a person for all this Kray Twin manipulation.

'No, Ron,' she said, somewhat too meekly for my liking.

Oh dear. Elaine's future unrolled before me. She didn't drive, Ron had already alerted me to this when he'd informed me that I'd be running her home. He would expect Elaine to run back and forth from Broadmoor with list after list of orders, things to do, people to see. It wouldn't be easy for her. But, selfishly, I knew it would take a bit of pressure off me.

'So when are you going to do it, Ron?' I enquired.

'Soon. Soon. But I wanna ask you something. 'Ow much d'you think the newspapers will pay?'

Then and only then did the penny drop. That was why he'd wanted us both there.

Her to say yes and me to get the ball rolling with a newspaper auction.

He'd already checked, as I've mentioned, that I could act as a liaison between him and Fleet Street. In those days, if you knew people working on the tabloids you could walk into the office and ask to see them, have a chat. By then I had several friends and contacts on various papers. It was no problem, really, for me to go in and talk to people about Ron Kray's latest venture. At that point in time, neither of the twins had sold any major stories to Fleet Street. But this one, Ron calculated, would excite them: Crazy Killer Kray Marries Mum of Two Inside Broadmoor. Different, I grant you.

'Could you get married in church, Ron?' I wondered.

Elaine nodded vigorously. She'd definitely like that.

But Ron had already sorted that one.

'No church. We can get married 'ere. There's a beautiful chapel 'ere. We can 'ave food, champagne, anythin' I want.'

Same old Ron.

He could have been talking about Westminster Abbey rather than a prison hospital for the criminally insane . . .

Chapter 14

Marriage

The idea of marriage preoccupied the twins once Violet had gone. The way they saw it, it made perfect sense: publicity, of course, and a caring woman on hand to run around doing 'errands' at their beck and call.

Not that they didn't find plenty of willing women on the outside to do this for them without a legal tie. With every year that passed, their fame – and their fan club – increased. But of course, as someone they'd known so long, who'd been close to their mum, once I'd divorced Terry in 1984 my name came high on their list of prospective candidates.

The first proposal came on a visit after Reg had been sent back to Parkhurst. He brought the subject up one day out of the blue. What did I think about marrying him? Years later, an old friend dug out a Christmas card that Ron had sent to his twin that year. Scrawled at the bottom was the comment: 'You've GOT to marry Flanagan.' So between the two of them, this idea had obviously been mooted back and forth again and again.

'I'll have to think about it, Reg,' I told him, playing for time.

Violet had never said it in so many words, but she'd hinted once or twice in later years that she thought I'd have made an ideal match for her Reg. It must have been a huge comfort for her to imagine me committing myself to her 'lovely' son. But while I picked up the signs, I dismissed it at the time. All mums have their secret wish-list for their son's perfect spouse, don't they?

But I was a mum too, with a son to consider. JJ was about ten then. He'd met both twins and liked them but the fact was that JJ came first in our lives. Did I really want our name to be Kray? I knew what was involved in bearing the name Kray from the old days. Look at Frances and the Shea family. She legally changed her name back to Shea but it didn't make any difference. She was always to be connected to the Krays. As were her family.

Reg got huffy that I hadn't said yes straight away. Typical of the twins, he expected his every whim to be satisfied on the spot. Sometimes you couldn't help thinking they believed they were still in Vallance Road, ordering everyone around.

'What's to think about?' he demanded.

'I can't say yes straight away,' I warned him. 'It's not just about me, is it?'

Reluctantly, Reg nodded. He'd wait.

Two weeks later, I wrote and said yes. I'd really thought

it through properly: I'd focused on the fact that I'd still be leading my own life and I'd be helping Reg. He could only have so many visits, couldn't he?

Obviously, Reg then alerted Charlie who turned up hammering at my front door at eight one morning, waking me up, holding a caravan made of matchsticks by Reg in Parkhurst.

'Reg's serious about the marriage, Flan,' Charlie warned me.

'You'd better not be doing it just for a laugh.'

Perhaps Charlie knew me better than I thought and realised I hadn't looked too carefully at the implications. He of all people knew what it would mean.

Then I did stop to examine all the angles. So much so that I discussed it with my ex, Terry. We were still on good terms, despite everything, and I knew he'd be totally honest with me.

Terry didn't think it was a good idea at all.

'He could get out one day, Flan,' he warned me. 'You're independent, you're bossy. I don't think those attributes go with being Mrs Reggie Kray. With Ron, you might never have him on your doorstep. But you might with Reg.'

Terry, despite his faults, had a sharp brain. OK, JJ liked the twins. But changing his name to Kray was another matter. His dad was his dad, after all.

Even so, I was a bit scared to tell Reg my decision on my next visit. You never knew how he'd react.

Out he bounced into the visiting area, all happy and

smiling, shaking hands with everyone, his usual Mr Celebrity routine.

'Sit down, Reg. I've made a decision,' I said, pretending to be all businesslike but quaking a bit inside. 'I've decided I'd rather be a good friend and the sister I've always been to all of you,' I blurted out. 'Don't want to be a wife any more. Doesn't work for me, does it?'

Silence. Reg stared at me, that quizzical look I knew so well.

Oh God, please don't let him get into a strop.

'OK, then.'

And amazingly, he just changed the subject.

Why didn't he lose it with me, I wondered later?

I was pretty sure I knew why.

He didn't want to lose me as a friend. His brother was in Broadmoor, his mum was gone. Reg knew all too well that we went back such a long way that ours wasn't the sort of friendship that was easily replaced. He wasn't about to fall out with me. He was far too shrewd for that.

But Ron still nagged him endlessly. A couple of years later Reg mentioned marriage again in front of his friend Steve Tully on a visit. Yet again, I stalled. Then when I next saw Ron, he started going on about it. Talk about a dog with a bone.

'Do you really think he can be bossy with me, like he is with everyone else, Ron?' I said, wanting to shut him up.

Give Ron his due. Despite his illness, there were times when he could be very astute.

'Reg is not insane, he's a model prisoner. And you're well known, you can get the campaign going for his release. As his wife, you could get him out.'

He was right. But I wasn't going to marry Reg, not even when the papers got hold of the proposal and started making a big deal out of it.

'Well, at least I'd know where he is at nights,' I told them. That was all I could do, make a big joke out of it.

I did continue to campaign to get Reg released: petitioned the Home Office, wrote to the Queen. (You always get a politely worded answer from Buckingham Palace.)

But I was never going to be Mrs Reggie Kray, not me. The twins weren't going to get their own way on that one.

As for Elaine, I became the go-between with Fleet Street for the story of the wedding. Ronnie insisted he wanted £20,000 for the exclusive. The papers could pay the money to Charlie. In the end, he had to settle for £10,000. Naturally, the paper insisted on sending a photographer, which kind of shocked Ronnie – he thought he was just selling a story. The paper, of course, wanted the photos: they could syndicate them abroad after publication and recoup their investment.

So, with the deal arranged, I went to see Ron again, accompanied by his friend Jack Leigh. Jack made a huge mistake that day. He went to Broadmoor wearing a beautiful black and white herringbone overcoat with a black velvet collar.

Ron insisted on trying it on. Not realising what this meant, Jack dutifully handed it over. Yes, we agreed. Ron looked marvellous in the coat.

'I wanna get married in this,' he told us.

'OK,' said Jack. 'Borrow it for the wedding and I'll get it back afterwards.'

Jack never saw his beloved coat again except in the newspaper story of the wedding. The paper photographed Ron wearing it on his wedding day. Elaine, for her part, got married in blue, after consulting Ron, who informed her that it was Violet's favourite colour.

The newspaper glammed Elaine up by hiring a white-fox stole to be draped over her beautiful blue dress. She did look a treat. My belief always was that she'd become genuinely fond of Ron and wanted a husband, even one who was locked up for life. In the end, of course, she'd be worn out with all the to-ing and fro-ing – Ron insisted that she should visit Reg at Parkhurst. The rules around phone calls had become more relaxed then, too. So Ron could phone his new wife every day. Though he was somewhat bewildered when a thoughtful friend left a paid-up phone card for him one day. Everyone used phone cards in the early 1980s after they were introduced. But of course, having been shut off from the world for nearly fifteen years, Ron hadn't a clue how to use a phone card.

Elaine's children met Ron, of course. She insisted they call him dad: Ron quite liked that. He'd happily buy them toys, books, games. He loved giving kids presents. When I'd first taken JJ to Broadmoor to see him, Ron had been at his kindest.

He ruffled JJ's hair and gave him fatherly advice, talking about the things in life all young boys should respect. Then, the next time JJ came with me, Ron would ask him to repeat, word for word, what Ron had told him, essentially Ron Kray's code of behaviour for youth (he never saw the irony in this, for had the younger Ron followed this advice to the letter, he might not have wound up locked up for life).

Essentially, Ron's mantra was:

* Make sure you get into some kind of sport, it gets you off the street – and away from trouble.
* Don't ever take drugs. You need to be in charge of you.
* Always respect and look after your mum. Your mum is your best friend.

Sometimes on these visits with JJ, one of Ron's 'slaves' would produce, on Ron's instructions, a special gift for JJ, purchased from the Broadmoor shop. Each time, the gift was the same: a fluffy toy. Not exactly appropriate – it meant little to an East End kid like JJ.

As a consequence, I learned to coach JJ about these daft gifts before we left home.

'Don't say a word when he hands it to you. Just say

"Thank you, Ron." We'll take it home and give it to someone smaller than you.'

When I look back at it now, those trips to Broadmoor were often an entertainment in themselves. Ron could be much more fun than Reggie, who tended to take life a tad more seriously. You had to laugh at Ron's obsessions and demands because they could often be completely over the top. Frequently, total strangers wanted to meet the twins and I'd wind up as the go-between, trying to steer people away from Ron's more acquisitive behaviour.

I didn't always succeed.

Take Ron's obsession with watches. He loved to collect them, like a little kid. So if I was taking someone new to see him, there was always the danger that Ron would somehow manage to cajole the person into handing their watch over to him. Which could turn into quite an expensive day out for those with pricey watches.

I'd warn new visitors beforehand.

'Don't wear your expensive watch,' I warned them. 'Go and buy a cheap watch in the market, otherwise he'll have the good one off you.'

I knew Ron's little routine. He knew exactly how to play it. How he loved sartorial splendour. Monograms were one of his passions. His shirts had embroidered pockets with R on them, his cufflinks too had to be embossed with the initial R. With new visitors' watches, he was a human jackdaw. The minute he spotted it, he'd swoop.

'Oooh, that's a nice watch,' he'd say. And before you knew it, the unsuspecting visitor would find themselves in an embarrassing situation.

What could they do but hand it over? Few men felt comfortable saying 'no' to Ronnie Kray. And it wasn't always a watch. Gold cufflinks, shirts, ties: he'd admire something and usually manage to get it off the person. He'd play the game, be all coy and refuse the first offer. Then the person would have to insist he take it. It was pure extortion. He'd defy them to speak up and say: 'Hey, give it back to me.'

At Broadmoor, Ronnie Kray got everything done for him. Not by the staff, of course, but by the other inmates. One slave would happily clean out his room. (Naturally, it had to be spotless.) Another was designated to Violet's old job – washing and ironing his shirts. Another guy would polish his shoes to perfection – they were so shiny that you could put your make-up on while looking into them.

I'd frequently be despatched to Ron's favourite tie shop in the East End where they'd let me have a selection of ties to take to show Ron in Broadmoor. On loan. And so on. Essentially, he ordered whatever he wanted. Pork pies from Harrods Food Hall were a particular favourite.

Though there was one thing he coveted madly that he couldn't have: my younger boyfriend, Mitchell.

I'd taken Mitchell to meet Ronnie when we were an item. Mitchell was really eager to meet him. I agreed – somewhat cautiously, I might add. I knew Ron would fancy him like mad. Could Mitchell cope? I didn't really want to find out, to tell the truth.

But Ron could behave impeccably when it suited him and the visit went well. Sure enough, when Mitchell left the visiting room briefly to go to the loo, Ronnie leaned across the table and hissed:

'You're a very lucky girl, Flan.'

I knew exactly what Ron was capable of doing. He'd start writing to Mitchell, playing up to him, suggesting he come and visit him without me. Or suggesting he could introduce him to someone famous.

I didn't think Mitchell would fall for any of it – he wasn't daft – but he was young and I suppose I was extra-protective of him, more so than if he'd been around my own age. So I warned Ron in no uncertain terms.

'Don't you *dare* start writing letters to Mitchell,' I said. 'He's straight. And he's mine!'

To his credit, Ron didn't push it. For once.

If Ron did fancy someone in Broadmoor, he'd woo them with expensive gifts. At one point he despatched me to a shop in Denmark Street, Soho, to buy a pricey guitar for Charlie, the handsome double murderer. Or the gift might be an expensive Gucci watch. Or a gold chain he wanted to give to another lust object. Then it was down to me to drive round to the East End to see some of the old 'faces' and collect 'Ron's Christmas money' from his pals, a few quid from this one, a fiver from another, till I'd collected enough to buy the gift. Of course, there were always deadlines. At one point he said: 'I want a football and I want it signed by George Best. Get the football here before Friday.' It took a lot of phone calls and running around but I managed it. It was exhausting.

In the early years after the twins went down, a movie called *Villain* came out with Richard Burton playing the part of a sadistic homosexual gangster who doted on his mum. The movie had been based on a best-selling book and it was obvious that the character of the gangster, Vic Dakin, had been based on Ronnie.

One day at Broadmoor I happened to mention the movie to Ron. Big mistake.

'Bring 'im down 'ere next week,' was the response.

Richard Burton was a huge movie star. 'Ron, how am I gonna get him to come to Broadmoor?' I entreated.

But, of course, Ron wouldn't listen. He'd made up his mind. There was no turning back. On and on he went. He wouldn't stop until you did what he wanted.

'Find 'im, Flan.'

As it turned out a friend of a friend of Ron's knew someone who was a big agent. The guy contacted a couple of other agents and one of them got in touch with Burton. And he agreed! Unfortunately, I didn't manage to be there for the visit.

Ron told me afterwards that when Burton walked in and they shook hands, his comment was: 'Well, I'm taller than you, Rich' – that was typical of Ron. He really could be very funny at times.

The twins had always wanted to see their life story as a big movie, which it was eventually. (They hated it, just the same as they'd hated *The Profession of Violence*, John Pearson's book about – among other things – his time with them before they went down. Though they could never understand that the book really set them on the road to being celebrity crims when it came out in the early Seventies.)

At one point in 1984 I found myself at the Duke of York's Theatre in London's theatreland in Al Pacino's dressing room. He'd given a rare and exciting stage performance in David Mamet's play *American Buffalo*. There'd been a lot of talk at the time that Pacino and Dustin Hoffman were keen to play the twins in the movie of their life. Ron had asked me to go and find out more.

After the performance, I managed to persuade the doorman to let me into the star's dressing room, mainly because the actress Frances de la Tour had also seen the play and had been invited – unlike me – to visit Al after the show. I stuck to Frances at the stage door – she was far too polite to say 'Er . . . who are you?' – and we were both ushered through.

There was Al, sitting at the mirror, taking off his make-up. I dived straight in.

'Mr Pacino, is the story true that you and Dustin Hoffman have been approached to play the Kray Twins by an English film company?'

Yes, he said, it was true. Then he started asking me lots

of questions about the twins. How different were they in temperament? Were they approachable? Which one was more likeable? What was Broadmoor like?

He seemed astonished when I told him that I went to see Ron there every month and had done so for ages.

'You actually *go* to this place?' he said.

'Oh yes, and it would be very easy for me to take you there if you wanted.'

But Al Pacino was no Richard Burton. He shook his head. No, he said, he didn't think he'd be going. It wasn't likely that the movie would happen, anyway.

So Al, one of Hollywood's biggest names, turned down his chance to play one of the twins. Imagine that, taking Michael Corleone to meet the man who'd modelled himself on Al Capone. I could see that Pacino was fascinated by the twins. But not, alas, fascinated enough to meet one of them in Broadmoor.

But if Ron was very good at getting everyone to run around him at his beck and call, there was one thing he couldn't control: the existence of one Broadmoor inmate whom he loathed and detested – the serial killer Peter Sutcliffe, the Yorkshire Ripper.

Sutcliffe had brutally murdered thirteen women and continues to serve a full-life sentence for his horrendous crimes. He was initially sent to Parkhurst in 1981, then to Broadmoor in 1984. Ronnie hated him. He didn't want him anywhere near him. Or his visitors. He'd killed women, you see. And in Ronnie's somewhat confusing rationale, the murder of any woman was a crime too far.

On one occasion, I was visiting Ron with some friends when he suddenly realised that Sutcliffe was at an adjoining table with a visitor.

Ron started to go potty. The other visitors froze. I grabbed his hand, managed to calm him down a bit.

'I can SEE that slag behind you!' Ron thundered.

Hastily, I moved my chair so that Sutcliffe was no longer visible to us. Ron didn't even want the back of my head to be angled at the Ripper. ('Slag' was his favourite word for someone he despised.)

If Ron's existence in the late 1980s was enlivened by his first marriage, Reg was still having a difficult time. In January 1987, we learned that Reg had been moved to Gartree Prison in Leicester. After nearly twenty years behind bars, he was now a Category B prisoner, no longer high-security.

That was, in itself, progress, cause for hope of release after the thirty years was up. Yet Gartree was horrible. A prison in a prison was one way to describe it then. The wardens at Parkhurst had seemed kinder. And, of course, Reg had made close friendships at Parkhurst. Now, yet again, he was on alert for the tearaways who wanted to take out Reggie Kray. He'd be permanently watching his back.

'The only thing I like about it here is being able to turn

the light on and off in my cell,' he told me. Which, when you think about it, is a terrible thing to say.

The twins wanted their visits to each other to be extended beyond three times a year – and they wanted them to be more private. They were always surrounded by guards who could hear every word. They were fed up with it.

Reg asked me and Charlie to talk to Ron's psychiatrist at Broadmoor, Mr Tidmarsh. Maybe he could help them. Tidmarsh was kind and diplomatic when Charlie asked him if Ron would ever get better.

'He's better off in here than in a prison. It'd be unhealthy for him,' he told us.

And sure enough, not long afterwards, the twins were allowed more visits to each other. Charlie and I then campaigned for more privacy on the visits. In time, that happened too.

In the four years of Ron's marriage to Elaine, I'd often spend time with her. Sometimes she'd come home with me for dinner after a visit. I could see that Elaine genuinely cared for Ron in a motherly sort of way but, typically, once the excitement of it all had worn off, Ron's interest dwindled. Which is not that surprising when you consider that he was a gay man. Even had he not been, conjugal visits were not permitted at Broadmoor.

Elaine was often broke, what with having two kids and having to travel to and from Broadmoor all the time. Her only job, if you like, was this marriage. We all did our best for her. Charlie took her out sometimes to functions. Jack and I would chip in with a bit of cash if we could. Briefly, she too became 'one of the family'.

Neither she nor Ron ever really told me what happened, why it ended. Charlie said she'd gone to see him one day and Ron asked her: 'Do you want a divorce if you're fed up with all the travelling?' and she agreed.

Elaine, alas, had worn herself out. The divorce came through in 1989 and she drifted out of his life. She kept in touch with me for a while, then I stopped hearing from her.

In the meantime, another woman had come into Ron's life before the divorce. Kate Howard had been writing to Reg and visiting him in Gartree.

Reg liked her. 'I've met this girl called Kate, she's very much like you, blonde, makes me laugh, saucy,' he wrote to me. 'I've sent her to Ron.'

History was repeating itself. Kate has a big personality. Reg knew she'd breeze in and enchant his twin, make him laugh with all her stories of being a Kissogram girl. And she did. Kate brought a lot of sunshine into Ron's life.

Ron decided he'd marry Kate after her second visit. She just laughed her head off when he asked her. At Ron's insistence, I went to meet her at Broadmoor. The three of us sat there in the big visiting hall, joking, mucking around and laughing ourselves silly. She was fun.

'Were you safe doing that Kissogram stuff?' Ron wanted to know.

'Yeah. I had a minder.'

'Oh, I had a minder,' said Ron, harking back to the bad old days. 'He was me driver too.'

I was really pleased about Kate. I knew, immediately, that she'd do her own thing. She was very down to earth. She'd been married twice. Third time lucky?

Yet before they tied the knot in 1989, I'd had more loss in my own life.

In 1986, Terry had been rushed to hospital after a heart attack. We still had a great friendship and JJ spent a lot of time with his dad. But Terry had never stopped partying – one very good reason for the heart attack. In the hospital, Terry told us he needed an operation. All his arteries were blocked.

'Oh, a bypass?' I queried.

'No. They've suggested a heart transplant.'

Terry waited ten months for the transplant. We saw him every Sunday but he was obviously deteriorating. One Friday night I got a call from him.

'Tonight's the night,' Terry told me.

He was going to Harefield Hospital for the transplant.

Somehow, he lasted for another twenty-two months. But in March 1988 he died in Harefield. Terry was just forty-three. He had continued his party lifestyle right to the last. Terry wasn't the sort of guy to sit in the garden, looking at the roses.

JJ was coming up to thirteen that summer. Along with

Terry's two other sons, I had to watch my own son carry his dad's coffin at the funeral. I'd long forgiven Terry for what had happened. But this was another heartbreaking time for me and JJ.

To this very day, I remember Terry as the one big love of my life. Other boyfriends would come and go. But it was JJ's dad who had won my heart right from the moment I'd clapped eyes on him in that East End pub.

Thankfully, Ron didn't ask me to get involved with selling stories to Fleet Street about his wedding to Kate in 1989. But I thoroughly enjoyed the wedding reception that he'd organised at the Bracknell Hilton. It was an amazing bash. About 100 guests enjoyed free-flowing champagne, a pianist and a magnificent buffet. But, of course, the groom wasn't there.

The lavish reception was a gift from a friend of Ron's, Jeff Allen. Charlie had to climb into the hired Rolls-Royce after the ceremony at Broadmoor and accompany the bride – and the wedding cake – to the reception. (Ron took his chunk of cake to eat in his room.) Naturally, the bride and groom had wanted Reg there and he'd been given permission to attend. But he didn't.

I was pretty preoccupied then. Most of my time was spent worrying about JJ. He'd turned into quite a rebellious teenager after losing his dad. He had no interest whatsoever in anything except music.

Every time I hear that Phil Collins song, 'In the Air Tonight' – 'I can feel it, coming in the air tonight, oh lord' – I go straight back to my son's teenage years. That song – and that bang-bang-bang drum solo – came out of his bedroom constantly, he and his mates would just play it over and over again. Or I'd be out on the street near our house, pacing up and down at ten p.m., terrified that something had happened to him, a typical mum of a teenager really. A mum who was still learning how to be both mum and dad.

Chapter 15

Movie stars

When the Kray movie finally came out in 1990, the twins were furious when they finally got to see it. They were upset that the actress playing Vi, Billie Whitelaw, swore. Vi never ever swore.

Charlie got the blame for the swearing. They'd all earned money from this movie – around £100,000 between them. Charlie's deal was that he would be technical adviser on the movie. His contract said he had to be on set every day while they filmed. But there were too many times when he just wasn't there.

'Oh, they can do without me,' he told me. I didn't think that sounded right and of course I told him so. But he just laughed it off.

Of course, his brothers knew he'd been absent from the set – far too many people continued to run back and forth to them with bits of gossip – and were convinced that he could have prevented the swearing. (That's a moot point: a technical adviser is there to point things out but the director and producers have final say.) So there were even more rows with Charlie, though, to be fair, he'd brought it on himself.

For my part, I was disappointed that the Vi in the movie didn't portray my Vi, the woman I'd known, always singing and happy. The Kemp Twins, Londoners and pop stars as they were then, didn't project the sheer menace of the twins in their heyday. But that's movies for you. It wasn't a documentary, after all.

Yet for me, the funniest consequence of the movie money was the story of Ron's bill at the Broadmoor canteen.

I was with two of Ron's closest friends, Jack and Laurie O'Leary, one afternoon at Broadmoor. We were just leaving when we were approached by a rather nervous man, an employee at the hospital.

'Er . . . would you be able to do something about Ronnie's canteen bill?' said the man. You could see he was very embarrassed by all this, tackling Ronnie Kray's friends for the readies.

'Sure,' said Laurie, ready to produce a £50 note or two to help out his childhood friend. 'How much?'

There was a slight pause.

Then the poor man 'fessed up. 'It's £7,000'.

Ronnie had clearly been ordering up big-time in anticipation of his movie payout.

'I think you ought to talk to Ronnie,' said Laurie tactfully, handing over a couple of £50 notes before we left.

Next time, I went with Charlie. We'd discussed the monster bill, of course.

Then we sat in the car park deciding which one of us would be brave enough to confront Ronnie about the bill.

'Go on, Flan, you're a good actress, he won't shout at you,' Ron's not-so-brave brother told me. 'If I tell him, I'll get called all the slags under the sun.'

Out Ron strode, fifteen minutes late as usual.

'New suit, Ron?' I quipped.

'Yeah.'

'New cufflinks?'

'Beautiful, eh?'

Time to be bold.

'Ron, last time we were here they gave us your canteen bill. They said you owed them seven grand.'

A very long silence – never a good sign when you were around Ron.

'Is it?'

'Look, Ron, Jack and Laurie left £100 last time. But how do you get a bill like that here? Is it something to do with what you order in your room?'

'Yeah, I 'ave to 'ave me pork pies from 'Arrods, don't I? I 'ave my friends in my room on Saturdays. Four of us.'

Clearly, Ron regarded this little weekly party, courtesy of Harrods Food Hall, as his right. Just like you would on the outside if you invited the neighbours round.

'What else do you have sent in, Ron?'

'Well, wine. I'm allowed 'alf a bottle.'

309

I'm not good at adding up but it dawned on me then that these in-room orders were only the tip of a very big iceberg.

There were the huge bouquets of flowers that he'd order, via the canteen, often for total strangers to take home to their old mum. Or for their sister who'd just got married. Or had her first baby.

Then there were the toys he'd buy for visitors' children, so he could give them out on visits. The generous orders for sandwiches, drinks, cakes for his visitors (bear in mind, he'd often have visitors twice a day, most days of the week). And, of course, his expensive clothes, the crocodile shoes, the Gucci watches and gold chains for the objects of his desire. Ron kept up appearances on a very grand scale.

The oddest thing was, so much of it was down to Ronnie's crazy, impulsive generosity. He loved to give. He did have a very compassionate side, especially for the underdog, the little person who'd had a raw deal in life. But he'd never in his entire life known limits, didn't want to know them. Someone, somewhere could always pick up the tab.

So what happened, you might wonder, to the huge canteen bill?

Dead right.

His friends the visitors paid it off. In instalments.

That day I confronted him, he demanded that Charlie should pay some of it from his film money. In fact, Charlie was already in debt, borrowing against the film-money payday.

'Everything is very *expensive* out there,' Charlie told his brother. 'It's not like the 1960s. All the visits to you and Reg, they cost money.'

'Yeah. And you're always in nightclubs spendin' *our* money, using *our* name,' was the response. 'Slag. Don't tell us 'ow much you spend on visits. WE'RE IN 'ERE!'

Charlie wasn't lying, though. He was permanently broke. By then his relationship with Diana had soured and he had a new lady friend, an attractive woman called Judy Stanley. Once the film money came in, he spent it as quickly as he got it Like his brothers, Charlie liked the good things of life, especially champagne and nightclubs, so Ron's jibes weren't entirely misdirected. Only Reggie, of the three, could be more careful with money. Though in later life he too would be very generous with cash gifts to some of his prison pals.

That same year the movie came out, I found a new love, Derek Francis, a chauffeur from south of the river and a good friend of Charlie Kray who'd introduced us. Once Derek came on the scene, he proved to be a bit of a calming influence on JJ. By then, such was JJ's dedication to pop music that I forked out for him to go on a special DJ course in London. That helped, too.

In the next few years, I maintained a fairly regular routine with the twins and the visits. The campaigning for parole for them continued: there was no point in letting up on it now.

If I didn't visit, they'd ring me sometimes – Reg had a

very annoying habit of phoning first thing in the morning – and Charlie kept me more or less up to date on everything else that was going on. By then, he was living with Judy and her family.

But the summer of 1993 proved to be a bad one for Ron. He attacked another patient: his illness was worsening and they'd had to switch his medication around. What with one thing and another, I didn't get to see him for a few months. I was told he looked terrible. So when I did visit again with Charlie, I was already very worried.

He came out angry. By then, he was much thinner too. As he marched towards us, you could see he was in a terrible mood. Something had gone wrong.

No peck on the cheek. His brother, as usual, was virtually ignored.

'What's wrong, Ron?'

'You read the book?' he snarled. He was referring to Kate's book, *Murder, Madness and Marriage*, which had recently been published. In the book she had mentioned her relationships with other men.

'Yes, I've read it, Ron. What's the matter?'

'She's makin' a fool of me. She didn't 'ave the right. I told 'er she could 'ave boyfriends. But why 'as she put it into print?'

I had to lay it on the line to him. The truth was, he *had* given Kate permission to have a normal life. Someone had to set him straight. But of course, by mentioning his agreement in a book and detailing her relationships, Kate had told the world. To Ron, hypersensitive, always proud, it was a nasty betrayal.

'NOW EVERYONE KNOWS!' he hissed. 'I ain't 'avin it!'

The Krays could be very odd sometimes. Really old-fashioned, as I've said. Ron might talk openly about the men he fancied. But he'd never talk openly to a woman about sex, for instance. Reg too was funny that way. They expected women to behave in a certain way. Me posing topless? Well, that was fine because it was me and it was publicity, a bit of a laugh. But strangers discovering that Ronnie Kray's wife had other boyfriends? That wasn't a laugh. That was taking the piss. Bad for the image.

Condemned as he was to a lifetime in an institution, marriage to Ronnie Kray was never going to be easy whether the woman was an easygoing, gentle housewife and mum or an adventurous young woman who grabbed life with both hands. Somehow, that day, between the two of us, Charlie and I managed to steer him off the topic of Kate's book. It wasn't mentioned again.

Yet, that autumn, Ronnie started divorce proceedings . . .

Chapter 16

A farewell

I ripped open the envelope that'd been lying on the mat. Reg. What now?

'At last, I can see a light at the end of the tunnel,' he'd written.

Really good news this time. It was March 1994 and the authorities had decided Reg could now be sent to Maidstone Prison. This meant all sorts of things. Maidstone, of course, was much closer to London, just one hour by train. He'd be allowed six visitors a month. The environment there was much more relaxed, too. Reggie could even earn a small sum of money: £5 as a cleaner.

'See, Ron,' I told his twin next time I got to Broadmoor. 'Reg's move means it's getting towards the end. In a couple of years, if we keep up the parole campaign, you'll both be released.'

'No, Flan. Don't bother with the campaign for me. No reason why they shouldn't release Reg. But me, I'll never come out of 'ere.'

I blinked. What was Ron on about? The parole campaign for both of them had gone on for years. Now, after all this time, it really did look like there was a small ray of hope.

'Don't say that, Ron. Even if you have to do the full thirty years, you'll be released one day.'

Ron leaned forward. He sighed heavily. Then he reached out, grabbed my hand. Held it tight.

'Flanagan. I'll never leave Broadmoor.'

Ron had never ever spoken to me like this before in such a definite, emphatic way.

What on Earth does he know? I wondered.

Afterwards, I made it my business to contact Dr Tidmarsh. He was, as usual, incredibly tactful: 'Ronnie is better here with us.'

Ronnie knew something that none of us, even the man treating him, knew.

Naturally, I told Reg of this strange conversation when I went to Maidstone. Not so surprisingly, Ron had said exactly the same thing to his twin. But unlike me, who saw it as something of a chilling prophecy, Reg didn't take the negative view.

He'd told Ron he was wrong. 'We will walk the streets again,' he'd insisted.

'Is there any reason why they could keep you inside after thirty years, Reg?' I wanted to know.

Despite his optimism, Reg's response was born of the wisdom he'd acquired after a quarter of a century inside the system. He'd attended those parole meetings year after year.

The answer was always 'no'.

'Flan, they can do what they like. And anyway, you can't go from Maidstone straight to the outside. I'd have to be moved to another prison where they can let you have days out first.'

Just before Christmas 1994, I took Ronnie his Christmas present, a tie made of red and navy silk. It had to be Italian and, of course, it had to be the finest pure silk. But that day, I realised that something was very wrong with Ron.

He didn't look at all well. To me, he looked a bit spaced-out. Not quite all there.

He did thank me for the gift when I told him I'd put it in his box. But there was something quite listless, even lethargic about him. There was no real conversation either beyond the usual. Had I seen Reg? What was I doing? Then he cut the visit short after I'd only been there about half an hour, most of which had been spent waiting for him to walk into the visiting room. He wanted to go to his room, he said. Which I took to mean that he wanted his medication.

I watched him walk off, as slickly suited as ever, but from behind he looked defeated, all confidence gone. I felt uneasy. Slimmer, paler than I'd ever known him, it was difficult to reconcile this Ron with the guy I'd sat laughing my head off with not that long ago. He was ill.

One of the Family

The minute I got home, I phoned Charlie and told him exactly what I'd seen. Over the Christmas break, Charlie saw Ron. He too saw what I'd seen: a sick man.

'I just think it's all takin' its toll, Flan,' Charlie said sadly. Much as he was routinely abused by his brother, Charlie was troubled to see Ron in this state, reduced to a sort of drugged passivity.

The truth was, some people who'd been visiting Ron for years had now stopped going to see him. A few old boxer friends had died. Ron's situation, after twenty-five years inside, had taken its toll on his friends too. Yet even then, I brushed off my fears, chose not to see the obvious. Maybe the medication needed some serious tweaking. He usually bounced back, didn't he?

What I didn't know until afterwards was that early in March 1995, prison doctors had been called to examine Reg who was feeling dizzy and having chest pains. Nine days later, Reg told the authorities that he knew his twin was ill. He wanted to see him. Now. Request refused.

Every 17 March, St Patrick's Day, I make it a point to go out and celebrate my part-Irish heritage. The day of the wearing of the green has always had a special significance for me. That night, as I was getting ready to go to a party, the phone rang.

It was Jack Leigh.

'Ronnie's dead,' he said.

I struggled to take it in at first. But it was all too true.

He'd died at nine that morning. I didn't even want to think of the state Reggie'd be in – but I managed to get through to a very stricken Charlie. He'd be seeing Reg the next day to organise Ron's funeral. He wasn't looking forward to it. Laurie, Ron's oldest friend, would go with him.

So Ronnie had been right. He'd known, somehow, that the end was coming, it was all over for him. At least, I comforted myself, he'd died in hospital and not in Broadmoor. But the saddest thing was that he'd been on his own. No family member or an old friend there, someone whose company he'd cherished.

It turned out that he'd collapsed in his room at Broadmoor and had been taken to Heatherwood Hospital, Ascot, where he was treated for exhaustion and anaemia. Then, back in his room at Broadmoor, he had complained of feeling unwell again and was taken to a specialist unit at another hospital, Wexham Park in Slough, where he'd died.

Charlie had even managed to get there to see him the day before. When he'd left, he didn't think that his brother was dying. But the reality was that the next morning Ron died from a massive heart attack at the age of sixty-one.

Ron was no health nut: he was an eighty-ciggies-a-day man throughout his life. He had been on all kinds of heavy medication since his twenties, which he'd recklessly combined with huge quantities of alcohol for many years.

One of the Family

Long before he was imprisoned, doctors had warned him about the dangers of mixing alcohol with the heavy-duty drugs he had to take, yet he'd blithely ignored them. When you thought about it, it was a miracle that he'd survived as long as he had. As for the effect of the massive intake of nicotine, I never once heard him even cough. Or talk about giving up, come to that.

Two days later, my phone rang at eight a.m. I knew who it was.

'It's Reg,' said the familiar soft voice.

I didn't really know what to say. I started to say how sorry I was . . .

'Heart attack. He should never have been put back in his room. Come and see me. We need to talk about the church.'

'Look, I'll be there. What about the church?' I wondered.

'I want you to do the seating. Don't want a man doing it. And I don't want the funeral directors doing it because they won't know anyone or where to sit people. Everything's got to be perfect. Ron's gonna 'ave the funeral 'e always wanted.'

I knew exactly what he meant. Ron had always been extremely vocal about the fact that he wanted a lavish East End funeral, the sort of funeral they used to have in the nineteenth century with six black plumed horses drawing the hearse carrying the coffin. An old-fashioned extravaganza.

'I've got a hundred and fifty security men,' Reg told me.

Huh? I got the idea of the plumed horses, that was typical Ron. But what on Earth did he need all those men for?

'It's all sorted. I want the cars and the hearse to go along Bethnal Green Road like a king, so everyone can say goodbye to him. So I need the security. Twenty of 'em will go inside the church.'

At that point I had to stop him. It was Ron's last farewell and of course it had to be just right but I didn't like this last bit. It was far too over the top.

'No, Reg. There's no need for security men in the church.'

'Yes, there is. People will try to sit where they want. They'll rush down the front. Or they'll turn up late. And they'll all want to see me, speak to me.'

Then I understood. This was Ronnie Kray's last performance. Reg, if you like, was the director, working from a prison cell. The stage, the props, the extras, the lines, the music – all had to be exactly as he wished at St Matthew's Church, Bethnal Green. I was the assistant stage manager. But I could see very clearly where my role would come in.

'We'll only need *one* security man on the door, Reg. I'll be standing at the church door and I'll let people in, twelve at a time. I'll know where you want them seated. Because you're gonna give me a list.'

'Are you sure you can handle this?' Reg asked, all suspicious. He knew me well enough to know I could cope with all this. Yet he had to be a hundred per cent sure.

'Yes. It'll be done with dignity, Reg. We don't want twenty minders in a house of God. The priest won't like it, for one thing.'

'Well, if you think you can do it . . .'

Of course I could.

'No security in the church,' I warned him before he hung up.

Don't get me wrong. I'd never done anything like this in my life. But my long association with the family meant that I knew all the people who were coming into the church who would want to sit in the front rows. Whatever people might say or think about my association with the Krays, I'd been part of this family for a long time.

And on the day of the funeral, everything that Reg had planned from his prison cell worked like clockwork. Ron got the funeral he wanted. Twenty-six big funeral limousines stopped the traffic in the East End, while the beautifully plumed black horses bore the coffin on the long ten-mile journey from the church to the cemetery at Chingford Mount.

The huge crowds massed along the streets were a sight to behold. Vi's funeral had been a big event but this was massive: the funeral cortege was virtually an exercise in mass hysteria, people running into the road to tap on the windows of the cars, TV cameras recording the entire event. An East End funeral like no other. Because it was Ronnie Kray.

At the door of the church I stood there, list in hand, as the mourners arrived, directing them to their seats as per Reg's instructions.

There were far too many people. In the end, many were left outside with the cars lining the streets and the security teams accompanying them.

As people came into the church, I had to use my discretion as best I could. Really old men, old friends, would want to see Reg, touch his hand. It was the first time Reg had left the confines of prison since Violet's funeral. I took them down the front row for a quick handshake. Dozens wanted that handshake so much.

It's difficult for some people to understand how two men who became so notorious for violence and murder touched the hearts of these crowds of onlookers on the street. 'You knew what you was getting with them,' people used to say. 'They didn't murder women or old people – they helped a lot of people,' they'd insist over and over again.

There was some truth in this. But essentially, this was London's East End and the old time-honoured code of the East End was based on loyalty, sticking together.

Times had changed beyond recognition but the people that turned up that day to say goodbye to Ronnie didn't give a fig about that. The twins, whether you saw them as evil or benevolent, represented a lost world to so many. They 'belonged' to the East End. Call it misplaced loyalty, call it what you like, but the old East Enders were fierce in their attachment to their dark corner of the world, despite its violent history and the tough rule of the street.

The Twins' obsession with image and publicity had now turned them into icons. twin icons inextricably linked to what had become, through wartime history and violence, London's most iconic area.

It's all about sentiment, really, a rosy, idealistic picture of a community that barely exists any more. But it's difficult to dismiss how powerful it can be in people's minds.

The church service took about forty-five minutes. I looked at Reg throughout, over the aisle. He just sat there, staring at the coffin. Then came the hymn, 'Fight the Good Fight', followed by Reg's voice over the loudspeakers. It had been recorded because he didn't trust himself to speak. He knew he'd break down.

'My brother had a vicious temper and many other faults. But at the end of the day, I remember him as a man.'

Succinct and to the point. Then, when the service ended, the sound of Whitney Houston singing 'I Will Always Love You' echoed through the church. As the four pall-bearers representing the four corners of London picked up the coffin, we all saw Charlie reach out to Reg and they clasped hands over the coffin. Only then could you see Reg's tears.

After the long journey through the crowded streets to the cemetery, our time at the grave was short. After the priest gave his blessing, twelve of us threw roses into Ron's grave.

I wondered, as you do, as I looked across to Violet's grave, what she'd have thought if she'd witnessed all this. It was a blessing, I thought, that she hadn't survived to see this saddest of sad days.

Reg was refused parole again, that Christmas. He was sixty-two and had been inside for twenty-seven years. The authorities said he could be moved to a Category C prison. But he'd still have to wait.

He wasn't in a good way, as you'd imagine after he'd lost Ron. Then, in January (1996) came yet another terrible blow for the family: Gary, Charlie's son, was seriously ill. Terminal lung cancer. The doctors informed Charlie that it was a matter of weeks, not years.

Poor Charlie. I found myself spending quite a lot of time with him after Ron died. We'd catch up with each other at least once a week, maybe where he lived in South London or we'd meet up at a nightclub called Scarlett's in Croydon. Often, I'd suggest that we'd meet in the East End in pellicis.

Charlie wasn't really bitter about the past, about what had happened to him. When we did sit down for a heart-to-heart, he'd always tell me that all their lives would have been happy and successful – if it hadn't been for Ronnie's taste for 'killin' people'. Sad but true.

As soon as Charlie told me about Gary, I rang Jackie and we dashed off to see him. Jackie had known him as a kid, when they were growing up. Gary didn't know he had just weeks to live – nobody was going to tell him. He was painfully frail but as sweet and uncomplaining as ever. We pretended to be breezy and cheerful. But our hearts were already heavy for this harmless and most loving of men. Losing him would surely break Charlie's heart.

'When you're better, Gal, we'll take you for a night out to Stringfellow's,' I promised him. The trip to the West End club, still my favourite haunt on a Friday night back then, was, I knew, a promise I'd never keep.

The next thing we knew, Gary had been moved to St Christopher's Hospice in Crystal Palace. When we got there, we found Charlie by Gary's bed, holding his hand and weeping. We combed Gary's hair. Cleaned his glasses. Gave him some magazines. Chatted to him about this and that. He was so gentle, one of life's innocents. How cruel was this?

Four days later, I felt a strong urge to see him again. Derek came with me this time. Derek sang to him that day – he had a marvellous voice. He sang an old song, a song the old East End grannies used to sing. I remembered Vi singing it too.

> I don't wanna play in your yard.
> I don't like you any more
> You'll be sorry when you see me
> Sliding down our cellar door
> You can't holler down our rain barrel
> You can't climb our apple tree

> I don't wanna play in your yard
> If you can't be good to me.

'Your nan used to sing that song,' I told Gary, who loved it and asked Derek to sing it all over again. Two days later, Charlie rang and said, 'I've lost my baby.'

Gary was only forty-four years old. Reggie organised his nephew's funeral, paid for it, everything. Less than a year since Ron had died and one empty car was driven right behind the hearse as it made its way to Chingford Cemetery – Reg's idea. He wasn't allowed to go, of course, but he wanted to show his love. After all, the twins had known Gary since he was born.

Later in March, Reggie rang me early one morning. I half-expected him to want to talk about losing Gary but no, he was all businesslike. A woman called Roberta Jones was coming to see him and her company were planning some sort of video interview with him. The video was a tribute to Ron. Could I possibly bring this lady with me the next time I came to Maidstone?

I rang Roberta and it turned out she lived nearby, on the Kingsland Road. Derek and I went to pick her up. She seemed quiet and quite shy, but obviously intelligent. Slim and attractive too, in a very natural way. She asked me about Reg on the way to Maidstone, how long I'd been visiting him. I warned her: 'He will talk non-stop and probably give you lots of orders.'

Yet the visit went extremely well. Reg charmed her,

managed to draw her out. He liked professional women
– and this lady was definitely involved in her work, knew
what she was talking about.

'So. What do you think of him?' I asked Roberta
afterwards.

'Exactly as you described him. So much energy. And
he doesn't want to dwell on the past, does he?'

She also seemed impressed at how fit Reg looked after
all those years inside, thanks to his regular gym workouts.

Would she go again? I wondered.

'If he asks me, yes.'

Later, at home, I thought about this new woman,
Roberta. If this did develop, I thought selfishly, Reg would
have someone else to do his bidding, work off his lists. Life
would be a bit easier for me, that was for sure.

Maybe she'd be a good influence. I'd been a bit worried
about Reg ever since he'd gone to Maidstone two years
before. Charlie had spotted it first.

'You're drunk,' Charlie told him one day when we were
visiting.

'Just a little bit of hooch – someone brings it in to me,'
Reg said.

This was daft. He'd endanger all his chances for parole
if he was caught boozing.

Charlie, of course, was all too quick to point this out.
No, Reg insisted. It was OK. It was only once or twice a
week.

Then I'd started to pick up on it on my visits without

Charlie. Reg would come out into the visiting area and you could see he'd been drinking. I'd spot it straight away. A kiss hello and a whiff of booze. This was no once-a-week drinking. Maybe it had already started in Parkhurst but in Maidstone it had definitely got worse.

Later, someone told me that Reg and some of the other men really went for it on a Saturday night. Lots of dope-smoking, too. I put it down to the fact that he was in the company of a lot of young men. They were doing short sentences. So why should they care about ignoring the rules?

Just the same, I was surprised that Reg wasn't clever enough to see ahead. He was normally so shrewd, so calculating. And the drinking did get reported in his reviews. It would have been impossible for it not to be noticed.

As for Charlie, Derek and I did our best to brighten the gloom for him, take him out for dinner, try to make him laugh. But you could see all too plainly that for Charlie losing his son was a tragedy that he couldn't come to terms with. His mum and his brother, well, it was tough but they were older. But he'd never expected to bury his boy.

Perhaps it was this terrible grief he was experiencing that led to his disastrous downfall, I could never be sure.

He'd certainly mentioned the nice invitations he'd been getting from this total stranger up north, a man called Jack, who was being so generous to him. He'd even suggested that me and Derek should go up to Birmingham to a party to meet these new friends. But in the end, I didn't fancy going.

When Charlie came back and told us about how this man and his friends had wined and dined him, given him a gold lighter, made a huge fuss of him, my first question was: 'Who are these people?'

To me, it all sounded very odd. Charlie was the ultimate people person – but you could read that as the ultimate party person too. He loved to be in a crowd of people, all drinking and laughing. He had no money at all. He was permanently skint. But he was used to people being around him, buying him drinks all the time because he was Charlie Kray. It's a sad truth that this became his entire social life in the last years of his life.

After it all went wrong for Charlie, I did wish I'd gone to that party. I'm pretty sure my intuition would have kicked in, told me that these guys he didn't know were up to something. Perhaps I wouldn't have instantly known that the strangers were, in fact, out to entrap Charlie: maybe I would just have said, 'I don't like these guys.' Who knows?

But the fact was that these 'new friends' were undercover cops. They bugged all his phone calls from the hotel where they'd put him up. And they had him taped talking about drug deals: cocaine. A class-A drug.

In July 1996, Charlie and two of his friends, Ronnie

Field and Bobby Gould, were arrested and charged with conspiracy to supply two kilos of cocaine, worth £63,000, and conspiracy to supply 520 kilos of the drug.

Bail was refused.

'It's a set-up,' Derek said. 'He'll get off.'

I could imagine many things but not Charlie arranging big drug deals. His talent, if you like, was putting people together: Charlie always knew someone who knew someone. When they arrested him at Judy's house, they found no drugs at all. All they could find to take away was a packet of white pills: contraceptive tablets.

He burst into tears when he saw me at Belmarsh as he waited for his trial. He looked terrible: scarily thin – nothing resembling the Charlie of old.

'I put two people together, not knowing what they were gonna do, Flan,' he sobbed. 'Now I'm supposed to be masterminding a cocaine deal worth millions. It's ridiculous.'

It was crazy. But to many who knew the Krays it looked like there was a determination, on the part of the police, to make sure that with one Kray brother dead and the other heading towards eventual parole, the remaining Kray should be taken off the streets. One undercover cop had been sent to attend Gary's funeral. He'd never even known Gary. But he'd driven hundreds of miles to be there, Charlie realised afterwards.

When the case went to court the following summer, I went into the stand as one of many character witnesses for

Charlie. When asked about drugs, I told them emphatically that Charlie had never taken drugs.

'If he's got a drug, it's champagne,' I said.

That got a laugh. But it didn't help. They'd recorded him in hotels saying: 'I can get you anything you want.' In the end he got a guilty verdict and a prison sentence of twelve years.

What a shock for everyone. He'd be in his eighties by the time he got out, I reasoned. If he lived that long.

I knew Charlie wouldn't survive this. Even before it happened, he was already a broken man. Whatever his failings, he didn't deserve to be sent to Parkhurst, across the water, the place where his brothers had battled it out in the early years of their imprisonment.

It was a cruel stroke of fate for a harmless man who lived for laughter and good times.

But the Krays were nothing if not tough and Reg was still determined to move forward in life. I knew Roberta was visiting him regularly and that he liked her a lot – he told me that. But he surprised me that summer when he rang with one of his dawn calls to say he was getting married.

'Who to?' was my initial reaction. I hadn't realised it was that serious.

But Reg needed a wife and he knew he'd found someone who loved him.

'We get on like a house on fire,' he told me that morning. Yet he wasn't in any way sympathetic to Charlie's plight.

In fact, he was angry. Charlie's situation could now affect Reg's own chances of parole. Even the prison guards at Belmarsh had warned Charlie of this before he got the twelve-year sentence.

I didn't get an invite to Reg's wedding to Roberta in July 1997, not long after Charlie's sentence started. I wasn't in any way put out, though I would have liked to have seen him tie the knot after all those years. But it was definitely love. And that, in the end, is what really counts.

When I heard that Reg had been moved to Wayland Prison in Norfolk, a Category C training prison, the month after the wedding, I sent him a note of congratulations: this was the step forward that he and Roberta had been waiting for. Now, as a happily married man, he had much to look forward to.

Or did he? For quite some time after the marriage and the move to Wayland I kept thinking back, re-running my memory of the last time I'd seen Reg, at the beginning of 1997.

I'd quite deliberately arranged to go and see Reg on my own. I had a lot I wanted to say to him.

I had to choose my moment, of course. On a visit, getting Reggie's attention was often difficult: he'd keep getting up from our table and running over to the other visitors' tables, kissing old mums, being introduced to new visitors. Constant table-hopping, glad-handing people, the habit he'd never relinquished since I first saw it that night at the Astor so long ago.

Now, here he was, hair cropped in a very short crew cut, a wiry energetic man of sixty-three. The familiar coiled spring.

'You look like Spencer Tracy, Reg,' I quipped as he finally sat down.

Oh, he liked that. But he didn't like what came next when we discussed his next parole review due at the end of the year. The thirty-year sentence would be up the following year, in May 1998. Yes, Charlie's troubles didn't bode well for either of them. But still, he didn't see the need for any more 'free Reg' campaigns. They'd let him out after thirty years, he felt sure.

I took a deep breath and went straight into my spiel. I'd been rehearsing it in my head in the car. A big-sister talk.

'People keep telling me you're still drinking, Reg. And smoking dope. This will prevent your release. All they need is a reason to keep two Krays locked up – they don't want even one Kray on the street. And what about these young guys, the company you keep?'

'They're my friends,' said Reg.

He clearly hadn't been expecting any of this, probably because not too many people were prepared to give the truth to him, straight to his face. These prison mates were all over him because he was Reggie Kray. There was huge kudos in just knowing him. What did they care about his release?

'Reg. It all gets reported that you surround yourself with young guys. The authorities don't like it.'

The sad thing was that, in the past, the authorities had worried about Reggie influencing other prisoners. Which was a fair assumption, really. But now it was the other way round. Reg, I'd learned from a number of people who visited him, was under the influence of some of these much younger men.

Reg took my hand, tried to lighten it all up.

''Ave you come 'ere to nag me, Flan?' he joked.

I wasn't having this. 'Listen, Reg. I'm talking like your mum. She'd be praying every night for you to be released next year. By now, they should have moved you to another prison and you'd be getting home leave. But they haven't, have they? Don't you think there's a reason for that?'

'I only 'ave a little drink once a week,' he said. Which was pathetic, a real boozer's lie.

'No, you don't, Reg. I *know* you don't.'

'Stop talking about me, Flan. What's *your* news, eh?'

'Don't want to talk about me. I'm free. You're not. The cannabis you smoke: that means more trouble than the drink.'

'I never smoked it in the other prisons.'

'No. Of course. Know why? It's only the young guys that smoke it – all youngsters do it.'

Then, in an attempt to shut me up or maybe distract me, he produced a photo taken in his cell. He seemed to be proud of it, just Reg and a handsome young inmate. Having a drink.

I wanted to rip it up. Why was he being so pathetic?

'Reg, you always tell people to concentrate on one thing at a time,' I told him.

'That's how you organise yourself,' he said.

'Think of just one thing now. You. And your release, not all these other people and what you can do for this one or that one.'

Oh dear. Once I'm on a roll, there's no stopping me. But as I said, I'd done a lot of serious thinking about Reg and how he'd been in recent years. People talked to me all the time about Reg, told me stuff about what he was up to, gleaned from their visits and phone calls. You had to discount some of it as just gossip. But a lot of it was true. A few had told me about his drunken phone calls, phones slammed down in anger. Reggie Kray wasn't the only networker on the planet to pick up snippets of information and come to their own conclusions.

'Reg, you should be nearly out now. We should be planning your party,' I snapped at him.

The brows knotted quizzically, the way they always did.

Reg had never seen me like this. To him and his brothers I'd always been good old Flanagan, a living reminder of the good years. Our mother's friend. The Page 3 girl with the heart of gold. The go-between with Fleet Street. The sister they'd never had. Someone to cheer them up, make them feel good. But I'd never ever sounded off at either of the twins the way I did now.

Why did I sound off? I was angry. At the time, Charlie was in Belmarsh, waiting for his court case. Yet Reggie was now putting his own chance of freedom in jeopardy because he wanted to hang out with younger men, smoke and drink with them.

I'd understood for some time about the gay relationships that he'd been having. Charlie, in fact, had first pointed it out to me when we went to Parkhurst together: the over-attentive behaviour towards a young man who'd turn up on a visit, the endless correspondence with young men. OK, so Reg had physical relationships with men in prison. It's hardly unusual. It happens.

But something had now changed with Reggie Kray. It had been going on for quite a while, maybe since Ron had died. It was hard to say what it was. It definitely wasn't Roberta. She was clearly a force for good. And he hadn't let himself go physically: he'd maintained his fitness, like the ex-boxer he always was. He'd never miss his visits to the gym.

Whatever it was, Reg wasn't about to confide in me on that day. As we made our way through the visiting room as I left he kept stopping, trying to introduce me to other people. But I wasn't my normal friendly self.

'Remember what I said, Reg: focus on your release, not on anything else,' I told him before I walked away.

He tried to brush it off with a joke.

'Blimey, Ron used to say you was bossy. Never realised you was *so* bossy, Flan.'

'Yes. I used to tell him not to smoke eighty fags a day but did he listen?'

One of the Family

We laughed. Better to end a visit that way.

'OK, I'll stop now.' I grinned. Then we hugged goodbye.

It turned out to be one very memorable visit. Because I never, for a minute, imagined that this would be the last time I'd ever get to see Reggie Kray . . .

Chapter 17

2000

Millennium Eve, 1999. As Big Ben chimes in the year 2000, London explodes in a whoosh of joy and celebration: the most spectacular firework display the city has ever seen. One million pounds' worth of fireworks soar across the night sky, watched by the two million people who have lined up beside the River Thames to witness the magical first minutes of the new century.

It's a big moment in time, a night to remember, and Derek and I are among the revellers, champagne glasses in hand, watching the dazzling display high above London from the balcony of a friend's penthouse flat overlooking the Thames.

Life at that precise moment was, at long last, on an even keel. At fifty-nine, I was still working occasionally as an extra in film and TV, my little granddaughter Scarlett had just turned four and her dad, JJ the D-J, was working at the Ministry of Sound. After nearly a decade, Derek and I didn't live together and we rarely crossed swords or argued. Good times galore.

Six days into the New Year and my world collapsed.

I'd spent the day shopping with Derek. At about ten p.m., he dropped me off at my flat. The plan was for us to have dinner the next night.

On his way home, Derek decided to have just one quick drink at a pub in Blackfriars, one of his locals. He'd walked into the bar, ordered a Scotch and coke, lit a cigarette and started chatting to the guvnor.

Then he'd collapsed onto the floor.

They'd called an ambulance and whisked him to St Thomas Hospital nearby. But he'd already died – it was a waste of time. By the time I'd got a call from the pub to say he'd collapsed, it was too late. At the emergency department there was Derek, lying flat on his back in a single bed with a sheet up over his torso, one hand on his chest. He was still warm when I touched him.

There had been no warning sign whatsoever. Derek hadn't had a day's illness in all the time I'd known him. Yet that night in the pub he'd had a massive heart attack. It would've been his sixtieth birthday in March. We'd planned to celebrate it in Tenerife.

I was, as you'd imagine, stricken with shock and disbelief. For the next couple of months I was in a complete daze. My family kept me going through the early days of grief: it was a case of 'one foot in front of the other' every day, just going through the motions. I couldn't tell you how I got through his funeral – I don't remember too much about it.

I do recall that Charlie had managed to send a message from prison to the priest to read out: Derek and Charlie had been friends for years. Diana, now back in Charlie's life, managed to get to the funeral too.

After the funeral, Diana gave me Charlie's news.

It was all bad. Initially, he'd developed a cough and it had got progressively worse. Then he'd stopped eating. His legs and feet had swollen so much that he couldn't walk. Now in Parkhurst, he was just getting worse by the day. Terrible breathing problems.

The following month, the authorities decided Charlie was so poorly that Reggie was allowed to be taken to Parkhurst to see him: the doctors had said Charlie had advanced heart disease, weeks to live. They even let Reg stay on the island so he could see his brother more than once. By then a shrunken, gaunt Charlie was hospitalised, heavily medicated and fading fast. I was gutted to hear all this from Diana. How vividly I remembered him telling me, when I'd last seen him at Durham Prison: 'They're not gonna let me out till I can't walk any more, Flan.'

Then, at the beginning of April, Diana called me. She was in a rush. She was just about to leave London to get the ferry over to the Isle of Wight. Charlie was now semi-conscious in the hospital. 'I hope I get there in time,' she told me.

She did, thankfully. He hung on for her. He died holding her hand. Charlie was a ladies' man all his life. But Diana Buffini was his one true love.

One of the Family

Yet again, as per Reggie's instruction, I stood at the door of St Matthew's and guided the mourners to their seats. I watched later on as Charlie was buried alongside his beloved son, his brother and his parents in what was now known as 'Kray corner' at Chingford Mount.

Reg remained his usual dignified self, his close-cropped hair now snow white, handcuffed to a prison officer, Roberta at his side. There was no time to exchange a word with him – he was whisked away immediately afterwards in the prison's people carrier back to Norfolk.

It had been the briefest of sightings but Reg didn't look ill to me on that April day when we saw Charlie laid to rest. Yet by then, I realised later, he must have been in considerable pain, though he'd never said a word to me about the stomach problems and pain that had been plaguing him for ages. Tests had been carried out but proved inconclusive: the doctors said it was diverticulitis, an intestinal inflammation.

Again and again, Reg asked to see the prison doctor. Each time he was told to take over-the-counter medication, that there was no serious problem. Only at the end of July, four months after Charlie's demise, did the prison doctors decide to send Reg to Norwich Prison Hospital for tests. Again, nothing conclusive.

But in August I got a call from Reg's friend, Wilf Pine. Reg was in the Norfolk and Norwich Hospital. He was having an emergency operation. On his stomach.

It was bladder cancer. Very slowly, Reg regained some

strength but as Roberta and their solicitor set the wheels in motion to apply to the Home Office for compassionate parole, Reg took a turn for the worse and needed a second emergency operation.

This time the prognosis was terminal. After thirty-two years in prison, unless something happened very quickly, Reg would die behind bars.

In my mind, I couldn't see why they couldn't let him out to spend however long he had left in freedom. Surely, I argued, they couldn't hang on to him now.

But fate had its own plan for the last of the Krays. Reg was already a dying man when he and Roberta learned he'd been granted compassionate parole at the end of August. He died, technically a free man, in the old Town House Hotel, Norwich, on 1 October just a few weeks before his sixty-seventh birthday.

Reggie Kray's last days, the BBC-TV interview he gave from his bed and the media circus surrounding his demise are already well documented. I didn't stay away from it all by choice: it was just a very different scenario that Reggie found himself in during those final weeks.

The odd thing was that his funeral, carefully planned by Reg as ever, though it got the newspaper and TV coverage he expected and the event itself more or less mirrored his twin's extravagant farewell – the security men, the stately cortege of limousines making their way to the cemetery at leafy Chingford – the impact on the public didn't resonate in the same way.

One of the Family

Times change quickly. Five years ago, 60,000 people had turned up on the streets of East London to say their goodbyes to Ron. Similar numbers had lined the streets to watch Violet's last journey. Charlie's funeral had drawn a much smaller crowd but you might have expected that.

Yet for Reggie, just a few thousand people stood on the street to watch the cortege, though the church service was exactly as Reg wished, dignified and sincere.

For the second time in six months, I took my place by the church door and greeted those who had come to mourn a Kray brother, showed them where they'd be seated before the service started. At the end, Reg's coffin was carried out of St Matthew's Church to the sound of Sinatra's 'My Way'.

The thing was, I realised afterwards, the people who came to mourn Reg now were no longer just a tightly knit group of East Enders or hard men from their past who'd known the Kray family all their lives. There were now much younger people who had shared Reg's last few years, supported him, whose concern he trusted, believed in: the two groups were more or less from different planets. Even the wakes after the funeral were in separate venues: that kind of thing isn't the East End way at all.

So there was a very poignant note to Reg's funeral, even beyond the inevitable sadness of this end of all the lives of all the Kray family members I'd known. Let's just say the East End loyalty that always meant so much to the twins was now coming from too many different directions, with different agendas. I do believe quite a lot of it was pure self-interest. It was the association with Reg that seemed to matter to some, not the man himself. That, I guess, is what can happen when you become a celebrity.

Perhaps if it hadn't ended so badly for Reg and Charlie and if I hadn't lost Derek that year, I might have spoken up at the end, what with all the feuding and bitching that went on around me.

But I'd told Reg the truth as I saw it that last time I'd seen him. Right or wrong, that would have to suffice.

I was exhausted afterwards, the kind of emotional exhaustion that needs time and a complete change of scenery. Over the years I had often stayed with a really good friend who lives in Tenerife. I love the place and she was more than happy to put me up for a couple of weeks. A sympathetic welcome and a large dose of sunshine always manage to have a healing effect, even for a short time.

Sure enough, by the end of the first week there, I started to feel a little bit better.

Wandering around the shops one morning, I decided, on impulse, to get my hair done. That's very unusual for me, as I've always done my own hair. But a bit of pampering never hurt any woman, any age. And for once I had the freedom of time to spare.

'On holiday?' the girl doing my hair chirped, once I'd been washed and gowned.

I looked up from my copy of *Hello*. The accent was pure

cockney. She was an extremely pretty girl, blonde hair cropped fashionably shoulder length, beautifully tanned, tiny skirt, tiny waist and long, long legs. But I really wasn't in the mood for the usual kind of upbeat hairdresser patter.

'No. Visiting,' I said quite curtly. 'Just blow-dry it straight, that's all. I used to be a hairdresser.'

She laughed. 'OK, better be good, then.'

Then she set about her job, not seeming to pick up on my unusually abrupt manner. She kept chatting away to me regardless. So I got her story without asking.

Martine had been living in Tenerife for over a year. An Essex girl, she loved the Spanish sunshine, the relaxed way of life. She had a Spanish boyfriend who managed one of the big hotels. They were living together, officially engaged, saving hard for their future.

'How d'you fancy a Spanish husband?' I finally asked. This girl could take her pick, no mistake. It must be love. Or something.

'Oh, he's gorgeous. He's crazy about me. Only thing is, he's really jealous. Waits outside the salon after work, that sort of thing. Goes potty if I'm not home on time.'

Well, of course, I thought to myself. Any guy, Spanish or otherwise, would go crazy for Martine: she had the looks and the familiar, chatty personality for the job she was doing. But she had a real problem on her hands if she'd tied herself up with some smouldering Mr Insecurity. As I knew all too well.

Normally, I'd have opened my mouth to say more or

less what I thought. Ben Jones always used to call me Motormouth and it's true, that's who I am. Usually. The normal me would have said: 'Get rid of him' or 'Forget the jealous ones, they're more grief than you need.' Or something like that. A bit of motherly advice.

But I wasn't the normal me. In less than a year I'd lost too many people, people who'd all played a significant part in my life in different ways. As a result, I'd been doing a lot of thinking lately, mostly about the past. When you see sixty coming round the next corner, you do tend to dwell on what your life was, where it took you, why you did what you did or said. Three funerals in one year tend to have that effect, don't they?

So maybe I was too heavily weighed down by it all or maybe it was just Martine, her youth, her blind unspoken assumption that life would roll along exactly as she planned it. But there and then, as the hairdryer hummed away and she smoothly finished the job, I saw myself in vivid flashback, exactly as I was at her age, the blonde girl with the jealous husband and the chatty manner.

The girl who dismissed her mother's warning not to marry, ignored her husband's temper to secretly wander, hairdryer in hand, into forbidden territory, the girl who thirsted only for glamour, excitement and the allure of what she believed was a glittering world out there.

I didn't listen to anyone back then – and I was pretty sure that Martine was cut from similar cloth. After all, she'd struck out for life in the sun, taken an initial gamble.

One of the Family

There was no point, I thought, as I tipped her generously and exited into the sunshine, in giving any young woman like Martine advice based on what I'd learned about life, about men, no point at all.

For like me back in 1961, on that afternoon when I'd wandered into Violet Kray's world, Martine would only follow her strongest instincts.

With any luck, just like me, those instincts would take her far beyond the safe, conventional parameters of her background and lead her into rich experience and a certain kind of wisdom, knowledge that we can only acquire through surviving the roller-coaster ride of success and adversity in life.

You have to live it to understand it, I thought to myself as I made my way back to my friend's apartment. But the wisdom of age tells you too that you are never ever going to understand all of it. Or accurately predict what might happen.

Knowing the Kray family for all those years, watching their story unfold from what was essentially superficial glamour shielding criminal activity to what ultimately became human tragedy had definitely taught me that . . .

Chapter 18

Today

So here I am now, a seventy-four-year-old with four grand-daughters and a son who, just like me, has determinedly followed his own path. I did all I could as he grew up to steer JJ to all manner of jobs. But all he was ever interested in was music. He definitely inherited that single-mindedness from his mum!

Today, half a century on from Vallance Road, the Astor Club and the fish-and-chip suppers with Benny Hill, I continue to live in London's East End. I've watched it change dramatically from a rundown, shabby, undesirable part of London to a vibrant, diverse and ultra-fashionable area.

Once-derelict old buildings are now fabulous places to walk through, eat and shop in. Tourists from all corners of the globe pack those narrow Dickensian streets, pose for selfies outside the Blind Beggar. Tour guides show people round the streets where the Krays lived out their early years. And the Kray myth itself? It lives on, to be endlessly recreated on the big screen, the small screen, the stage – you name it. As successive generations discover it, it remains a compelling story for many.

Finally, Ronnie and Reggie got what they wanted: enduring fame and celebrity. They certainly worked hard at it through the years of incarceration. The relentless quest to be known as criminal superstars, gods amongst men, never let up, right to the end.

Yet at the same time the twins also got what they deserved for their crimes. Over-analysed their lives and story may have been, but there is no condoning what they did, the reason why their freedom was taken from them for the rest of their lives. Yes, they were tough. Ron, I knew, never gave in to self-pity for the path he'd chosen. Reg, it seemed, regretted much later on in life. But they still paid a terrible price for their fame.

I hope my side of their story gives some sense of what drew me into their world at the time and why I chose to maintain those links with them down the years. When I look back at it, it was the warmth and generosity of one East End mum who lived only for her children that was the true catalyst for my involvement with it all. And then, when Vi had dedicated her later years to doing whatever she still could do for them and was worn out by it all, it was, in the general scheme of things, a very small thing to honour her last wishes.

Of course it would have been so much easier never to go near the Krays again when Violet had died. But I knew just how much her boys meant to her. Certainly, they'd done terrible things and they'd expected others to pick up the pieces for them, stay close-mouthed about their crimes no matter what. The trouble was that in their freedom years they believed in that kind of blind loyalty where you keep your mouth shut, full stop. 'Respect' was a kind of religion for them. But how respectful is it to blast a man to smithereens, knife him to death or order his execution? Theirs was a very twisted logic.

Violet, in turn, was blindly loyal to her boys. She believed in them implicitly. As she believed in me, listening to my problems with all the concern of a mother. I had a fantastic mother, so I was doubly blessed to know Violet too. I never saw myself as Violet's daughter. But that was the way she treated me.

The twins were users of the first order. I had my eyes wide open about that. They didn't single out certain people to manipulate: they were like that with everyone. As I've said, I was one of many women who wound up running back and forth at their behest once they were locked up. Some of them have chosen to remain silent about their involvement with the twins. Which is perfectly understandable. But I wouldn't like anyone to believe that I saw myself as having some sort of exclusive relationship with the Kray Twins – that never existed.

People from all walks of life who had never met them queued up to visit them in prison when the rules permitted. And all the time, the twins deployed networking skills that any public-relations person would envy to bring the world to their front door – even if it was a locked one. As the years passed, of course, I came to represent 'the old days' and the mother they loved. Ronnie Kray, more than his twin, needed to hang on to those sentimental fragments of his past. He needed them: they were part of who he was.

If you consider the Kray Twins' most significant relationships through their lives it always comes back to the same thing: their fixed bond was with each other and with their mother – as a trio they were bonded until eternity. But beyond that, when it came to loving anyone else, it was far more complex: Reggie, I always felt, confused love with possession, control, manipulation.

For complex reasons that only he knew, he set himself up in public as the bereaved loving husband of his young wife, Frances. Yet that relationship, sadly, became distorted because of his own possessive nature – and the possessive nature of his twin, who only wanted Reg to himself.

Both men became wiser in later years, certainly, because they had all the time in the world – and then some – to ponder the past. But in the end, without his twin, Reg was blinded by his obsessive need for celebrity, constantly maintaining and reshaping the status he'd acquired over the years from behind prison walls. You could say, in the end, that the image he so cherished took over the man.

As for Ron, superficially he is always seen as 'the mad one', but paranoid schizophrenia is a serious illness. Like all mental illness it remains widely misunderstood by most people: to me, underneath the scary exterior Ron, as an individual, was a softer, kinder person than many would ever imagine.

As a younger man, he'd been driven by fantasy and delusion. Yet finally, when Ron stared the truth about his situation in the face, he could acknowledge it openly.

It has to be said too that it was easygoing, affable, Champagne Charlie of whom I was fondest. I like a man who enjoys the company of women, relishes showing them a good time, and that sums up Charlie: he was the best person to be with when you were out enjoying yourself. Deep down, I always maintained a strong feeling of sympathy for his plight. By all accounts he was weak and foolish, took the easy route of riding on his brothers' celebrity when he might have walked away from it all. Yet violence to others had never been Charlie's game: he suffered just because he was their brother. Everyone who knew him would agree with that.

You can argue that nowadays the twins would never have wound up serving such punishing prison sentences. I hear that all the time, the stuff about those committing far worse crimes now walking free. It's a valid point. But you can't have sympathy for the twins: they wrote their own ending. As for Violet and Charlie, I do strongly feel that in many ways their lives were eventually destroyed by the twins. It's the old, old story: the effects of violent crime rebound on the innocent families of both the victims and the perpetrators.

One of the Family

People who knew the Krays often insist that the outcome might have been quite different had Violet been a harder type of woman. Or that somehow she might even have been to blame for it all because of her obsessive love for the twins, placing them far above her husband and her other son.

I don't believe that. I've always maintained that the twins were two halves of the same whole – one followed the other. Had she thrown them out of the house at sixteen – as some mothers do – they already knew then what they wanted to be. They were a force that couldn't be stopped by their mother's love. So the outcome would have been exactly the same.

I learned much about life from knowing Violet Kray. I came to understand how resilience will always triumph, no matter what the world throws at you. She too was weak in some ways. But in others she was the backbone of that little household. Totally committed to her family.

From being close to her, of course, I understood too about the sacrifices that motherhood can entail. I knew some of it from my own mother, an early widow making huge sacrifices to bring up three children on her own. Then, when I was left alone with JJ and we lost our home, I too found myself making tough but necessary choices, juggling three different types of work at one point to keep us going. The modelling work, by then, was pretty limited. So I returned to home hairdressing, bleaching and cutting. And I went out and bought a load of clothes from the wholesalers and I'd tote them around in the Mini with JJ in the back, selling the stuff to everyone I could. Any mum who loves her kids will do what they can in a tight corner.

The other big question that fascinates people is how much Violet really knew about the twins' violent activities. Some would have her as a cockney Ma Barker (branded Public Enemy No. 1 by the FBI in the 1930s, the machine-gun-toting mother of a legendary gang of murdering sons) scheming at their side, eyes wide open to the worst of their endeavours. Others say Violet was a complete innocent, naive and blameless.

She was neither. In the end, as I've written, she did have to confront the truth. But I do believe she found it easier to survive by blanking a lot of stuff out in the early days. She'd believe what she wanted to believe. Otherwise, how could she keep going? In her mind, she could counteract the good things in her precious cuttings book – the stories of the charity handouts, the good deeds of the twins, the celebrity photos – with the bad: the newspaper clips about the prison sentences, the frauds and the bloodshed.

This long relationship with the Kray family has often led to me being pilloried, mostly because I've always been willing to talk openly about my relationship with them.

But that's the thing with the Kray Twins: their story, their legend, their twinship, with its blend of East End history, 1960s glitter and dark deeds has an uncanny way of polarising people. You're either fascinated by it all or you can't stand the very idea of them but the myth will continue with more books and films.

People have often said: 'Oh, you're a strong person, you could have pulled away from it all at any time.'

That's very true. But as I hope I've made clear in this book, I tend to go by gut feeling. And that feeling unfailingly told me the same thing for all those years: keep your promise. So I did.

Maureen Flanagan
East London, 2015

Acknowledgements

I wish to thank Ajda Vucicevic, my editor at Century, for taking a chance on me with this book. My thanks also to Jacky Hyams for all her hard work in helping me tell my story and reliving the memories with me. I am hugely indebted to David Riding at MBA Literary Agency for all his ongoing support and help, on my behalf.

Finally there is one person in my life who has shared so much with me – my son JJ. Long may he continue with his radio station, Kool London 96.4 FM.

Photographic Acknowledgements

Page 2 – Joe Louis with the Kray Twins photograph ©
          Kenneth Newman

Page 3 – At No 10 seeing Mrs Thatcher photograph ©
          Daily Star/
          N&S Syndication and Licensing

Page 5 – East London Advertiser article printed 29th
          January 2009

Page 5 – 50th birthday party celebration with Charlie
          Kray photograph © Chris Barham

Page 7 – Ron Kray's wake photograph © Sass Tuffin

All other photographs are author's own.

Every reasonable effort has been made to contact all copyright
holders, but if there are any errors or omissions, we will insert
the appropriate acknowledgment in subsequent printings of
this book.